Bc

AN AUTOBIOGRAPHY

BY

ROBERT FORMAN HORTON

M.A., D.D.

LONDON: GEORGE ALLEN & UNWIN LTD.

RUSKIN HOUSE   40 MUSEUM STREET, W.C. 1

First published in 1917

Reckon thy life by loss instead of gain,
Not by the wine drunk, but by the wine poured forth;
For love's strength standeth in love's sacrifice,
And he who suffers most has most to give.

H. HAMILTON KING.

FOREWORD

IT would not, I think, have occurred to me to write an account of my life if a publisher had not asked me to do so ; for, except that the life of any one written with sincerity would have a certain value, I did not think that mine was worth recording. But, after revolving the proposal for a year, I saw it in a different light. My life, I reflected, belongs not to me alone, but to God, and to my fellow-men ; if God commanded, or if my fellow-men demanded, I had no right to hold it back. The demand of the public was made clear, in so far as a publisher does not propose to publish what the public does not want. And as I waited and pondered, it seemed to me more and more that the command of God was not wanting. I was thankful to have an opportunity of recording, however slightly, my tribute to the most loyal and inspiring friend, that, I should imagine, any man ever had, the friend to whom, for nearly forty years, I owed all my best and most effective impulses, the friend who even now from behind the veil continues to rally and urge me on to the goal. And as I began to review my life I became almost startlingly aware that it had been under the control and direction of a higher and wiser will than mine ; and if readers should perceive what to me is clear, this record might have the effect of helping them to recognize, and to submit to, the guiding hand.

> My bark is wafted to the strand
> By breath Divine,
> And on the helm there rests a hand
> Other than mine.

R. F. H.

CONTENTS

ILLUSTRATIONS

AN AUTOBIOGRAPHY

CHAPTER I

MEMORIES OF CHILDHOOD

1855–1874

How curiously distinct are the memories of childhood. After nearly sixty years, vivid as if it had occurred yesterday, is this : a little boy crying in spiritual distress, a longing for salvation, for peace, for something, he knew not what ; a mother's arms thrown round him, drawing him to her bosom ; the yearning inquiry, what was the matter ; the childish confession, " I want to be saved " ; and then the eager, tender words about the love of Jesus ; and that warm embrace and crooning love, seeming then, and seeming now, though a lifetime lies between, the demonstration that in the same way God enfolds the soul, and none can pluck it out of His hands.

Equally vivid is another memory : the boy, ten or twelve years old, I surmise, listening to his father preaching (my father was the minister of Queen Street, Wolverhampton ; a new chapel was being built, and the services were held in a bare, comfortless Corn Exchange, with shifting and rattling chairs), and a vision coming in that singular temple ; he heard the call to preach, and recognized that in that activity might his own life ultimately find expression. In the light of that definite memory of childhood the call of Samuel, and the call of Isaiah, have always seemed quite intelligible.

But bitter experiences lay between those first movements of the spiritual life and the work to which they
pointed. I was thrown among boys at school who
opened my eyes to the shame and sin in our own bodies.
The heavens darkened ; conscience awoke ; I felt myself
a guilty, unclean thing. In secret prayers I wrestled
for pardon and assurance. I had a little sister, Annie,
my first companion—sweet child, she died of typhoid
in her sixteenth year. We, as children, had often knelt
and prayed together, and peace had fallen on our hearts.
But now among boys, in the discovery of sin, all peace
was gone. I seemed to myself degraded, and was often
ashamed to look people in the face. My head master
at Tettenhall School, Alexander Waugh Young — I
remember him with reverence and gratitude—saw that
something was wrong ; I know now what it cost him,
but he had me to his study and spoke wise words
of warning, quoting to me the words that the body is
the temple of the Holy Ghost. I wonder why he did
not tell me of Christ's power and readiness to save ;
perhaps he did not know it ; but Christ Himself did
what my master could not. The hymn we used at
that time to sing in the school-chapel—

> Saviour when in dust to Thee
> Low we bow the adoring knee,

haunts me still as the expression of repentance which
breaks from the soul in the first consciousness of sin.

In the Fall Christ comes. I learnt at the beginning
how the Kingdom of God is entered only through the
lowly gate of penitence, how Paradise is lost before
it is regained ; how sin enters and drives the prodigal
to the swine trough in the far country ; and the deep
meaning of life is the awaking in shame, the resolution
to return, and the welcoming embrace of the Father.
Still I stand in perpetual wonder at the grace of God
which lifted me out of the slough, which did not weary

in my relapses, but sought and held me, until I learnt the truth of Victory in Christ.

I do not think that any one tempted me ; the tempter was within. Rather, I remember boys, not good or pure boys, trying to save me, and perhaps themselves. The inwardness of our spiritual wrestle became familiar to me, and I found, long before I knew or thought anything of the Atonement, or had even known a question about Christ's Person, that Christ is not a Being who stands without, but One who effects an entrance into the secret places of the heart, and achieves His conquest there.

Even in those earliest days, before I was sixteen, the Spirit had convinced me of sin, righteousness, and judgment. I knew in my own body the horror, the sinfulness, the loathsome fascination of sin ; I looked out towards a righteousness which seemed unattainable, and discovered that if it was ever to be mine, it must be given me ; and Judgment lay heavy upon me. Though I never doubted the infinite love and goodness of God, I felt that His goodness must be angry with my sin, and His love, in order to save me, would have a sacrifice to make, how long, how lifelong, I did not then, of course, know.

I ought perhaps now to explain that I was born in the bosom of the Congregational Church. My father, as a young minister, had married Ellen Forman, of Derby, and had entered on a brilliant ministry at Tonbridge Chapel in the Euston Road. In a house, Egremont Place, which was demolished to make room for the St. Pancras Hotel, I first saw the light on September 18, 1855. My father's father, who had been a Methodist minister, lived with the young married couple, and I was told that he used to carry me about in his arms, relating to my unheeding ears the incidents of the Crimean War, which then possessed the public mind. But before I reached the period of earliest recollections the family moved to Reading. There my out that such a decision should be made at the age of sixteen, because if not made then it was as a rule never made at all. That also has been a guiding thought in my pastoral work from the beginning.

It was in my sixteenth year that an influence entered into my life, the strength and beauty of which it would be impossible to exaggerate. Among my schoolfellows at Tettenhall was the son of a distinguished Congregational minister, Dr. Mellor of Halifax. In boyish admiration of the head of the school he asked me to go and spend three weeks of the summer holiday of 1871 at his home. Every detail of that visit is impressed on my mind, for it all had a determinative effect on my life, on my religious faith, on the choice of a career, and on the development of my thought and character. Arriving in Halifax on Saturday, I went with some of the family to a large Temperance demonstration at Shibden Hall. My friend's eldest sister, who was called Rosa, seemed the centre of the party. As we sat on the sunny slope and watched the procession pass by—and a banner bearing the announcement that sixty thousand drunkards die annually attracted general attention—I looked up and saw that face, which from that day forward shone upon my life with a light which seemed to come from another world. She was at that time twenty-two, and to my boyish eyes seemed a mature woman. It was a very beautiful face, with large brown eyes, that often looked like the pools on the seashore, the depths of gleaming seaweed lit up by the sun. Her hair was very dark, and broke into little curls around her ears. Her complexion was clear and rosy. But the countenance was all aglow with pity for the sufferers whose lives were brought before her by the procession, with swift and radiant thought, and with a flashing humour, which gave charm and piquancy to everything she said. All this I saw at once ; the powerful influence of woman as the guiding star and inspiration of a man's life had flowed in

upon me, and rapidly flooded my whole being. The
next day, returning from a service at the beautiful church
which Mr. Acroyd had built in the town, she had left
something behind, and her brother went back to fetch
it. We two walked home alone, and as we approached
the house, Shaw Royd, which lay in a delightful garden-
hollow beneath a railway bridge, for me thenceforth
a place of enchantment, she turned brightly to me and
said : " I think we shall be friends." It was a
prophecy. Before I returned to school that friendship
had been sealed. Recognizing at once what it meant
to me, she told me that she was engaged to be married,
and that we could only be friends if I recognized the
nature of the friendship. This did not trouble me at
all. To have her friendship and her interest was all
that I desired. For nearly forty years, until she was
taken away on Christmas Day 1910, I had that friendship, unaltered, except that it ever grew better, undimmed and only strengthened by all the vicissitudes
of our mutual life. It was three years later that she
married, and her husband became a devoted friend and
helper. He has lived with me since 1902, and we
cherish together the memory of the beautiful being,
who to him as wife, and to me as friend, was the
guide and star of life.

She took me at once into her care and imparted
to me her interests and her tastes. She had brilliant
intellectual gifts. It was only in her later days that
she published, under the *nom de plume* of Mary
Beaumont, *The Ringby Lass, Joan Seton,* and *Two
New Women,* in which her passionate love of Yorkshire, her intense moral convictions, and her interest in
Italy, and indeed in all humanity, found a beautiful
expression. But in those early days she was already,
writing poetry for some of the magazines ; Dr.
Guthrie and Dr. Arnott were eager to take anything
she would send. Her father was a man of rich literary
culture, and her friends in Halifax and in Liverpool

had introduced her into intellectual circles not often
open to one so young. She was overflowing with the
interests of the British Association in those great days
of Tyndall and Huxley, when science was to be the
religion of the future. She loved sketching, and had
the most discriminating love of art. She sang, and was
sensitive to music in an unusual degree. Ruskin was
her delight ; Browning she forced me to read and to
understand. All the world of poetry, romance, thought,
and travel, art and literature and science, opened out
before me, and she seemed to move in it freely and
easily, a beautiful being acclimatized and regnant there.

But what made this great new influence so decisive
was that she had an ardent religious faith and deep
convictions, which made all that I had hitherto known
seem comparatively shallow. She had a class of boys,
some of them as old as herself or older ; and through
her teaching and personal influence they became
Christians and leaders of the Church. She had wrestled
with the early doubts which come to a vigorous
intellect, and had attained a faith which always widened
and deepened, but remained true to Christ, and com-
municated itself to others, partly by the singular force
of her reasoning, but still more by the charm of her
own character which seemed to result from it.

I can never sufficiently praise the wisdom and love
of God that brought into my life, at the critical age
of sixteen, this transforming and inspiring influence.
Her health was delicate, and the next year, as a result
of sorrow, it broke down altogether. I remember in
a room at St. James's, Carey Crescent, Torquay, going
to see her, that she might break to me the news that
she was going to die. She was on the couch, frail
and lovely ; and the evening fell. She told me how
she had wished to help me, and how my mother, who
was very ailing, had asked her to watch over me and
never to give me up ; and then she said that the
doctor offered her no hope of life, and I must resign

myself to God's will and let her go. She did it so gently, so persuasively, so magnanimously, that I left the house in a brave resolution, and seemed walking in an upper air.

She was spared. Thirty years later she and her husband came to live with me when his business had failed, and it was thirty-eight years later that I had to summon that early resolution, and grasp with all my might the faith she had given me, to let her go.

When I returned to school after that memorable summer holiday of 1871 I had a friend. The letters began then which continued without intermission until 1902, when she came to share, or to make, my home. Those letters and her influence were my constant help, and they were soon greatly needed. By the advice of Mr. J. E. Courtney Bodley, an old Tettenhall schoolfellow, who came to visit my father, I was sent to Shrewsbury School that I might be better prepared for the university. The life at Shrewsbury was a sore battle for me. Entering in my seventeenth year I found it difficult to adapt myself to the new ways. As a Liberal and a Nonconformist I was eyed with suspicion by the boys. There was an office in Doctor's Hall, that of crier, which required the holder of the post to prefix announcements with " Oh yes, Oh yes, this is to give notice," and to end them by the pious adjuration, " God save the Queen, and down with (it had until recently been damn) the Radicals." The genial spirit of my persecutors determined to elect me to this office, that they might have the joy of hearing me denounce my political friends. From this ordeal I was only saved by my remove, after my first term, into the Sixth ; sixth-form boys were exempted from election to the menial offices of the Hall. But that was by no means the worst trial. The school life was incredibly rough and coarse. It is surprising, as I look back, to realize how comparatively pure it was morally ; but it was at all points a trial to a sensitive boy who had been brought up in a Puritan home.

Mr. H. W. Nevinson, my contemporary at the school, has given in his book, *Between the Acts*, the most lifelike picture of Shrewsbury in those days. He was in Rigg's Hall, not in Doctor's, and therefore did not know the special customs of the head master's house ; but the picture, as a whole, is one of the best pieces of description I have ever read. It brings out the finer elements of the system which had been made by the classical enthusiasm of Butler and Kennedy. But there were elements of coarseness, humiliating situations, sharp antagonisms of thought and practice, which might easily have crushed me. My friend's letters kept the ideals bright, held me in touch with the world of high thinking and pure living in which she moved, and taught me to get a personal grip of religion, which began to be to me a sure refuge and strength in the practical struggle of my life.

A vivid memory abides with me which sheds some light on my own spiritual life then, and more upon the school and its ways—a light on the school not unbeautiful. I shared a study with a boy who was an extreme ritualist, and with one who is now a Roman Catholic priest. In the curious fervours of boy-life we began a brief service of prayer in the evening before tea. One after another joined the circle, until the study was thronged with a reverent crowd that joined in the prayers. This excited persecution, and one evening there was a throng outside the door that received the dispersing worshippers with scoffs and buffets. Something of an uproar occurred. Next day the head master, the Rev. H. W. Moss, appeared suddenly in Hall and addressed the boys thus : " I hear that some boys have been meeting in a study for prayer. The school-prayers in the morning and the evening might be enough. But if there are boys that require or desire more, they shall not be molested."

The persecution ceased, but, alas ! the prayer-meeting ceased too.

I look back on the old school with much gratitude. It was entirely owing to the severe drilling in classical scholarship, which then made Shrewsbury famous, that I was able to enter successfully at Oxford. But the peculiarity of the school was that its most famous boys, Sir Philip Sidney and Charles Darwin, achieved distinction in things which the school did not teach them. I am so far from the Shrewsbury tradition that the art of writing Greek iambics, which I acquired at school, did but little for me. I owe to Shrewsbury chiefly the antagonisms, open or concealed, which brought out all my powers of resistance, and made me realize that I must stand alone, and never expect to float down the easy current of things.

In the winter of 1873 I went up to Oxford, and sat for a scholarship at Corpus. I was not elected ; but next week the examination at New College was to take place. I thus spent a fortnight in the city of dreams, and stood upon the threshold of what seemed a golden portal opening into vistas of glory. New College gave me a scholarship of £100 a year for five years, and when that expired elected me to a Winchester fellowship, which I held, in accordance with the new University regulations which then had just come into force, for eight years. A year earlier, and I might have held my fellowship until I married, which, in my case, would have been for life. But, as it was, I was kept in close contact with Oxford life for nearly ten years ; what I owe to that I should labour in vain to express.

When I came back to Shrewsbury to report to Moss that I was a scholar of New College, Oxford, I think he was pleased, but his only remark was, " Well, one never knows what they will do at Oxford." He was a Cambridge man, and thought little of Oxford scholarship. Nevertheless, when he retired from Shrewsbury, he went to live, not at Cambridge, but at Oxford. So subtle is the charm of " our friend, the enemy."

But just before my election at New College came the first crushing sorrow of my life. In the first days of September 1873 my little sister Annie died of typhoid fever. She was in her sixteenth year, and had been my closest and dearest companion through our childhood. It almost broke my heart when she said on her deathbed : " Of course I know you loved Nell best, but I always loved you best." I had never weighed the love of the elder and the younger sister, but the sweet child whom I had loved with all my boyish heart slipped from me. On her bed was found a hymn which she had been copying out—

> When wounded sore the stricken soul
> Lies bleeding and unbound,
> One only hand, a piercèd hand,
> Can salve the sinner's wound.

She had written in pencil as far as the line—

> 'Tis Jesus' blood that washes white,

and there the dear hand had failed. But the little incident brought untold comfort to us all ; it seemed an assurance from within the gates of death that she was with our Lord. My mother had nursed her with untiring assiduity ; and on the following day, when she was broken with sorrow, she saw Annie come to her radiant and well, assuring her that she was very happy. My mother's grief was calmed, but she was worn out ; I remember flinging my arms about her and silencing some apprehension that she too might be going, by crying, " O, God will not give us that added sorrow." But she went away for a change to her sister's in Derby, and there the typhoid developed. We were sent for, and saw her in her semi-consciousness ; but we were not allowed to stay ; and presently the telegram came from my father : " The lovingest heart in Europe has ceased to beat." That is the fond illusion of devoted love, that the one we love is the most loving in the world. But whether it was my father's authority, or my filial partiality, I still have the feeling that no one ever had such a gift of loving as my mother had. She had a gaiety of spirit and a power of rallying her friends which brought sunshine into every society she entered. I thought I could never smile again when she died. But she left in me some of her own happy spirit, and ever since she has seemed to me to be watching my life and taking the deepest interest in it. Once only she had expressed the wish that I might, like my father, enter the ministry. That wish lay in my heart, and though it was for long repressed and put aside, it proved to be the most decisive influence in choosing my career. It left me also with a conviction, which I have never quite surrendered, that the thoughts of a mother, and the work to which she dedicates her child, shape the child's character and the development, and therefore, if a mother in prayer and faith consecrates her boy to the ministry, that will, as years go on, prove to be a call ; and if the mother has passed away, the call will resound with a commanding authority from behind the hills of death.

CHAPTER II

OXFORD

1874–1878

IN July 1874 I went up, with others who had matriculated at New College, to sit for the examination in lieu of Responsions. It was a delightful arrangement. We were lodged in College rooms, and we dined in Hall. We thus had our first taste of Oxford life under very favourable conditions, and there was an opportunity of forming acquaintances before we should come into residence in October. One friend I found then for the first time, Nathaniel Micklem, afterwards K.C. and M.P. for Herts. We drew together immediately, for we had both been brought up in Nonconformist homes. We found much more in common ; and all through our undergraduate life we held together. He was captain of the Boating Club in his second year. We rowed in the same boat, and we carried New College from the bottom to the place from which it afterwards became head of the river. We had a wonderful reading party together at Grasmere in 1877, and when we went out of college we had lodgings together in Holywell. We were together at the Union. It was my friendship with him which led, as I shall relate at the end of this chapter, to the decisive step which brought me into the ministry. I married him in 1885, and his eldest son, now in the ministry, was my bright and delightful companion in my Indian tour 1912-13. This, therefore, was a rich immediate firstfruit of Oxford life. But

the memory of that first July week in the university city
abides as a romantic possession, a foretaste, too, of what
an entrance into another world may be. I remember
the charm of the rooms, the names of the men over
the doors, the speculations about the undergraduates
and dons who would in October throng the College.
The Hall, with its high-pitched roof and stained-glass
windows, and the paintings of William of Wykeham
the Founder, and Waynfleet and Earl, and numerous
other dignitaries of the past in Church and State, filled
me with vague aspirations. Proud as I was to belong
to a society lodged in so stately a building, I already
dreamed of adding to its glory by my work and my
career, not knowing then that I should be called to
a life in which no earthly honours are to be, a life,
therefore, which would bring no recognition from the
College, which at once I began to love.

I remember above all the College Gardens in those
glorious July days, when the work of examination was
over. The great trees were at that time unfallen along
the city-wall, which formed the eastern boundary of
the garden. The glorious copper-beech was in its un-
diminished splendour. And the still summer air, alive
only with the rustling of the leaves, was shaken every
quarter of an hour by the exquisite meditative chimes
from Magdalen Tower, which led the tuneful choir of
the steepled city. Quickly the ear became insensible
to this recurrent music. But the first and most
permanent impression of Oxford in those quiet days,
when all the men were down, and the city in summer
glory could make its undisturbed appeal to the
imagination, was that of a modulated orchestra of
silvery and harmonious chimes. Deliberately as time
slipped by Oxford shook out upon the air her record
of the centuries that had passed away, her musical
acclamation of the boys who from generation to
generation had come up to haunt her quadrangles and
cloisters, and then had gone out to carry her learning

and her discipline, and the undying love of her beauty
into the world.

Over the wrought-iron gate of the garden was the
motto of the founder, " Manners makyth man." I did
not then know that the grammar was correct and
strictly Chaucerian, not because " manners " is singular,
but because " makyth " is plural. I had not yet considered that " manners " stands for " mores," and might
as well be " morals." I took the motto only on its
face value, and I found that a suggestion had sunk into
my mind, a suggestion which has run all through my
life as the primary gift of Oxford to my thinking,
that good manners, courteous behaviour to all, an easy
bearing, and ready speech, are the determining qualities
of life in civil society. No doubt William of Wykeham
meant a great deal more than this, and what he meant
I have partly learnt. But there on the threshold of
Oxford life was a standard of conduct, an ideal to aim
at. I was made aware of a long tradition of culture.
The two St. Mary Winton Colleges, the one at
Winchester, and this at Oxford, called New College
because five hundred years before it was new as
compared with Merton, came into my life, or rather
I came into theirs. The meagre streams of Shrewsbury
were widened, and I began to feel what the age-long
culture of our country means. The familiar story of
the American who asked one of the gardeners at New
College how they got so smooth and even a lawn,
and received the crushing reply : " You have to weed
and roll it for a thousand years," had another meaning
for me. I had hitherto been brought up in circles
which took little heed of the past, circles which
thought of England not as what it had been, but as
what it might be made by vigorous and effective
reform. That progressive spirit of Liberalism in which
I had been born and bred had entered irrevocably into
my blood ; but here came its necessary corrective. The
England, the country which I already loved with a

passionate and unreasoning enthusiasm, was the product
of long evolving time, freedom slowly broadening down
" from precedent to precedent." The storied past, and
all the precious memorials of it, seized my imagination.

New College—the delightful misnomer, ironical like
the obscure approach to the ancient gateway along the
crooked lane that bears the college name—with its five
hundred years of tranquil history, its main quadrangle,
hall and chapel and cloister and campanile, remaining
substantially as they were originally built (only an upper
floor was added in later times to the one side of the
quadrangle, and in that upper story I passed my last
four years at Oxford), the whole foundation with its
memories of Wykeham, his episcopal crosier, and the
injunction on the windows to pray for his soul, inspired
me with a passion for all the records of England's past,
which are to be found everywhere in England, accessible
though unvisited. In my journeys all over the country
during thirty years I have had an eye for the old buildings, churches, castles, manor-houses, or the quaint streets
of towns, an interest which I owe largely to the College
of which I was a member for those eleven years ; and
the love of England means for me a profound gratitude
for the past, a careful cherishing of its monuments, an
unwillingness to surrender its distinctive qualities, and
a conviction that the future of the country depends
on our leading her life on, expanding, deepening,
refining, to become the England that is yet to be.

I have no prejudices against other universities, but
I am grateful to be an Oxford man. When I went
into residence in October 1874, I was allotted a room
in the tower of the new buildings which Gilbert Scott
had begun to erect for the college along Holywell
Street. On that staircase Alfred Robinson, one of the
tutors, had his rooms. An excellent statue of him in
stone surmounts the inner gate of the now completed
buildings. It always strikes me with a new chill of
surprise, there ranked with the monuments of the past,

the image of the man whom I came to know when I first entered the College. Subsequently as the bursar he became the main leader in that expansion of the College which was beginning just at the time that I went up.

But in that room, overlooking Holywell, occurred a spiritual struggle which left a lasting mark on my life. While I was still at Shrewsbury, in my seventeenth year, I had asked to be received as a member of my father's Church at Queen Street, Wolverhampton. My mind was sufficiently turned in the direction of Christian life and service to make me enter at once into such evangelical societies and enterprises as existed at that time in the University. But I had not yet come to close quarters with Christ ; personal faith in Him was up to that point a name rather than a reality. But in that room, entering on the independence and solitude and responsibility of college life, I was brought sharp up with the question, Was I a Christian? Had I found Christ? There was no voice, no companion, no book, that initiated the struggle. I cannot therefore seriously doubt in the light of what I now know that it was Christ Himself approaching my soul. I was greatly agitated, and paced my room late into the night. My Bible was on the table. I came across the words : " Him that cometh unto Me, I will in no wise cast out." I did not notice the context. I only flung myself on my knees at the table, and cried : " O Christ, I come unto Thee, I am persuaded that Thou wilt not cast me out." Nearly fifty years have gone by since that crisis ; but I cannot question that there, in that room newly built in New College, at the very outset of my University life, a definite transaction between Christ and my soul took place, on which He has not gone back, notwithstanding all my lapses, wanderings, and unbelief. He took hold of me then, and by His grace, no one has hitherto been able to pluck me out of His hand.

The time when I entered the University was one

of great spiritual upheaval and consequent unrest.
Positivism had attracted some of the most brilliant men
of the past generation : Congreve, Beasley, Frederic
Harrison ; and though the religion of Comte—and its
worship in Fetter Lane, with its " three persons and
no God "—had certainly not gained a footing in
Oxford, its negative principle, its relegation of theology
to the first and lowest of the three stages of human
progress, had produced an impression that no one could
hold the Christian faith and be abreast of the times.
The sensation-philosophy of the Mills had captured the
schools, and though lectures turned largely on the
criticism of Mill's metaphysics, Thomas Hill Green had
not yet gripped the best men of the university in the
interests of Idealism and Religion. " Supernatural
Religion " was read by undergraduates, who scored and
underlined it to show how the old dogmas, the truth
of miracles, the infallibility of the Bible, the claims
of supernatural revelation, were entirely discredited
among the thinkers, and those " true religious leaders
of the day," the men of science. Tyndall had claimed
to find the origin of life and of thought in matter.
Huxley had triumphantly floored the great Bishop of
Oxford at the meeting of the British Association in
Oxford, and had proved conclusively the derivation of
man, by evolution, from lower forms of life. Thus
undergraduates in Hall sneered at the Hebrew my-
thology, and if any scholar of Balliol or a University
prize man was a Christian, and contemplated taking
Orders, he was regarded as a freak.

Not long ago I had a singular experience which
threw my mind back to those days of stress and doubt.
I was speaking at a Bible Society meeting in
Nottingham. The vicar of the parish took the chair,
and explained that he had come in order to meet me,
because he had been at Wadham in the seventies, and
he remembered how his set of men, in the general
doubt and agnosticism of the time, fortified themselves

in believing by saying that if Horton of New found reasons for being a Christian they might be content. When I heard this remarkable statement I was overwhelmed with the evidence of the way that, all unknown to me, Christ had kept me, and even used me, through the ordeal of my undergraduate life. The whole trend of thought was against faith, not only against Christianity, but against Theism. Materialism had a glamour, a kind of fascination, owing to the brilliance of its advocates : Tyndall, Huxley, and W. K. Clifford. Romanes spoke the mind of his time in his anti-Theistic argument.

The literary and artistic influences of Oxford were almost equally against religion. Swinburne, with his matchless though empty music, led the fierce revolt against Christ—

> Thou hast conquered, O pale Galilean,
> And the world has grown grey with thy breath,

was the language which pleased undergraduates. Or Morris was throwing a veil of pensive beauty over the paganism of the past, and calling his age to substitute a better paganism for an effete Christianity in *The Earthly Paradise*. The atmosphere so cleverly caricatured in *The New Republic* was the breath which reading men drew in at Oxford.

I found myself for the first time brought face to face with doubt ; everything that I had believed seemed open to question.

One of my earliest friends was Arthur Lionel Smith, who has lived to win universal recognition and honour as the Master of Balliol. In 1874 he was a young Fellow of Trinity. I had met him in Halifax, where he had been the tutor of Sir Savile Crossley—now Lord Somerleyton. He very kindly asked me to his rooms, and talked to me the language of Oxford. He showed me Arthur Hugh Clough's poems, and the picture of Jesus like a phantom seated on his tomb, recognizing that his resurrection was no longer believed in. I left that room in Trinity with the whole world giving way under my feet, wondering whether it was possible to think and yet to believe.

It is a wonderful fruit of time to live to see my friend, the Master of Balliol, issuing the Report of the Archbishops' Committee on the relation of Church and State, the brilliant and capable advocate of Church Reform, and to know that his whole life makes for faith and practical Christianity.

But as this new and difficult atmosphere had to be breathed, it was a singular fortune which brought my friend, I might well call her my guardian angel, to see me in that first term. She had married John Oakes, and they were returning from their wedding-tour in Italy. They came to the "Randolph," and for two days I had the joy of seeing them in my rooms, and showing them Oxford, so far as I then knew it. The brief visit enabled her to realize my life and its demands ; and the home that she and her husband formed at Lightcliff, near Halifax, later on at Southwood, and finally at Wood Hall, was my refuge and retreat up to the year 1902, when they came to live with me. Oxford fascinated her ; all the problems I was facing she faced too. As doubt assailed she seemed miraculously forearmed with weapons and arguments to face it for me. Never shall I forget one of the early vacations, when I had been sorely shaken by the weight and variety of the assaults on the faith. I was telling her all the difficulties, and she quoted a verse which up to that time I had never noticed : " If any man wills to do God's will, he shall know of the doctrine, whether it be of God," She had an extraordinary vigour and precision of language ; she was logical without studying logic ; and she spoke out of the experience she had gained in her own inward wrestles for faith. Those words sank into my heart, and became like a chain-armour fitting closely to the body. I got the conviction, which has deepened ever since, that Christ's doctrine is not established by external arguments, nor by an authority which guarantees Him to us. I had not thought it out then, but the principle was discovered which leads to the conclusion that Christ's doctrine is not proved by an infallible Bible or an infallible Church. But when a man wills with all his might to do God's will, he finds that the doctrine of Christ is of God. She taught me that principle, not on that first visit to Oxford ; but the few days with her gave me heart to face what was before me.

The religious life of Oxford at that time was to be found in Puseyite circles. Pusey was still living, a venerated and saintly figure. Canon King followed him at Christ Church as the friend and spiritual guide of a certain section of undergraduates. The Evangelical party maintained a genuine but feeble life. Canon Christopher of St. Aldate's was its most zealous leader ; Chavasse, now the Bishop of Liverpool, supplied the more intellectual and scholarly side. Christopher invited all freshmen to a missionary breakfast at the " Clarendon." It was impossible to resist his charity, his warmth, his love of souls. But he was a poor speaker, and very deaf, so that it was not possible to talk to him. Furthermore, the long ear-trumpet thrust to the lips of the speakers on platforms or in Convocation was apt to provoke amusement ; and when in a prayer-meeting after service he and the verger, who was equally deaf, both prayed together, neither hearing that the other was speaking, the amusement became serious enough to thwart an influence which in itself was absolutely good. There was also Bazley ; I think he had been a Presbyterian minister. His zeal was overflowing. He would stop the men as they streamed up from the river and offer them tracts ; he would tackle any of us with unfaltering courage and devotion. But he, like the other Evangelicals, seemed to present religion as the negation, or the crucifixion, of the intellect. And to be quite candid, the evangelical atmosphere in the university was stifling and unattractive. There was a daily prayer-meeting even then, which I attended, and in my turn conducted. There was also a society of undergraduates who visited the slums, taking with them tracts, which they exchanged weekly. This society I joined. I visited a street in St. Ebbe's parish, and later a district in Headington. It was a valuable experience ; there I first came into contact with the vice and the crime of the slums. There, too, I experienced a crushing rebuff. Calling at one house I was received by a young woman with a superior air, who told me that they were informed that I was a Methodist, and they were Church of England, they did not therefore want my visits. I did not go there again ; but I continued the work for years ; the incident only left upon me an unhappy impression of the exclusive and superior airs of the Church of England. I was a scholar of New College ; I was sacrificing my boating, and incurring criticism from the men of my College to make these visits ; they cost me more than this young woman could even imagine ; the Tract Society was a Church of England institution, and we visited with the full consent of the vicar. But the malicious and untrue rumour that I was a Methodist disposed the girl to give me this rebuff.

I did not give up visiting. Nonconformity had no recognized place in the university, and I could only get Christian work to do by joining with the Evangelical Churchmen. But it gave me an unpleasant shock. And the evil was deepened shortly afterwards. The secretary for the C.M.S. at that time was Knox of Merton, who is now the Bishop of Manchester. As he could find no Churchman to collect in New College I gladly undertook to do it. Going to one of the men to beg, I was met by the chaffing reply : " I don't mind giving you what I won at cards last night—twelve shillings." I thought it tainted money, and would not take it. But when I reported to the secretary, he silenced my scruples, arguing that the money was of the same value, however it came. It was one of the many things which made me realize the difference between religion at Oxford and the Puritan atmosphere in which I had been brought up.

In my later days at Oxford I attempted to teach in the Ragged School, which gathered together the roughest boys of the town. There I came into contact with youthful crime. I appeared before the magistrates to get off one of my boys who had been stealing, and I got him to a school in London. It is often a surprise to me to realize how my experiences even at Oxford were preparing me for the work, at that time undreamed of, which was to occupy my life.

One other feature of the religious life in my under-graduate days must be mentioned. As representatives of the Oxford Christian Union, Mitchell Carruthers, and, I think, Barnes Lawrence, and I, paid a visit to Cambridge. We were amazed with the far richer religious life at the sister University. I always remember, and have often told the story, of young Wright from Cheltenham, who startled us all with the fervour of his speech. I found that he had been a careless lad, attending his father's confirmation classes, and would come out, throw his cap on the pavement, and horrify his companions by pouring out a volley of oaths. But when the time came for the vicar to decide who should go forward for confirmation, the boy and his sister stood at the study door awaiting their turn to enter.

" What shall you say? " he asked.

" I shall say that I wish to be confirmed," was her reply.

" And what shall you say? "

The boy paused a moment and thought that some day he would wish to be a Christian ; why not now? And he suddenly astonished his sister, who knew too well what he was, by saying that he too should ask for confirmation.

" And you," said his father sadly, when his turn came to enter the study, " what must I do for you, my boy? "

Promptly he replied : " I wish to be confirmed."

" But when did you arrive at that decision? " asked the father incredulous.

" Five minutes ago, as I stood at the door."

He was confirmed, and the result was that zeal which gave promise of a useful life. He died shortly after ; but the incident opened my eyes to the fact that the decision for Christ is an act of the will. I had supposed that conversion was due to the operation of the Holy Spirit, a change wrought without the co-operation, almost without the knowledge, of the subject of it. Now I found that the pressure of divine grace on all human hearts is constant ; God's will to save is always there, Christ stands at the door of every one and knocks ; but the decisive point is where the will awakes, opens the door and lets Him in, responds to the infinite and universal love of God, yields to the steady, though gentle insistence of redeeming grace.

That experience in Cambridge therefore marked a very distinct stage in my spiritual life.

An even greater influence entered in during those early Oxford years.

The visit of Moody and Sankey to England roused a very general curiosity. My aunt, Mrs. Robertson, who since my mother's death had tried to take her place to me, and was my kind and generous helper all through my college life, was deeply interested in the mission. Her second husband, David Robertson, was a minister, whose health had broken down, and he had won her hand by a promise to help her in the work of Bible distribution on the Continent, which developed into the Association for the Free Distribution of the

Scriptures. With these two I spent much of my vacations. They took me to Scotland in the summer ; and when the American Evangelists were holding their mission in the Agricultural Hall, Islington, my aunt invited me to stay. Day after day I saw that vast throng of twenty thousand persons listening to Moody's heart-piercing addresses, or to Sankey's extraordinary solos. The great gallery of the hall was an inquiry room, and any one might go among the crowds of inquirers and point them to Christ. The scene was one which stamped itself on my memory. I took my Bible and went among the people. I was able to bring several distressed souls to the joy and peace of believing by showing them how the new birth, of which Christ speaks in John iii, is explained by Himself as simply believing in Him.

That great experience made me desire above everything, not to preach, for that had hardly entered my head, but to win souls to Christ. I had preached in the summer before going up to Oxford in the private chapel of my aunt's house, that Cliff House, Curbar, which she afterwards gave as a college for the training of industrial missionaries. And in the summer after, when we were in Edinburgh, I had ventured to give an evangelistic address one Sunday evening in the great Free Church Assembly Hall. I had also spoken in the High Street to the pitiable crowd from the Wynds. But it was not preaching which drew me ; it was the thought of saving souls by bringing them to Christ. The result of these early experiences was that preaching never seemed to me more than a means to an end ; the end was to get into touch with individual souls and help them to make a decision for Christ.

It was quite a new light when, many years after, an old minister told me that my real power was in preaching. Gradually I learnt that God uses " the foolishness of preaching " to save men, and that the ardent desire to speak to others about their souls was not the only way of reaching men. Even my aunt, who was indefatigable in speaking to all, in trains, buses, and by the wayside, assured me later that, while that was her way of winning souls, mine was by addressing large audiences.

But to return to the Oxford life. I had taken to boating at Shrewsbury, and at New College I was quickly enlisted for the boats. My friend Micklem deserted cricket, of which he was an adept, to help the College on the river, where it occupied an inglorious place. Together we worked to bring the boat from the bottom to the top : he was captain and I was treasurer of the club. It is not worth while expatiating on those achievements. Still in my study hangs the oar which helped to carry the boat up in 1887, when we made seven bumps in the eight nights ; and still my section of the victorious boat, the sixth thwart, occupies a corner in the room as a cupboard to hold my missionary books.

The drawback of boating was that it required me to be down at the river every afternoon, to row in the Fours, then in the Torpid, and then in the Eight. When I was not rowing I was coaching. I rowed in the Eight five years running, once, of course, after I had taken my degree. But this absorption in one form of exercise prevented me from knowing Oxford itself, and from entering into other pursuits while I was an undergraduate. I occasionally attended Ruskin's lectures, and heard him denounce the rows of ladies for coming, and the absent undergraduates for not coming, to his lectures. Occasionally I got a walk over Shotover or Cumnor Hill. But I remained for my four undergraduate years almost blind to the beauty of the city and of its surroundings, seeing only the river and the pulsing boats on its tortuous course striving for headship.

There was, however, one outside interest which gradually invaded my life. Without any intention of speaking at the Union, I was stung into speech by a

motion about the burial of Dissenters in churchyards.
A Bill was before the House of Commons to give
Nonconformists the right to bury their friends with
their own burial service. A gross scandal had just
occurred at Cowley ; the minister had lost his wife,
and when he brought her to the churchyard he found
that the place allotted for her was a rubbish-heap in
the corner. All the blood of my Nonconformist
ancestors was roused, and I made a speech in the Union
which immediately drew the attention of all the undergraduate world. I spoke from time to time, and
earned, as the *Undergraduate's Journal* expressed it,
" a unique reputation for bold politics and consistent
eloquence."

In my Union days the speaker who won the greatest
fame was Mr. A. A. Baumann, who, starting as a
Liberal, turned round and supported Mr. *Disrĕāli* (as
he always called him) against Mr. Gladstone, who was
rousing the country on the subject of the Bulgarian
atrocities. Baumann's manner was cool, imperturbable, sarcastic, and, with the exception of Lord Rosebery,
whom he somewhat resembled, he was the ablest
political speaker for a cultivated audience that I ever
heard. Milner was the speaker of that time who made
the greatest mark afterwards. He had a somewhat
foreign accent, and never struck us as quite English,
but his intellectual mastery was the prophecy of his
famous career. He would begin in a low tone, and
when the House shouted, *more suo*, " Speak up, sir,"
he would lower his voice further and wait until there
was silence and a breathless attention.

My Union experiences were not without their value
in opening my eyes to the nature of English public
life. When I was President my predecessor and
successor were Lymington (now the Earl of Portsmouth)
and Brodrick (now Lord Midleton). Thrown a good
deal into their company, I found out the slender equip-
ment with which the governing classes, by the weight

NEW COLLEGE, OXFORD, OLD CITY WALL, AND CAMPANILE, SEEN FROM THE NEW BUILDINGS.

of their traditions, could be carried to the highest places. I saw the men, *quibus etiam dormientibus* (to use the words of the upstart Cicero) *honores populi Romani deferuntur*. I think it was in Brodrick's rooms that I met Lord Aberdare, and heard him tell anecdotes of Disraeli (e.g. Disraeli, now in the House of Lords, asked : How do you like it? replies : " It's death " ; then with a long-drawn breath of satisfaction, " but it's Elysium "), and felt a little of the fascinations of public life, which began to draw me. I had dreams of going to the Bar, entering Parliament, rising to be a member of a Government, or to " shape the whispers of a throne." Mr. Asquith, whom I got to know in Hampstead, had just left a great Union reputation behind him when I went up. Milner was taking his first steps through journalism, and a private secretaryship, toward political life. I remember, too, meeting some brilliant agnostic Jews who heard me preach in my father's church, Bradford. " Do you know what we shall see you, Mr. Horton? " said the lady, Mrs. Hertz. " We shall see you one day a brilliantly successful barrister."

I do not now remember how those political ambitions died down. Doubtless a strong hand was upon me. The desire was only an ordeal, a test. But it is strange that all my subsequent experience of the House of Commons and of Government circles led me to think it among the greatest mercies of my life, that I was not tempted by Union successes to enter the arid arena of politics. It was, as Nehemiah would say, " the good hand of my God upon me."

Far more delightful in memory than the stormy debates of the Union are the Saturday meetings of our Essay Society at New College. As president of that very select society, I enjoyed, on the whole, the happiest hours I spent in Oxford. An essay was read by a member, while the rest smoked and lounged. Then coffee and muffins came in. This was followed by a discussion, and the president summed up in conclusion. I think I see Webbe (the University bat) start up in pious horror, because Cook (now Sir Edward Cook) had compared Shelley, for his passionate love of love and eagerness for truth, to our Lord.

" The idea," cried Webbe, " of likening an adulterer and a suicide to Christ ! "

" A suicide ! " retorted Cook, who had a curious acidulated heat in debate ; " I know that Shelley was drowned by accident in the Bay of Genoa, but this is the first I have heard of his committing suicide."

Then Webbe, hot and fuming : " I have no doubt that he entered the boat with the intention of committing suicide." The session ended in convulsive laughter.

In the New College Essay Society was the salt, the Attic salt, of college life. Never since have I found just that flavour of intellectual interest, of solid discussion, of serious aims, mingled with the high spirits of youth. Buckle, afterwards editor of *The Times*, Ogle, editor of the *Standard*, and E. T. Cook, one of the most famous journalists of his time, were modest lights in that high-hearted circle. E. D. Morshead, the translator of the *Agamemnon*, was an old member, who would revisit us and enthrall us by the brilliance of his essays. The essays I wrote for that society were my earliest efforts in research and in literature. I would give much to have an Essay Society in these later days ; in the future world I am convinced I shall find it reproduced ; and I trust that I shall meet there all the old members, even the melancholy Gossett, who confined his speeches to references to Théophile Gautier, or any other foreign author whom he was sure that none of us had ever read.

The value of Oxford life in those days was by no means to be measured by schools and degrees. Yet as an incident that side of the experience may be mentioned. I entered for Classical Moderations in the

Michaelmas Term of 1875, and got my First, but narrowly, my tutors told me, owing to some glaring faults of taste. I think the worst was that I translated the Horatian *luculentus* by the semi-slang word "fit." I intended to read for Mathematical Mods. after—for at Shrewsbury I had taken the mathematical prize in the Sixth. But life had become too crowded and interesting in my second year. I turned therefore to Greats. In that school of *Literæ Humaniores*, as it was in the seventies, I found myself. For Mods. no lecturer had impressed me except Bradley, the Master of University College, afterwards Dean of Westminster. He lectured on Latin prose in the College Hall, and on Greek plays, in a way which was but imperfectly rewarded by the appointment to follow Dean Stanley at Westminster. But for Greats I found some really stimulating lecturers. Bywater was most edifying in lisping about Plato, and the current story of his agnosticism gave piquancy to his lectures. "When I wath a child, I wath vacthinated and chrithened ; neither of them took." Pelham, afterwards President of Trinity, inspired me with enthusiasm for Roman history, which took form in the first book I ever wrote —*A History of the Romans* for schools. Courtney (now the editor of the *Fortnightly*) came back to Oxford to lecture on Philosophy, and as a fellow of my own College he not only taught me, but allowed me a measure of personal friendship which I have retained to this day. And, most decisive of all, I attended Thomas Hill Green's lectures on Kant, and came into close personal contact with him. Never can I forget his expression when one day he found that I had a real and vivid faith in Christ. His own faith was philosophical and ethical ; but Christ, as a Person, had been dissolved by criticism. "You are very fortunate" was his brief, intense comment.

All the reading for Greats fascinated me. At the College Collections, just before my finals, Alfred

Christ transcends it ; and to enter the Church of England would seem to me a contraction, a plunge out of the open air, where the winds of God are blowing, into a building with stained-glass windows which do not open and the musty smell of dead centuries.

The tour in Switzerland, however, had this decisive result, for which it had incidentally prepared me : Cecil Curwen's father was a stockbroker, living in Hampstead. There, though his health was failing, he had been deeply interested in founding a Congregational Church. An iron building was erected in the Willoughby Road, on the Carlyle Estate, which was just being cut up for building purposes. By the invitation of Cecil I went to visit their beautiful home, Westridge. Mr. Curwen, seeing that my mind was turning towards the ministry, but drawn aside by competing claims, conceived the idea of persuading me to come and take the charge of the nascent Church, which at present showed no signs of life, but only signs of failure ; the community, gathered by the earnest efforts of Mr. French, had broken up and melted away.

In January 1879 I was elected to a Fellowship at New College, and this opened a possibility of remaining in Oxford to do tutorial work. When, therefore, I was asked by Mr. Curwen to go and preach to the handful of people at Hampstead, my mind was drawn strongly in another direction. At the same time the family at Westridge fascinated me. The mother was an exquisitely gentle, but firm and strong, personality, who had brought up her ten children in such a way that they obeyed her slightest behest. Her influence over them was amazing. She had taught them Sunday by Sunday herself, and notwithstanding a great variety of character and disposition, they were all of one mind on matters of chief concern. The eldest daughter was just married to Mr. Eliot Reed, and lived hard by ; but the five sons and four daughters at home formed as happy and complete a family as could be imagined. The two

ROBERT F. HORTON, 1880.

eldest boys (my friend was the second in age) carried
their father up and down stairs, as his heart was affected.
The mother seemed to control the whole house with a
grace and courtesy which made an atmosphere. There
was gravity in the home, but constant cheerfulness. There
was conviction without harshness, and strength of principle without intolerance. After visiting the home and
preaching in the little church, Westridge remained in
my mind as a centre of light and warmth in Hampstead,
to which I continually reverted. And chiefly through the
attraction of this one home I entered into an engagement
that I would come for a longer visit. The College
agreed that I should be away for a year on the understanding that I should then return, and lecture in Roman
History for the Greats men. Naturally I should have
gone abroad to study at a German university, but I
was drawn by the ties that I have described to settle
down in Hampstead for a year, only going up to Oxford
for the College meetings. My uncle and aunt settled
down at Dunedin, Oak Hill Park, for my sake, and I
lived with them after a few dreary weeks in lodgings.
The whole arrangement was tentative ; the work at
Oxford seemed not only more attractive, but far richer
in possibilities of Christian service.

When I settled down for the year 1880, I was very
far from having decided the sphere of work to which
I would give my life. Here was an empty building,
approached by an unmade road, and here was a small
group of families that wished to worship in it. I was
asked to minister to them from Sunday to Sunday, and
I undertook to do so as an experiment, while I was
preparing for my tutorial work at Oxford.

But God leads us by a way which we know not.

Directly I began to preach regularly, an unknown
gift developed. The sermons came of themselves. The
people gathered round me eagerly. Their first desire
was to begin work amongst the poor ; and as Hampstead
was overworked in a parochially religious sense (Mr.

Hugh Matheson, in answer to my question, what could be done for the people, said : The best thing that could be done would be that all the Churches should let them alone for five years), we began work in Kentish Town, taking as our district Litcham Street, which at that time had an evil reputation. Mrs. King, who was the leader in this work, was a woman as remarkable in her way as Mrs. Curwen was in hers. George Macdonald was her brother-in-law, and she breathed an atmosphere of art and charitable effort which quickly drew around her a band of workers. Welford House, where she and her husband, three boys, and a suffering daughter lived, speedily became a centre of religious and philanthropic interests. At that time Edward White was at the acme of his great ministry at Hawley Road ; he had begun to give a monthly lecture to artisans, and the effort had been crowned with success. On the first Sunday evening of July I announced a lecture to working men. That monthly lecture has continued ever since. In October the worshippers, who attended the Iron Church, asked that they might be formed into a Church. From fifty to sixty entered into the covenant of a Church fellowship. Thus the year in Hampstead had raised a great difficulty. My work as a lay-pastor had developed, and the promise of success opened out great possibilities.

So strong was the attachment formed between me and the people that when the time came for me to return to Oxford, in January 1881, it seemed impossible to break the newly formed ties with Hampstead.

I was myself in the greatest uncertainty. I could not see my way. For three years I strove to do both works, though either was quite enough to demand all my energies. I continued to carry on the Church work in Hampstead by being there during vacations, which meant six months in the year, and by coming up on the first Sunday of each month, that the continuity of the lectures might not be broken. But at the same time I was in residence at New College, lectured in

Roman History, and prepared myself to become in due time the tutor for the Modern History School.

It was quite certain that this divided allegiance could not continue indefinitely, and indeed it only continued three years, because Dr. Kennedy, who had retired from his great ministry in Stepney, had come to live in Hampstead and undertook to fill my place while I was away in Oxford. But while I knew that a decision must be made, I remained wholly in the dark as to which direction it would take. For years afterwards I was haunted in my dreams by the agitation of that difficult time. I should fancy that I was in Hampstead when my work was calling for me in Oxford, or that the Church in Hampstead was waiting in vain while I was away at College. The matter hung continually in the balance, and inclined now to one side and then to the other.

I must now turn aside to recount what it was which made the claims of Oxford preponderate for so long over what were the far stronger claims of the ministry.

Oxford had become very congenial to me. Every visit I paid to famous cities in England, Scotland, or abroad, sent me back to her with a new sense of her loveliness. I began to know the secret beauties of her buildings and gardens. I went out to Elsfield, and saw her towers emerging like a lovely dream out of a bed of green foliage. I wandered with " the scholar gipsy " on Cumnor Hill, and saw the line of lights in Christ Church Hall, not with the effect of wishing to eschew the city of forlorn hopes, but with an ever-growing attachment to it. Often when I came up to London, and found myself in the Underground Railway, and even when I emerged on the breezy heights of Hampstead, my heart was sick to leave that leisured, cloistral calm, and that sense of the interests of a nation centring in its chief school of learning, for the confusion, the commonness, the obscure dinginess of London. My rooms in the front quad at New College, with the southern sun streaming in at one window, and the opposite windows looking out on the traceries of the Chapel of William of Wykeham, came to symbolize for me beauty and antiquity. I seemed there in touch with a great past, and yet looking out into a hopeful future. My heart sank within me at the thought of leaving it all for a suburb ; the historic interest of Hampstead had not yet touched me, and London had lost the charm and wonder which it had in childhood as the place of pantomimes and other shows. Oxford created in me a kind of nostalgia.

Then, as a senior member of the University, I found interests which were lacking to an undergraduate. All great movements seemed to seek Oxford for sympathy and help. Now it was the Co-operative Congress and the industrial leaders who came among us. Again it was Canon Barnett, advocating settlements and founding Toynbee Hall. Then it would be a bishop pleading for his diocese. All was full of interest. I remember Bishop Benson of Truro speaking one Sunday evening, with amazing eloquence, about his work in Cornwall. He implied that the Church was fulfilling her mission in converting the Methodists. I ventured to ask him afterwards if the Methodists needed conversion, for I had heard that, as miners and fishermen, they were rather exemplary Christians. He hinted that they were immoral, and that a " chapel case " was a familiar description of a scandal. I said no more, but next day I received an agreeable letter, saying that he did not know he was speaking to one of " another communion," and hoping that if ever I visited Truro I would go to see him.

Arnold Toynbee himself was in Oxford, and I numbered him among my closest friends. He was full of the Industrial Revolution, and was advocating a work for the workers which filled all his hearers with enthusiasm. I see the delicate pale face, I hear the cultured appealing voice, and I am always thankful that I felt his influence. We worked together on the Charity Organization Society, and tried to work the Charity and the Poor Law hand in hand. Phelps, now the Provost of Oriel, A. L. Smith, now the Master of Balliol, Arnold Toynbee, and I were the University representatives on the Oxford Board of Guardians. Well I recall entering the Board Room a little late, when Spooner, the present Warden of New College, was upon his feet ; we were just in time to hear him say : " The case of this boy came before us, you remember, *next* week." But that social work, animated by high ideals, made the friendships which last. Toynbee went too early, but the others remain, and a visit to Oxford still brings back the arresting charm of those early graduate days, when age had not brought donnishness, and Oxford seemed only the elect instrument for social reform and the salvation of the country.

Not only so, but my work in history promised to be a growing delight. As I wrote my History of the Romans, youthful as it was, a mere beginning, I felt that I should like to give my life to literary work. The publishers wished me to attempt a History of Latin Literature. And when the College asked me to prepare to be the tutor for the Modern History School, though I had only read for Greats, as A. L. Smith, who was only a Greats man, had become the Modern History tutor at Balliol, the prospect had every attraction for me. Freeman was still living, so was Stubbs. And John Henry Green was a living memory. I had a strong desire to work in that school and threw myself into the preparation with enthusiasm.

But what drew me to Oxford with a more imperative claim still was a religious interest which opened before me. There was a gap which, as it seemed, only I could fill. Since 1871 an ever-increasing number of men came up from Nonconformist homes. I found that in 1881 there were at the least two hundred in residence. Just at that time a rollicking Member of Parliament mentioned the fact, and said that these men came up to the University, became Churchmen and " respectable members of society."

I published a brochure, answering Mr. Collins, and invited Nonconformists in the University to come to my rooms. Joseph King, the son of my Hampstead friends, had come up as an undergraduate to Trinity College. He gave me loyal help as secretary. We formed a Nonconformist Union. Professor Bryce (now Lord Bryce) consented to be president. Mr. Acland was vice-president. We had the warm approbation of Jowett, the Master of Balliol, who was then Vice-Chancellor and the most influential man in Oxford. By his good offices we secured a room in the New Schools, in High Street, for a series of lectures by prominent Nonconformists. Dr. Fairbairn was one of the lecturers, and that was his first contact with Oxford. The origin of Mansfield College could be traced to that source.

The Union met twice a term in my rooms, which were often crowded. W. J. Ashley, now Professor of Commerce at Birmingham, was a prominent, though not always a congruous, member. J. W. Mackail, now the Professor of Poetry, took a tepid interest in it. And S. D. McColl, as a Presbyterian, lent a doubtful support. I tried to win the trust and friendship of these undergraduates. I encouraged them to remain true, through their Oxford days, to the Church in which they had been brought up, and I sought to show them the part that Nonconformity has played, and has yet to play, in English religion.

Before Mansfield came to Oxford and its chapel offered a spiritual rallying-point for Nonconformists, this Nonconformist Union had to do yeoman service. It seemed to me that I was called to stand in the breach, and I thought that in the course of time I might make the Free Churches really at home in the Oxford which I loved.

These, then, were the reasons which tugged hard against the call of Hampstead. And yet gradually Hampstead prevailed. The numbers in the Iron Church grew. There were 220 members. The building was often thronged, 600 people crowded into the space for 440. My friends began to move for a permanent building. The only site available in Hampstead could be secured by a syndicate purchasing a large plot from the Ecclesiastical Commissioners, just opposite St. Stephen's Church. Such a syndicate was rapidly formed, and the land was bought.

It was a matter of deep regret to seem in competition with St. Stephen's, a church which had been built mainly by Nonconformists in the previous generation. I remember Canon Mason of Cambridge coming to see me, when he had noticed my articles in the *British Weekly,* entitled " An Appeal to Young Nonconformists." I took him round Hampstead, and coming up Pond Street he noticed a large red Nonconformist church dominating St. Stephen's. " There," he said, " isn't that sad, to see such a rivalry among Christians ! " I had to say to him, " That is Lyndhurst Road, my church." His grief, however, did not prevent him, when I took him in to see the building, from kneeling reverently down by the Communion Table and praying God to bless the minister and the services held there. Well, as the only available site, this was taken. The most eminent architect of the moment, Alfred Waterhouse, was retained to draw plans to suit the rather unusual shape of the land. The money flowed in. In the spring of 1883 the foundation-stone was to be laid. Meanwhile my times in Hampstead assumed greater and greater importance ; the mission work rapidly extended. In every meeting of deacons or of the building committee I was pressed to come to a definite decision. One day in Oxford I received a memorial with about two hundred signatures, among which was that of Mr. Asquith, entreating me to come and undertake the work which was waiting for me. Mr. H. M. Bompas, Q.C., who had thrown in his interests with the young Church, argued in his peculiarly persuasive way, 'that if I wished to affect Oxford, I could do it best by establishing a position in London and in the country at large. The situation became very strained. The loyalty and zeal of my friends in Hampstead seemed each term more irresistible. Meanwhile I gave much of my time in Oxford to the study of theology. My first tutor in New College had been S. R. Driver, the great Hebraist, who became famous as Professor of Hebrew. He took a deep interest in my Hebrew studies. There was also a Jew in Oxford, named Piarritz, who had been ordained ; I took lessons from him. Pusey was still, though very old and infirm, lecturing at Christ Church ; and from that great leader of the Catholic movement in Oxford I got such help as his antiquated and prejudiced scholarship was able to give. I read for the Denyer and Johnson Theological Scholarship in order· to give direction to my studies, and though I only came *proxime accessit* to the two scholars elected, I got launched in that way on the systematic study of the Greek Testament, the Hebrew Bible, and Church History.

The openings for Christian work were on every hand. I was frequently asked to preach in Oxford and the neighbourhood. One Sunday I announced a sermon at George Street Congregational Church. The undergraduates, especially from New College, thronged the building. I had a project for preaching regularly in Oxford, and drawing the Nonconformists of the University into a close religious society. But this was not to be. The call from Hampstead became louder and louder.

In April 1883 Robert Moffat laid the foundation-stone of the church. It was the last public act of the veteran missionary, and his name drew a very distinguished company, who were entertained at luncheon in the Vestry Hall. There, the Rev. Joshua Kirkman, the Vicar of St. Stephen's, delivered a most cordial address, saying that the bells of St. Stephen's would ring in the two congregations. He was not able to maintain quite the same spirit when Lyndhurst Road began to fill. The story went that Bishop Temple came to preach for him one day, and as they walked to the church and saw the people entering Lyndhurst Road, he said : " You see, my Lord, where the people go ! " " Whose fault is that? " was the gruff answer. But we continued friends, and it has been a great object always kept in view, to preserve the brotherly spirit between the two Churches, which face each other as complementary rather than as antagonistic.

When things had gone so far, it was not fair to hesitate longer. With tearing of my very heart-strings I resolved to leave Oxford, and promised to settle finally in Hampstead with the New Year 1884, to be ready to take up with both hands the work when the church should be completed.

It was a curious accident, not altogether unfortunate, that an event occurred which gave to my leaving Oxford almost the appearance of an expulsion. I had as a resident don already examined in Responsions, and the next natural step was that I should examine in the Divinity examination which was still, at that time, compulsory for all who would take a degree. The subject of the examination was Biblical, but the Thirty-nine Articles of the Church of England were included, unless the candidate preferred to offer some alternative matter. I had myself taken the Articles, and passed in them. The Vice-Chancellor, Jowett, saw no reason why I should not do this piece of work in the natural course, although I was by now known as an avowed Nonconformist. Dr. McGrath, Provost of Queen's, who followed Jowett as Vice-Chancellor, offered me the post in the usual way, and I accepted, thinking that I could run up from Hampstead for the purpose, and pleased with the idea of still keeping in close touch with the University.

But an unexpected storm broke. Some of the strict Churchmen objected to a Nonconformist examining in Divinity. Opposition was raised in Convocation. There the authority of Jowett carried the day, and indeed the spirit of residents in Oxford was far from being illiberal. But the extremists demanded that Congregation should be summoned, that is the whole body of graduates. The tocsin was sounded, and the country clergy poured up in hundreds to save the Church. It was a storm in a teacup, but undoubtedly it was a storm. Canon Scott Holland and Dr. Locke (now the Warden of Keble) urged me to withdraw my name for peace' sake. The latter friend, who had examined me for the Denyer and Johnson, acknowledged that I believed the Thirty-nine Articles more than he did himself ; but he thought it indecorous that a Nonconformist should examine men in the distinctive Articles of the Established Church. I felt that to withdraw would be cowardly : how could the equality of Dissenters in the National University be maintained if a Dissenter might not be an examiner in an examination essential to an ordinary degree? My Oxford friends were courteous and reasonable, but I was deluged with insulting letters from country clergymen, which gave me a somewhat sad impression of what they called " the Catholic Church of England," which they maintained I was seeking to destroy by examining young men in the Articles of that Church.

But this outbreak of fanaticism had two results : it led to the entire abolition of the Divinity examination as a necessary part of the Oxford degree, and (a result still less foreseen by my antagonists) it gave me an unmerited prominence as I settled down to my work in Hampstead. The matter attracted wide attention. A leader in *The Times* brought my name before the whole country. The Edinburgh Philosophical Society invited me to go and give three lectures on *The Twelve Cæsars,* an honour bestowed at that time only on celebrities. And I entered on my work with the *éclat* which attends persecution and a violent contest. Unhappily there also remained in my mind a feeling of the intolerance and injustice of the Established Church, a feeling which I have tried ever since, with more or less success, to overcome.

The very day of the huge adverse vote in Congregation I left New College for good. Though my Fellowship, extended by a year on the ground of my service as a lecturer in the College, ran on for four more years, and that required me to attend the periodical College meetings, my long and happy connection with the College was broken. As a Nonconformist minister I was no longer of any interest to it. Even the Fellow whom I had myself had a share in electing, himself the son of a Congregational minister, changing into an orthodox Churchman, assumed the tone of a tepid toleration. When I went up in 1874 every one, from the Warden downward, tried to make me feel that I was received without any prejudice on the ground of my Nonconformity ; could it have been with the calm conviction that I should, in that charmed atmosphere, join the Church of England and " become a respectable member of society "? But when I went down in 1883, with my Nonconformist principles unchanged, and my life dedicated to the ministry in the Church to which I belonged, I had the feeling that the College repudiated me ; and though my relations with Oxford never ceased, I became a stranger to all in the College except to the porter and the servants, who remembered certain little efforts I made to secure their well-being.

The legal disabilities of Nonconformists can be removed. But no power known to man can alter the feeling which pervades the Established Church, especially in its stronghold, Oxford, that to differ from the Church and to seek Christian life and service outside its borders is not only schism or heresy, but a disqualification for mingling with polite society, if not for taking part in the life of the State. Burke said that he knew the political map of his time well, and was aware that the course he was taking did not lead in the direction of honours and preferment. In the same way I knew when I left Oxford to be the ordained minister of a Congregational Church, that the sunshine of social recognition and national appreciation was left behind. I took the step with my eyes open. And if sometimes, especially in reading Oxford biographies like those of Jowett or Principal Shairp, a suppressed longing revives, and I hanker after that atmosphere of culture, that centre of vivid interests, that open vista to the highest honours in Church and State, I have never had reason to doubt that I was led by the unseen hand, and was obeying the command of Christ who had met me so unmistakably in the room overlooking Holywell in my first term.

The first thing on settling finally in Hampstead was to arrange for my ordination. My father came up to offer the ordination prayer ; the neighbouring ministers, Edward White, Joshua Harrison, John Nunn, gave the addresses and the charge. My beloved friend came to stay with us at Dunedin, and gave me her blessing on the new stage in my life. I was spared the usual questions presented to ordinands, and was allowed to state, in my own way, that the whole object of my ministry would be to preach Jesus Christ—Jesus, His human life and death, Christ the exalted spiritual Saviour and Head of the Church. At that time, while one thing was sure, viz. salvation in Christ, other things were either unsettled or liable to much reconstruction, because they had not been independently investigated. I had been studying theology for four years, but I was not sworn to the formularies of any school. I had missed both the advantages and the drawbacks of a seminary. I have often wished that Mansfield had been founded in time for me to belong to it. But that regret is largely compensated by the thought that Oxford remained to me, a university, and not a wider interest dwindling into a narrower. I lost much, but I gained something. And Oxford had given me the methods and the habits of private study, so that I was equipped to work out my theology in a long course of years.

At that Ordination Service, influenced by the great example of Dr. Dale, I avowed my intention of declining the title of Reverend, and refusing to adopt a clerical dress. I think I expressed the latter determination in the form : " I shall wear no clothes to distinguish me from my fellow-Christians." An Oxford caricaturist caught at the words, and for long there appeared in Shrimpton's a picture of me soaring in the skies, and tearing off my clothes piece by piece. And underneath was my address to my flock, in the form : " I shall wear no clothes, to distinguish me from my fellow-Christians." That, I think, was the last interest that Oxford took in the work on which I now entered.

I do not now lay any stress on the refusal of clerical dress. But my innovation had one interesting result. A boy at the City of London School heard that there was a man preaching in Hampstead in a *red tie*. It was a curious mistake, but often repeated. He came to see this phenomenon. He was arrested, drawn to Christ, entered my class, joined the Church, and finally entered the ministry. He continues, in spite of impaired health, to do fine work for Christ. It is the only instance I know of definite good resulting from my uncanonical costume ; but perhaps it is enough to furnish a justification of it.

The church was to be ready for opening in the early summer. I seized the opportunity of the pause to make my first visit to Italy. My friend, Mr. Edward Curwen, who was already a deacon of the Church, and has continued in office ever since, was my companion. Full of the studies which had been necessary in the preparation of my Roman History, I found this experience of being in Italy and in Rome irresistibly absorbing. I shall never forget passing the Thrasymene

Lake in the train, and realizing Livy's description of
the famous battle. Siena, Perugia, Florence, Venice,
Milan, entered into my heart to abide. Notwithstanding
my dear friend's efforts to awake in me the artistic
sense, I had been too occupied hitherto to give my
attention to Art. Italy was therefore to me like a
new birth. From that time forward Art took its place
in my life alongside Religion, an interpreter of life,
a revelation of God. Subsequent visits to Italy, once
with my dear friend and her daughter, once with
Joseph King and Dr. Fairbairn, deepened my gratitude
for the work of the great Italian masters. Italy opened
to me our own National Gallery, and made me sensitive
to modern developments of Art.

When I returned, the building of the church was
far advanced. I used to visit the workmen in their
dinner-hour, and had with them many talks. One of
the men was a good specimen of artisan-rationalism.
I asked him to bring the things which he objected
to in the Bible, and I would try to answer the difficulties.
Next time I went with fear and trembling, for I knew
only too well how easily I might be floored. But after
a week's thought his charges were these : (1) that
the Bible taught infanticide ; in proof of this he cited
Pharaoh's order to slay the Hebrew children in Egypt ;
and (2) that it represented God as a liar, because
Jeremiah exclaimed in his bitterness : " O Lord, Thou
hast deceived me." This intercourse with the workmen set me to labour at the Bible with the hope of
meeting the objections of the Rationalist Press, which
at that time was more scurrilous, if not less active,
than it is to-day.

In reply to this particular artisan I wrote a tract,
" Why I am a Christian," the first of many which
the Religious Tract Society has published for me.

By July the church was ready for use : but that
opens up a new and crowded chapter in my life.

CHAPTER IV

TEN YEARS OF EARLY MINISTRY

1884–1893

ON July 3, 1884, Lyndhurst Road Church was ready to be opened. The building has been somewhat altered since that day : the stalls and choir screen have been added ; the organ has been greatly enlarged, and the keyboard brought forward into the area ; and an outer approach to the gallery was added at a time when the crowds made the egress too slow for safety. The large Institutional buildings were added only a few years ago. The cost, therefore, of the whole was nearly £30,000. But at the opening it looked very much as it does now. It seated 1,150 people. Dr. Fairbairn preached the first sermon, on " How amiable are Thy tabernacles, O Lord of hosts." Mr. Waterhouse told us all along that he could not guarantee the acoustical effects : he mentioned the case of two court-rooms in his great Town Hall at Manchester, built on the same plans, as duplicates ; in the one hearing was easy, in the other almost impossible. We were not therefore surprised, but greatly dismayed, to find that Dr. Fairbairn's voice echoed round the walls but was almost unintelligible. A sounding-board over the pulpit, and thick curtains under the galleries, which can be dropped, making the body of the church a small, compact, and very comfortable auditorium, holding four hundred people, largely met the difficulty ; the reefed curtains break the voice and deaden the echo. This, however, was the only drawback of the opening day. In the evening we had a memorable meeting. Professor (now Lord) Bryce, my friend of the Oxford Nonconformist Union, was one of the speakers ; Dr. Courtney Kenny, from Downing College, Cambridge, was another. But the speaker who left the most welcome impression was Dr. Fergus Ferguson, of Glasgow, who happened to be staying with us at Dunedin. He had a singular gift of impromptu versifying. As he sat in the church that first evening he composed some lines which he recited when he rose to speak. He pictured the future of the Church, and imagined an inquiry made of the angels who should be present at the services, as they returned :—

> One asked the angels on their heavenward way,
> " Was some one born in Hampstead Church to-day ? "

This messenger of God seemed thus to prophesy the purpose of the building ; it was to be one of which it should be said : " this one and that one was born there." In all the crowding claims of the next few years, this main object of Church-work was, I shall presently show, kept in mind.

On the first Sunday, Joshua Harrison, the honoured minister of Park Chapel, Camden Town, preached in the morning ; and in the evening I gave the Workmen's Lecture, which was by then an established institution. The subject was " A Welcome to the New Church." Every seat in the spacious building was occupied, and I remember seeing with pleasure in the gallery one of my old pupils at New College, who has since made his name as an historian, Professor Oman. It was a lingering touch with Oxford. That touch I tried to continue when our first literary society was formed, by asking my Oxford friends to come and give us lectures. I remember A. H. Gilkes, the master at Shrewsbury to whom I owed most, afterwards head master of Dulwich, coming to lecture on Socrates ; he made one remark as I walked down Fitzjohn's Avenue with him which has always remained with me. I was telling him how large a number of domestic servants came to the church ; one had actually given £5 to the building fund. Perhaps in the foolish pride of youth I secretly fretted that my congregation was not composed of intellectual people, and I had not then read how Stopford Brooke regarded it as one of the great successes of Frederick Robertson of Brighton, that he was peculiarly attractive as a preacher to servant girls. But when I mentioned the fact that I had very many of them, he said with conviction : " How thankful you must be ! " I was, and have since then been increasingly thankful. *Servus servorum* is the highest title that a minister of Christ can win.

Arthur Sidgwick of Corpus Christi came twice and lectured inimitably on Greek life. My friend, W. L. Courtney, who afterwards settled in Hampstead and was a frequent worshipper at Lyndhurst Road, came and spoke on Ibsen. Hereford George, of New College, lectured on Napoleon. Much later, another pupil of mine, J. A. R. Marriott, now well known as an historian and publicist, came to lecture on Jane Austen. In this way Lyndhurst Road has kept a precarious hold on Oxford. My love for both, the University which formed me and the Church which I was privileged to form, was the connecting link.

Before leaving the subject of buildings I must anticipate a little to show how the Church, as it gathered strength, extended its borders. The mission in Kentish Town steadily grew, until it was necessary to erect the large hall in Warden Street. Samuel Smith, the distinguished philanthropist and M.P., came to lay the foundation-stone. A deluge of rain fell, and it was necessary to keep him overnight. He amused me as he went to bed, when I asked in courtesy if he would require anything, by his reply : " Thank you, a loaf ! " A loaf was accordingly sent up to his room.

The collection of the money for those buildings was a very illuminating lesson for me, which I will mention when I come to speak of foreign missions. But at the opening of the new hall, Hugh Price Hughes, whom I had known at Oxford, and who was just then in the full tide of his great work in the West End, came and delivered an address which has never been forgotten. He told us that the people of Hampstead were going to Kentish Town to save Kentish Town, but knowing the perils of a suburban Church, he said that it was really Kentish Town that would save Hampstead. That proved to be the case. The demand of that mission, requiring nearly £1,000 a year in cash and a body of two hundred workers, was the making of Lyndhurst Road. All the capacities of the people have been drawn out ; all the forms of social service have been discovered ; the Church has never been allowed to sink into suburban complacency ; but it has recognized all along that her duty is to grapple with the social problems of London. When the buildings were finally enlarged they had cost about £20,000, and the generous way in which outsiders helped in that last effort was an evidence that the value of the social work was felt. When I ventured to appeal for outside help my letter was sent to Lord Winterstoke, who in earlier days had lived in Hampstead and occasionally attended the church. By a strange providence he was just considering what he should do with some money. He drew a cheque for £3,400 to pay for the larger site that had been acquired—and a few days after he was called to his account.

But while the Church was thus working in Kentish Town, it initiated another work at Cricklewood. The old iron church was transferred to that locality. Richard Drury Lown was among the workers from Lyndhurst Road who gave their strength to that forward movement. When a permanent building was erected it was called the Lown Memorial Hall, for this gifted young man, just engaged to be married, died very rapidly from strangulated hernia. But another worker was in preparation at Lyndhurst Road. Cuthbert McEvoy had come after a brilliant career at Cambridge to be a tutor at Regent's Park College. At Lyndhurst Road he heard the call to the ministry. He became the minister of Cricklewood, and under his beautiful leadership a fine church has been erected. I was allowed to lay the foundation-stone, and to rejoice in clearing off the last penny of the debt.

The building of the West Hampstead Church was not entirely the work of Lyndhurst Road, but £1,000 was promised to promote the building scheme, and the sisterly help of the older Church has been frequently acknowledged by the younger.

But I am describing the material works of Lyndhurst Road in her younger days before explaining how the power was gained for these and many other extended operations. The new church, except for the monthly lecture, was by no means filled. But the growth in the first five years was very rapid. Every church meeting witnessed additions. Sometimes there were ten or fifteen ; on one occasion twenty were received, and thirty were proposed for membership. Once, in 1888, after Dr. Macfadyen's mission, forty were received. But the members did not adequately represent the growth. The opening of the new church had been prepared for by a week of early morning meetings (from 7.15 to 7.45) for prayer. This became an annual institution. Ever since, in the corresponding week of July, the people have gathered morning by morning in large numbers to pray for the Church and the work. "Not by might, nor by power, but by My Spirit, saith the Lord," has been the fundamental idea. The meeting for prayer every Saturday evening has been similarly sustained. And my own irrefragable argument for the reality and power of prayer lies in what prayer has accomplished at Lyndhurst Road. That week of prayer annually, and that hour of prayer weekly, to one who sees the course of things extended over many years, furnish the explanation of all that has been accomplished. We know at Lyndhurst Road, and those who do not discover it never become incorporated in the life of the Church, that Christ in the midst fulfilling His promise and gaining for us the answer to our prayers has maintained us all these years and enabled us to do whatever has been done.

But now a further explanation must be given. Among those who joined us just after the opening was Ralph Wardlaw Thompson, who had just come to London to be the foreign secretary of the London Missionary Society. He kept us in close touch with the missionary work. Then a very remarkable thing happened. A Mr. Malcolm came to us from Union Chapel, Islington ; as an old United Presbyterian he was greatly interested in missions. For a year he sent me monthly Dr. Pierson's *Missionary Review of the World*. I became so interested that I took in the Review for years. The lesson I learnt from its articles and records was, that for the real prosperity of a Church, it is necessary that the minister should put the missionary claim first, and should keep it in the forefront of the Church's interest.

When I had grasped the principle I was subjected to a severe test. Mr. Malcolm was made treasurer of the Kentish Town Hall building fund. Strange to say, he came to me and proposed that in order to raise the necessary £6,000 we should for that year put the missionary appeal in the background. " But," I exclaimed, " it is through the Review that you sent me I have learnt the principle of priority : I cannot recede from it." He was silent but not convinced. I continued to press the claims of the Mission Field as usual. And this was the extraordinary result : the £6,000 were raised, and the building was opened free of debt, and the missionary subscriptions were increased by from one to two hundred pounds as well. That was God speaking with a clearness and emphasis which could not be surpassed by a voice from heaven. I suppose Lyndhurst Road has given something like £50,000 to the London Missionary Society, and has sent out about thirty missionaries. It is, I believe, the response to the direct guidance of God in this matter that has given vitality to our work.

But now I must explain how Fergus Ferguson's aspiration for the Church was fulfilled. In 1884 Moody and Sankey again visited London, and in a large wooden booth erected for the purpose in Fleet Road, close to Lyndhurst Road, they carried on a mission for three weeks. I heard Moody give the same sermons that he gave at the Agricultural Hall ten years before. The effect was now much reduced. But the memory of that former visit inspired me with the idea that the mission method, viz. the concentration of effort for the conversion of souls, with much prayer, and nightly appeals, and an inquiry-room in which inquirers could be personally dealt with, was most valuable. Its fault was, that in the hands of travelling missioners, it excited the people by drawing vast multitudes, and left a reaction, when the mission was over, which weakened rather than strengthened the Church.

Why should not every minister be his own missioner? I suggested the question to my Church. In 1886 I undertook, if the Church would help me, to hold a week's mission. I was only thirty-one, and had abundant physical energy. I read carefully Moody's addresses, and tried to get his directness, his fecundity of illustration, and his ardent desire to win souls. My people prayed much, and distributed invitations all round. On the last Sunday night in October the church was thronged ; and every night during the week I gave an evangelistic appeal. I took Peter's words in Acts iii, "Repent and be converted," etc. The six subjects were "Repentance," "Conversion," "Sins

blotted out," " Seasons of refreshing," " Christ Jesus,"
" The restoration of all things."

Each afternoon I gave a short Bible-reading, and
in the evening people came prepared. Some remarkable things happened in the mission, only one of which
I remember. There was a family in the church con-
sisting of three young men. I had found them reserved
and unapproachable. But one evening they went, quite
separately, to the mission, and the next day they told
their mother, each separately, that they had given their
hearts to God, and all joined the Church.

I never ventured to repeat the experiment at
Lyndhurst Road, but got others to come and take
missions for me. After the invasion of influenza in
1890 I could not command enough sustained energy
for such an effort in the midst of my own work. But
it led to one of the most interesting chapters in my
life, of which I may give a very incomplete record.
The report of my mission in my own church brought
me a request from Arnold Thomas to conduct a
similar mission at Highbury, Bristol. Invitation
followed on invitation, and though I could never manage
more than one in a year, there were very few years up
to the end of the century in which I did not attempt
a repetition of the Hampstead effort. I took the same
addresses and Bible-readings, which diminished the
strain ; but I returned after every mission utterly
exhausted.

The mission at Highbury taught me a lesson in faith,
and another in humility. Some saintly person wrote
me a criticism on my manner : I was too impetuous,
too restless ; I did not realize the power of the Spirit.
I thank that unknown critic to this day. One method
I ventured to adopt was to ask any one in the audience
who wished for our prayers, in order to decide for
Christ, to hold up the hand. My friend, Arnold
Thomas, said that such a plan would never do at
Highbury. To his surprise, and my gratitude, the first

who responded to the invitation was his own brother, whom he regarded with equal affection and solicitude. But humility came from another episode. Shortly after the mission, Silvester Horne, ten years my junior, preached at Highbury. A lady in the congregation with weak sight confused the two names, and supposed that I had come back for an aftermath. Her remark was : " How wonderfully Mr. Horton has matured in the short interval ! "

A mission at Sherwell Chapel, Plymouth, stands out with far greater distinctness. Mr. Slater, the minister, threw himself into it with all his soul. The students of Western College rendered yeomen's service. They took the college bell and went through the town ; pausing at favourable points, they rang the bell until a crowd collected, and then they gave brief invitations to the mission, followed by brief addresses on their own account. There was a very striking movement in the church, illustrated by an episode which is vivid in recollection. At the afternoon Bible-reading a wife asked for prayers on behalf of her husband, who was bitterly antagonistic to religion, and would never enter a church. " Pray," she urged, " that he may come to-night." After the address in the evening I invited all who desired to find Christ to rise and come to the vestry. The first who rose was a rough-looking man ; he walked unhesitatingly to the vestry ; God had found him, and he yielded to his Saviour. This was the husband for whom we had prayed in the afternoon.

These missions were very singular ; no two of them were alike ; sometimes immediate results were visible, sometimes the results only appeared after many days. Mr. Burford, a recent pastor of Sherwell, told me that the leading people in the Church were those who had been gathered in by that mission twenty years or more ago.

There was a somewhat similar experience at Dr.

Macfadyen's Church, Whalley Range, Manchester. He honoured me, when he was at the height of his great ministry, by asking me to take a mission in his church, and rewarded me by coming to repay the visit the next year at Lyndhurst Road. There were great congregations, for Macfadyen was not only a fine preacher but an ideal pastor, who visited regularly not only the members of his Church, but the homes of the Sunday School. But the shy Manchester people resisted all appeals to enter an inquiry-room. The mission seemed a failure. But on the last evening we distributed cards, on which was a declaration of faith in Christ. One hundred and fifty entered their names and addresses. And visiting the church in Dr. Goodrich's time I found that some of the leaders then were those who had decided in that apparently fruitless mission.

Another mission I took for Dr. Mackennal at Bowdon gave me a further impression of the reserve of Manchester people. But though I saw no fruit among the people, the letter from Dr. Mackennal at the close was one of the sweetest things in my life. His reserved nature opened and revealed a tenderness that was almost incredible. The simple addresses had gone home to his heart. In his subsequent leadership of the Free Church Council movement I was with him and understood him. He was one of the greatest men, though inarticulate, that we have had among us.

I had a similar revelation of shy tenderness when Dr. Bruce of Huddersfield asked me to take a mission at Highfield. The tears would pour down his cheeks as I was speaking, and when he saw his young men gather in the inquiry-room he overflowed with joy. One of those young men was named Carlisle. Intelligent and eager, he was sceptical, and disinclined to yield to Christ. But his heart melted and his intellect was convinced. He entered the ministry and went out to South Africa. The ordination was at Lyndhurst Road, and Dr. Bruce came to give the address ; it was carefully written and closely read, but it was by far the best ordination address that I ever heard. Dr. Bruce understood the ministry and its difficulties, and he knew the man through and through, and had watched with fatherly interest his development ; he brought the man and the ministry together in such a way that I thenceforth understood the value of ordination when it is in capable hands. Visiting Highfield, when Mr. Merlin began his ministry there, I was deeply grateful to hear him say that the leading people in the church then were those who had decided for Christ in that mission.

There are some happy recollections of missions in two other great Yorkshire towns. Because my beloved friend was a passionate lover of her native county, and because my father went to Bradford from Wolver-hampton, I always had a peculiar love for the straight-ness, bluntness, and warm-hearted loyalty of the Yorkshire character. One of these missions was at Nether Chapel, Sheffield. The men came in, grimy from the furnaces, and the message seemed to gather warmth from the pressure of life. It was there that I witnessed one of the most beautiful scenes of my life. A big lad, who had come into the vestry, anxious for salvation, was on his knees sobbing. I knelt beside him and explained to him that it was not by works of righteousness that he was accepted, but by the free gift of God in Christ Jesus. Presently the light broke into his soul, and he rose radiant. I saw a man standing near, who was his teacher in the Sunday School. When the teacher realized what had happened, in his joy he threw his arms about the young fellow and drew him to his heart. It was like the Parable of the Prodigal Son—the father waiting, the son returning penitent, and the warm embrace silencing the words of self-reproach. Sheffield was in those days a favourable field for Christian work. The people were unsophisticated and natural, and there was a warmth which even a stranger felt. In my youth, staying at Cliff and enjoying the soft murmur of the Derwent, the wooded hills, and the bold outline of the Curbar rocks, I used to hear of the neighbouring great town under its canopy of smoke. I thought of it as an inferno. But the sight of that young workman finding his God, and wrapped in the arms of his loving and solicitous teacher, seemed, and seems, to me more beautiful than all the glories of the Peak.

At Leeds, too, I had a wonderful time. The services were at Headingley Hill, where James Legge was the minister, and I saw there the direct power of the message to touch and win young men. Many years after Mr. Walters asked me to revisit the Church because the results of that mission were still seen. I was going, and the Church was prepared, and then Mr. Walters removed to Bristol, and the mission was not held ; but forty were received into the Church as a result of the *intended* mission, which did not take place. This proves what I suspected all along in these special missions, that the converting and ingathering effects do not come from the missioner, but from the preparedness and prayer of the Church. The most that the missioner can do is to stir up the spirit of seeking, and to concentrate the efforts of the people. His part, which seems most prominent, is really subsidiary. But an event occurred at Leeds which I love to recall. Each day at noon I spoke to business men in the Philosophical Institute. The men crowded in at the last moment, and were gone as soon as the address was over. It was impossible therefore to gather results. But one of those addresses was reported in the *Leeds Mercury*. Next Sunday, in one of the small towns near Leeds, a man, according to his wont, after breakfast took his pile of papers to wile away the day. He read that address, and it led to his conversion. When I heard afterwards of what had happened he was a member of the Church and had been elected a deacon.

But how much turned on the preparation, and how little on the preacher, was illustrated at Kidderminster. My devoted friend, Edward Smith, who afterwards wrote *Mending Men,* worked for the mission ; he and his helpers buttonholed the people in the streets, and brought them in. I was only able to be there three nights. But I learnt that forty were converted in that brief mission.

One other of these missions must be recorded. In November 1895 Silvester Horne invited me to visit Kensington. It was just at the height of his influence there, and I had the joy of staying with him for the week. He was a delightful character, full of a deep earnestness, which was not at that time veiled so much by his wit and his platform manner. He secured the Town Hall, and by his great influence he was able to get a series of professional singers to render solos. I recall Miss Evangeline Florence and Clara Butt among the rest, and some of the great results were due to that noble freewill offering of song. But the effect was very remarkable. Twenty years later Mr. Yates, the minister of Allen Street, urged me to pay them a visit, on the ground that the leaders of the Church were then the fruit of that mission long before.

I cannot forbear mentioning one of the strangest co-incidences I ever met with, which occurred at Kensington Town Hall. One night I had asked inquirers into the anteroom ; when I entered I saw two young men, one at one end and the other at the other end of the room. I spoke to the first, and found him an earnest inquirer. He seemed to find the light, and we prayed together. I went to the other man and had a conversation and prayer with him. Before leaving them I asked their names. " What is yours? " I said, turning to the last one. He replied : " Higgs." " And yours? " I said, turning to the other. He replied : " Whiggs." We were all, Horne included, to whom I told it just after, so solemnized by the spiritual movement going on that the odd incident did not produce even a smile at the time.

But I must now turn back to mention a great and beautiful influence that came into my life in the year 1887. The year before, my friends, Mr. and Mrs. Oakes, wished me to go with them to Norway, a new holiday field for us all. I was prevented by the illness and death of Mr. Robertson. He died at Ramsgate in the summer, a dear and good friend to me. He left me a generous legacy in his will, and some of the pictures he bought and loved hang on my walls. But better far than that, I believe his sympathetic prayers were among my best supports in that opening of my ministry. In deep sorrow for his loss, and longing to comfort my aunt, I took her to Switzerland instead of going to Norway. But in July 1887 my first Norwegian tour, the first of many, actually came to pass. Directly I reached Bergen I had the strange sense of being at home. Norwegian friends declared that in form and complexion I was clearly Norsk, and I got the settled conviction that I was descended from the fjord raiders who came to our East Coast, and settled there before the days of Canute. And at Balholm on the Sogn Fjord we found another Knut who became a dear and devoted friend. He and his brother, Ole Kvikne, kept the little hotel. He had been in America and spoke transatlantic English. Afterwards he was introduced by Edna Lyall into her book, *The Hardy Norseman*. Later still he married Miss Green, the sister of my old friend, Professor T. H. Green, the philosopher, and in devotion to her memory the two brothers built the English Church of St. Olaf's, and incautiously handed it over to the Society for the Propagation of the Gospel. But Knut Kvikne immediately became a valued friend. This Norwegian peasant was one of Nature's gentlemen ; he had a tender piety, and a delicate courtesy, that made him very congenial to our dear lady, whom he regarded with a reverential affection.

In a later visit, when the hotel had grown to a size which reminds you of Switzerland, and there were three hundred guests, there was a story going of a German who had gone into the office with the toothache, and asked Ole to halve his bill, on the ground that he had only eaten with one side of his mouth. That year Knut accompanied us, as our guest, back to Gudvangen, and at *aftens* I asked playfully if the story were true. "Oh yes," said Knut with grave sympathy, "the poor man suffered much." "And did Ole reduce the bill?" we asked. "Yes, I think," he said. "We was both feeling much for him." Still later, when the wife had come, and after one brief year had passed away, Knut put us in her boudoir, which he kept as a sacred place in the great hotel. He showed us her grave in the churchyard of 'Tjugum, across the Esse Fjord, and the tears stole down his face. Balastrand came to mean for us, not the scene of the Frithiof-Saga, but the place where these guileless men lived, the benefactors and friends of the whole district, unspoiled by their success, or by their contact with the commercial nations, the rich product of Lutheran piety, and the grandeur and loveliness of the fjords, the fjelds, and the braes. That first summer I threw into very simple verse the impression that Knut had made upon me.

> I joyed to meet, yet did not grieve
>   To leave him, for a sweet thought stole
> Into my heart : We cannot leave
>   One true and human soul.

> In covenant which cannot break,
>   By kinship older than the earth,
> True human souls for ever make
>   One line of lofty birth.

> When all the hills have passed away,
>   And the last sun has set,
> In God's great mansions these will stay
>   All undissevered yet.

I suppose I have met as great a variety of human beings in my life as most men of my age. But of all I have known and loved there is none who holds a more abiding place in my heart. One of his sweet words to my beloved friend and me was : " You have the same-way-feeling hearts." We included him in the company. Sad indeed would life be unless we had the assurance that we shall meet and know each other again.

> And we shall sit at endless feast,
> Enjoying each the other's good.

Norway completely captured all our hearts. We returned to it again and again. I do not know that I could go there now, without the beloved companion, who made the charm of it by her enthusiastic mastery of the language and the literature, by her books and sketches, and by her tender love for the grave and truthful people. But I learnt there what we so seldom realize in our own dear land, that the true aristocracy of a country is the peasantry, that courtesy comes not from courts, but from hearts, that men may be quite free from the love of money, and that a genuine democracy may be marked by real refinement and the noblest human relations.

It is not the grandeur of those precipitous mountains descending into the waters deeper than their heights, nor the exquisite iridescence of the light on the great bastions just swept by rain ; not the vast snowfields and the long glaciers blocking the narrow valleys with green walls of ice, nor the variegated flowers of the brief summer pying the fields and even the roofs of the *gaards* ; it is not the long drives in *stolkjaer* or carriole through pine woods, up zigzag roads, across the illimitable uplands ; not the deep, transparent rivers, rushing like liquid malachite down to the fjord, nor the fos leaping a thousand feet over the shelf of the tableland into the roaring chasm below ; not even the pleasant arrival for *middags* at the roadside station, and the new horse captured from the fields to trot us on to the goal for the night, the night which is never quite dark ; but what twines Norway around the soul of those who go to it capable of understanding it is the human worth, qualities which in us have been overlaid by our prosperity or our conventionality. The Norwegians always show us what we might have been, or even yet might be. We are akin, though so different now. We might get back to simplicity and courtesy and piety, we might learn again that money is not the true measure of wealth, but real wealth lies in qualities of heart and character which enrich human life and make living itself the chief good.

Norway worked wonders for me. It was like a new birth. In the weeks of the summer again and again I found all my lessons and plans for the whole year. I came back laden. In 1889 I made some notes, which show how the germs of thought were received in that pure air, in the quiet, and the happy intercourse of friends amid such surroundings.

After five Sundays practically without public worship (very often we were at places where the service, coming once only in three weeks, was not held), I have learnt to distinguish more sharply than ever between *religion* and *church-going*. Communion with God cannot be satisfactory on Sunday unless it is maintained daily, and if it is maintained daily the Sunday service cannot be regarded as essential ; it is of secondary use, but not indispensable.

In the long quiet thought, removed from the pressure of daily life, I have realized how our age is athirst for a Theological Reconstruction. The basis of Faith has naturally shifted, and the superstructure is one odd combination of eternal verities and casual accidents. One line has become clear : we need to base our religion on proved fact, proved spiritual fact ; dogma must in every age be brought afresh to the standard of experience for verification. The fatal flaw at present is that we suppose ourselves to base our religion upon a supernatural book, yet few have ventured to inquire into the meaning and the limitations of the supernatural in such a connection.

The long weeks have brought me a step further in humility. I see more clearly than ever that my own part in God's vineyard must be a modest one. He has given me not ten talents, but barely one, and that not very shining or unique. I must not expect or demand even so much as I have hitherto expected or demanded. I must not wonder if I work no deliverance in the earth, if thoughtful and cultivated minds turn from me disappointed, if strong men find themselves unable to learn anything from me.

I am not sure that I always returned from Norway with thoughts so just and salutary. But I know that I owe to that land of glooms and glories, not only the health which has enabled me to continue, but many of the inspirations and revelations which have come to illumine, my ministry.

But the quotation just made from the journal of 1889 obliges me to speak of the attempts which I had already begun to make by writing to influence the thought of our time. *Inspiration and the Bible* was published in 1888, and as it formed a pivot on which my life turned, it will be well to open a new chapter that I may give some account of it.

CHAPTER V

SOCIAL REFORM : THEOLOGICAL REFORM

THE eighties were a period of great industrial unrest and social upheaval. The Fabians were indoctrinating the people with Socialism, and the Social Democratic League was sowing seeds of discontent and revolt at every street corner. Coming from Oxford, where Toynbee was held to be the herald of a better day, I was eager from the very first to make the Church the champion of the people and the leader in economic progress.

> The Time's unrest an angel sent from God
> Troubling with life the waters of the world.

So I regarded it. *The Bitter Cry of Outcast London*, written by the Secretary of the London Congregational Union, Andrew Mearns, had stirred the country with compassion for the forlorn multitude that slept on the Embankment by night and haunted our streets and roads with ragged and hopeless figures by day. Henry George's *Progress and Poverty* had touched the conscience, if it had not convinced the understanding, of the time. Professor Marshall breathed a new spirit into Economics, and brought Ruskin's Idealism into the realm of practice. Every one felt that men and not money were the wealth of nations, and the tyranny of money over life must be broken. Many of my early lectures dealt with the social problems : the Unemployed, Social Wreckage, the Eight Hours' Day, the Housing Question ; and the eager crowds that gathered to listen made me long for a solu-

6

tion of the pressing problems. When William Booth published his *Darkest England and the Way Out*, I hastened to explain and commend the scheme. When Charles Booth surveyed London, and issued his volumes on Work and Labour in London, I tried hard to enforce the value and results of the investigation. I steadily urged that Christ's attitude to the rich and the poor, and His practical benevolence to the hungry, the diseased, and the outcast, should determine the attitude of the Church. We were as much bound to remedy the social condition of the people as to preach to them the gospel of eternal life in another world. With my friend Mr. Arnold White, who was for a time a member of Lyndhurst Road, I went to Medland Hall on a Sunday morning and spoke to those hundreds of ragged and homeless men ; on another occasion I went with him to the Home Secretary, Sir William Harcourt, who was credited with the saying : " We are all Socialists now "—and we took with us three typical men gathered from the Embankment, and urged on the Government the necessity of taking steps to put an end to this scandal of the homeless and the neglected in our streets. The more eagerly I entered into the situation the more I realized how little even the wisest understood the conditions of the problem. I could speak passionately of the evils, but when the remedies were demanded I became aware that no one could suggest them. I saw that the vague dreams of Socialism could not be embodied in a practical form, and that other remedies were partial, and at the best uncertain. But in the winter of 1889 I got the men who attended my lectures to form a Social Reform League, which met on Sunday evening after the lecture. Questions were earnestly, and sometimes effectively, discussed. And the League, before it melted away, accomplished two practical pieces of work. A Sanitary Committee was formed, which worked hard to get the law applied to the unsanitary dwellings of the neighbourhood. In the days before the London County Council came into being, and before our own admirable Council of Social Welfare had been formed in Hampstead, this voluntary effort was of some value. Mr. Snowdon Gard made the Committee a living power.

The other practical result of the Social Reform League was the introduction of the Adult School movement into Hampstead and Kentish Town. Mr. Allen Baker (now M.P.) came and instructed the League in the work of Adult Schools. A school was begun in Hampstead ; I went myself on the first Sunday morning and wrote my copybook, which was kept for long as a pledge of my interest in the movement. The school established in Lyndhurst Hall, Kentish Town, drew from a more populous area, and has continued to flourish and do good work up to the present time.

This and other movements which I began in the first ten years declined when my health began to give way in the early nineties, and when at the same time crowding outside claims, which must be explained later, began to tax my strength to the utmost, and to reduce my power to extend the home organization of the Church. Always when I designed a forward move came a temporary breakdown. When we formed a Settlement at Kentish Town, and three young business or professional men went to live in the house in Warden Road, I was myself arranging to live there, that I might be more among the people. A breakdown came, and I had to recognize my physical limitations.

However little this passionate desire to help Labour and the Democracy accomplished, it operated powerfully enough in alienating the rich from the Church. Hampstead was always a solidly Conservative district. Every time I pleaded the cause of the people the wealthy employers and successful professional men charged me with introducing politics into the pulpit. It had no effect in silencing me, but it constantly depleted the Church of that class which used to be the support of suburban Christianity.

If, however, I lost supporters because I advocated the Christianity of Christ, the loyalty of my people was still further strained by the course which I was obliged to take in explaining and (according to my intention) defending the Bible.

My theological work at Oxford had not opened to me the new reaches of Biblical Criticism. When Robertson Smith was expelled from Edinburgh for his article on the Bible in the Encyclopædia, so far as I understood the position I sided with his persecutors. The traditional teaching about the infallibility of the Book had not, for me, received any serious shock, and the intense and unreasoning faith of my aunt, with whom I lived, made me very loath to raise the question of the authority of the Holy Scriptures. When one evening in the Iron Church a man eagerly asked me if I believed in the Mosaic authorship of the Pentateuch, I knew Bishop Colenso's argument only by hearsay, and I had never read a book of modern criticism. I had heard Kuenen lecture at Oxford on Israel, and I was vaguely aware of the destructive criticism of the Tubingen School on the New Testament, that was all.

But this dogmatic slumber could not last. Directly I entered on my regular ministry I began a systematic study of the Hebrew Bible and the Greek Testament. The Revised Version gave a stimulus to that study by clearing up some difficulties and by showing how open to question the readings of the *Textus Receptus* were. I soon began to realize acutely the moral stumbling-blocks in the Old Testament, and the historical contradictions patent to any mind, undefended by dogmatic presuppositions, in the parallel works of Kings and Chronicles. My contact also with the infidel literature circulating among the working classes (" Saladin " then was at the height of his power—*God and His Book*, I carefully read), convinced me that the infidelity among the people rested on a view of the Bible which the best scholarship of the time did not support. Wellhausen's

History of Israel, Robertson Smith's Prophets of Israel, Archibald Duff's volume on the Prophets, Davidson's Introduction, opened a new world to me. I saw that the scholarship of our time, by applying the admitted canons of literary and historical criticism to the Bible, was not only giving a new and fascinating life to the Book, but also opening the way of dealing with the perplexing moral problems. As I continued my study I experienced an exhilarating emancipation. The Bible had been made to me a priceless treasure by getting rid of the dogmatic inhibition which forbade criticism, and of the dogma, for which there was no authority in the Bible itself, that the writings in the Canon were guaranteed against the mistakes and limitations to which all writings, however old and venerable, are liable. Reuss's History of the Canon showed me how precarious and late the settlement of the Canon had been. Directly the baselessness of the traditional dogma was revealed, I felt that the problem of our time was to shift the authority of the Bible from this crumbling basis to the indisputable quality and power of the literature itself.

I had no thought of discrediting the Bible. Quite the contrary, I felt that I was defending it from the assaults of infidelity, which acquired all their force from an erroneous conception of what the inspiration of the Bible was. Partly from the necessity of being quite honest, but still more in the belief that I was offering needed help to my own people, I gave in 1887 a series of addresses, explaining what Inspiration of Scripture means, as we discover it from the study of the Scriptures themselves.

At that time Mrs. Carus Wilson, the widow of a clergyman, and her daughter (now Mrs. Flint), were staying in Hampstead. Brought up in the orthodoxy of Church Evangelicalism, they found these addresses an extraordinary help and relief. They urged me to publish them in a book, I sat down and began to write them out. My old friend and tutor, Professor Driver, by this time recognized as the greatest authority on the Hebrew Bible in the country, most kindly read and criticized my MS. In this way I was assured that I had said nothing which was not approved by the best, most cautious, and most reverent scholarship of our time. This was why all the wild and frenzied assailants of the book were never able to point out any specific mistake in it. The invulnerability was what excited the fierce temper of the unreasoning orthodoxy of the day. But when the book was written, it was another matter to get it published. I was not known as an author or a theologian. Dr. Robertson Nicoll had invited my co-operation in the starting of the *British Weekly*, and I had written articles for him which were republished. I therefore turned to him, and offered the MS. to be published by Hodder & Stoughton. He was not prepared to face the peril of publishing a book which might shock the orthodox ; probably he had been too occupied with journalism and current literature to follow the course of Biblical scholarship ; in any case, with all kindness and courtesy he refused to take the book.

Then my friend Joseph King, who as a theological student himself, and an active member of Lyndhurst Road, was deeply interested in the venture, introduced me to Mr. Fisher Unwin. He was willing to publish the book at my expense. I think I paid him £40, which was, of course, repaid when the royalties began to come in. This was the only book I ever published at my own expense. The many that followed, more than forty in number, were all asked for by publishers. Not till 1915, when I wished to publish my book, *Reconstruction: a Help to Doubters*, during the war, was I forced again to seek a publisher. I was grateful then to James Clarke & Co., who had published many things for me in the interim, for undertaking the precarious venture.

But to return to 1888, when *Inspiration and the Bible* saw the light, it met with a very appreciative reception from a few scholars, who were hoping for a restatement

of the question of the authority of the Bible, and saw in
the book an opportune utterance. But the reason why
few were willing to undertake the task was plain from
the excitement which was occasioned in the religious
world. A fierce storm seemed to break from all sides
at once. I had been asked to preach the sermon for
the Baptist Union ; immediately the Secretary had the
difficult task of asking me to cancel the engagement.
I think it was not till twenty years after that I fulfilled
the engagement and preached for the Union at Huddersfield. This was the first sign of the storm which was
coming. Whether my assailants read the book or not
I could never tell. If they were reasonable, and in
any sense seekers after truth, I used to say to them :
" Well, point me out any mistakes and I will immediately
correct them or withdraw the book." Never on any
occasion could I get any one to render me the service
of a useful criticism. It was all wild, unreasoning,
fanatical denunciation. The orthodoxy of the eighties
was no longer defended by the intellect or the sanctity
of the Church ; it was left to the charge of those who
had not studied and were incapable of seeing the point
at issue. Dr. Parker, who lived near me, and was a
kind and appreciative friend, supposed that he was answering my book by publishing *None Like It*. It seems
presumptuous to say that the author of *The People's Bible*
was unacquainted with the work of Biblical scholarship,
but his book betrayed no knowledge of it. Because the
Bible is, as I for one allowed as unreservedly as he
did, a perfectly unique treasure as the vehicle of the
supreme revelation of God, he seemed to think that the
traditional view of its provenance must be maintained
at all costs. He thought, as the older generation had
thought, that the Bible was not able to assert its own
authority unless it were prefaced by a dogma to this
effect : " This collection of writings from Genesis to
Revelation is written by God, through the medium of
the ' sacred penmen,' and therefore every statement in

it is necessarily correct, and every opinion or judgment
in it is of binding authority." To raise the question,
But on what foundation does that preliminary dogma
rest? roused the orthodox of that time to a kind of
frenzy. They lashed out, they denounced, they called
the daring questioner a unitarian, an atheist, the worst
enemy of Christ. The reason of the fury became very
clear to me as time went on ; the dogma had no foundation. The Church had never formulated it, nor was
it derived from the Bible itself, except by the most
palpable wresting of two, or at the most three, scattered
texts. The dogma had crept in, unquestioned, in the
days when the infallibility of the Church was finally
disproved, and it became necessary to find another infallibility to take its place, the days in which no impartial
and searching inquiry had been made into the dates and
authorship of the Biblical literature. The opposition
was simple obscurantism.

Mr. Spurgeon was just then highly incensed against
the Down Grade theologians as he called them.
I was now included in their number. Such was
the fame and deserved authority of the great preacher,
that to lie under his censure was to forfeit the ear of by
far the larger proportion of evangelical Christians. In
later years I have formed an ever-increasing appreciation of the value of Spurgeon's sermons ; their freshness
and power, their concentration on the one end of bringing
men to Christ, their number and never failing interest,
set them amongst the greatest homiletical productions
in the world. I should not be surprised if Spurgeon
should be finally ranked with Chrysostom, Bossuet, Liddon,
in the very front of the masters of the Christian pulpit.
But the limitations of his mind are obvious from the
very fact that he continued all his life to preach absolute
predestination, and yet to offer to every one a free
salvation through faith in Christ.

One day I went to hear him in Exeter Hall uttering
one of his eloquent diatribes against the Down Grade

preachers, of whom in my humble way I was one. " If any man preach any other Gospel than that is preached, let him be anathema," meant, I found, that if any one took a different view of the Christian Gospel from that which Spurgeon took he was accursed. The rich mellow voice, the obvious sincerity, the religious fervour, the flashes of wit, made the whole address impressive. But it was a sad performance all the same. Afterwards I found myself at lunch by a young minister, who was one of Spurgeon's own students ; I asked him his opinion of the manifesto, and he told me that he thought it deplorable. Nothing is more pathetic than to see zeal, sincerity, Christian integrity enlisted in the cause of obscurantism. It seemed to me that there was a kindly providence in the removal of the great preacher shortly after, that he might be spared the sorrow, after a life of service in the cause of the Gospel and of humanity, of being numbered amongst the Lucifugæ, who fight against truth.

It was a curious fact, that when my father began his ministry in London in 1854, Spurgeon was the great sensation of the religious world, and my mother, newly married, was to be introduced to him. " And you," he said, " are one of the young ladies who wish to be introduced to me, are you? " My mother, who was a high-spirited girl, and intensely disliked bad manners, turned quietly away and declined the introduction. And just at the end of his life Spurgeon, a very different and much chastened man, was engaged in denouncing her son, who had undertaken the unpopular cause of explaining the claims of the Bible.

When my book was published there was a well-known evangelist in London who was a brave advocate of purity and a devout believer in the Bible. Without any education or knowledge of theological questions, he entered the field against me, and published a book full of crudities and errors, not only tearing my book to pieces, but overwhelming the author with ridicule and obloquy. He was well known, and I was practically unknown. His work was approved, and mine was in its infancy. While his book was of no value in itself, it succeeded in raising a prejudice against me, and in sowing suspicions in the minds of those who would have been my best supporters. I refrain from perpetuating the name of my opponent, just as at the time I did not think it worth while to enter the sordid arena by arguing with him. But he made my path thorny for many years. Parker and Spurgeon, however misguided, were high-minded and noble critics. But the coarse nature that throws mud cannot be touched, and yet some of his mud always sticks.

Members of my Church came to resign ; not caring to search into the question, they accepted the judgment of my ignorant critics, and believed that I was repudiating the Christian faith. I recall—and the pain of it comes back as I do so—two devoted women, mother and daughter, who came to see me, strung up by prayer and mutual exhortation to do their difficult duty. The elder woman was a tall, straight, strong-minded Amazon ; her daughter, equally tall, was beautiful and zealous, with the light of fanaticism always lurking in her eyes. The two entered my drawing-room and began at once to appeal to me in the name of my mother to recant my heresy and to withdraw my book. " But," I said, " it is from my mother that I get the love of truth which led me to publish it, and if she were alive she would be my stoutest supporter." Then the attack changed its face. " Why will you not be content to preach the Gospel, as you have done, without assailing the Bible? Look at Mr. Spurgeon and his great success ! " " But," I replied, " it is the wrong and indefensible view of the Bible which nullifies the preaching of the Gospel by exciting unbelief in the minds of the people. Only by recognizing what the Bible is can we see truly what the Gospel is. And though Mr. Spurgeon is a unique preacher, do you realize that South London, where he has worked all his life, is, broadly speaking, sunk in indifference ; Christianity is not even in possession, as a distinguished prelate has recently said." It was of no use, arguments fell in vain upon the triple mail of fanaticism, zeal, and sincerity. My friends left the room and the Church and I saw them no more.

But what rendered my position a veritable crucifixion was that my foes were they of my own household. Since my uncle's death my aunt and I continued to live together, and in January 1889 we moved into the house with the singular name of Chesils, which I have occupied ever since. We took it for six months because no other place was available. But her blindness, which was already beginning, made me unwilling to move when she had become familiar with the house, and then the rush of life made such a detail as where to live irrelevant ; finally, the dear presence of my best friend changed the whole atmosphere and character of the place. And thus, if the house holds together, I suppose that, notwithstanding its inconvenience and artistic solecisms, I shall remain here till the end, and die in the house where my aunt died in 1902, and my beloved friend died in 1910. The place where our best loved die becomes sacred, a house of God, a gate of heaven : there we see them vanish into light, and we cannot bear to leave the spot where the gates opened.

My aunt was an Evangelical of the Plymouth Brethren type. Her whole life was occupied in circulating the Scriptures, and in seeking by personal conversations to win souls to Christ. I am not sure that she ever read *Inspiration and the Bible* ; if she read anything it would be Dr. Grattan Guinness's *Approaching End of the Age*, or some work on the Premillennial Advent. Moreover, her sight was giving way, and she wanted what was left of it for her ceaseless writing on behalf of The Association for the Free Distribution of the Scriptures ; but her Plymouth friends assured her that my book was not on the right lines ; with unspeakable sorrow she counted me a heretic.

Partly owing to her failing sight, but chiefly owing to this credal alienation, she ceased even to attend the church. She did her very best to rejoice in such success as attended my ministry, and never, I know, lost her personal affection ; but there was a strain which only death relieved. I was forced to pursue my way with this sorrowful sense of cleavage in my own house. As book after book came out, and blessing after blessing fell on the Church, she accepted the situation more resignedly. But I fear she suffered acutely. She made her blindness an excuse for being away, attempting various methods of faith-cure. And when my eldest sister, whom I had the privilege of maintaining as a missionary in India, was obliged to be at home owing to failure of health, my aunt took that opportunity also to be much away. Indeed, I must (so unwillingly) have spoiled her home, certainly I had spoiled my own. And yet there stood I : I could no other.

And now I must pause to review this publication of a book which was so great a stone of stumbling to many, and so slight a cause of satisfaction to myself. I was driven to speak out by the sense of truth, I was convinced that to go on preaching, without declaring my position on this fundamental question, would vitiate my whole ministry. There was nothing for it but to say what was in me in supreme disregard of consequences. As always, my beloved friend was my one refuge and my most unfailing helper. She used to tell me that I was called to be a pioneer, and the ways of pioneers are always rough. She followed my work with intense sympathy and appreciation. She saw that, notwithstanding the outcry of the religious world, I was not an iconoclast, but was, in my own view, standing up for the Gospel of Christ, and liberating it from some hindrances which obstructed its progress.

I owe it to her chiefly if I was not alienated from the religious world which seemed so prejudiced and unjust, and continued to work cheerfully in my Church, notwithstanding the alienated affections of many. Our holidays were times of recuperation. I always returned from them forearmed against all the assaults of enemies and the betrayals of luke-warm friends.

There was one other help which I may gratefully record. *The Independent,* or denominational newspaper, was at that time in the hands of Mr. Herbert Stead, who afterwards made the great settlement at Walworth, called Browning Hall, and initiated Old Age Pensions and other noble schemes for the social uplift of the people. As editor of the paper he was to me a loyal friend. Himself an advanced scholar, he was able to appraise my work, and he delighted to accustom his readers to accept the new and truer views of the Bible by pointing out that the Biblical critic was also a prominent missioner. When Mr. Stead gave up the paper it fell into very different hands, and for many years I had the bitter chagrin of seeing my books treated with suspicion by the organ of my own denomination. If I wrote on questions of criticism, the review was put into the hands of some extravagant critic, who brings discredit, by exaggeration, on the work of Biblical scholarship. If I published books on the Trinity or the Atonement, the reviews were put into the hands of those who rejected and ridiculed those great fundamental truths of Christianity. My own experience of a denominational paper led me to think that papers like the *Christian World* or the *British Weekly* are more serviceable to a denomination than an organ devoted entirely to its interests. I know what the *Freeman* did once for the Baptists, and what the *Methodist Times,* in Hugh Price Hughes's hands, did for the Church which he loved. But Congregationalism was better served by the *Nonconformist,* under Edward Miall, than it has been by strictly denominational papers. No editor is equal to the task of writing and leading societies so varied and free as the Congregational Churches. And the paper, in order to live, must fill its columns with the pettinesses and personalities which please the lower elements in the Churches.

The reception given to *Inspiration and the Bible* was certainly not encouraging. But in looking back upon it I cannot doubt that I was obliged to publish it by that Power which directs our lives and arranges each piece of the mosaic. For, in the first place, I have met an extraordinary number of people in the last thirty years who have said to me something of this sort : " I came across your book just when I was beginning to think, and feeling the difficulties of the Bible ; my faith was saved by the truth I learnt from you." And perhaps better even than these very numerous testimonies, the young student, now a minister, who was my companion in India, discussing with me the various problems which occupied his mind, never, I noticed, referred to the difficulty of understanding the Bible. The questions which disturbed students in my early days had evidently been settled and were no longer disturbing. When I commented on this one day, he said : " No, I was brought up on *Inspiration and the Bible,* and therefore I never had difficulties on that subject." That is the justification of the book ; it brought obloquy to the author, but help to the reader. I do not therefore regret it. If I had kept it back for ten years it would have excited no such antipathy, for by that time already the scholarly view of the Bible had become widely diffused. Professor G. A. Smith in his famous *Isaiah* showed how the dreaded criticism which orthodoxy was denouncing gave new life and power to the Old Testament. And when in 1891 Professor Driver, my old tutor and master in Hebrew, published his *Introduction to the Literature of the Old Testament,* the whole situation was altered. The way of regarding the Bible, which in 1888 seemed to ignorance revolutionary and heretical, in 1891 was recognized as the result of a cautious and reverent admission of facts which could not be disputed. The extravagances of critics, especially of German and Dutch critics, have prevented the Church as a whole from acknowledging its debt to modern scholarship, but sober criticism has now finally taken its place as the only criterion by which we are to know *what that Book,* which we as Christians accept as the final court of appeal and the authoritative law-book of our religion, as literature is.

The effect of criticism on the Bible is happily illustrated by something which happened at Chenies some years ago. There stood on the green an old hollow tree, which was to all appearance dead ; some mischievous boys lighted a fire in the hollow trunk, which burnt for some time, and was with difficulty extinguished. But when the fire ceased, the tree burst into new life, and now flourishes among its neighbours. Criticism has had a similar effect on the Bible ; seeming to be destructive, it has proved to be restorative.

Another illustration occurred in the Great War. The German shells were pounding a Russian trench, where the tired and parched soldiers were in danger of dying from thirst. But a shell struck a ledge of rock and liberated a stream of water. Delicious and refreshing supplies poured into the trench and refreshed the weary defenders. Such is the only result of the most relentless criticism on the Bible ; it releases the living waters which abound in the Book, waters which are often bound by the rigid and 'deadening traditions of interpretation. The prophets hardly lived for the Church, except as the occasional utterers of oracles which seemed to be forecasts of Christ, until criticism inquired into the dates and circumstances of the several writers and found a chronological order in the writings. And in more recent years the Gospel narratives, subjected to an unflinching criticism, have yielded to us a picture of Christ, such as was entirely overlaid by the cobwebs and varnish of accumulated tradition. Such a book as Harry Emerson Fosdick's *Manhood of the Master,* bringing us face to face with the perfect character of Jesus, only became possible after a generation of criticism. The Gospels were treated no longer as sacrosanct oracles, guaranteed against the possibility of error ; the claim made for, never by, the evangelists, that every sentence they wrote was infallibly correct, was surrendered as a gratuitous assumption. The documents were searched and collated, precisely in the same way that we search Plutarch or Xenophon's *Memorabilia* to find out what manner of man it was whose life was there presented. And what was the result? From these memoirs, with all their limitations and fragmentariness, stands forth a Person who is unmistakable. The perfect balance in Him of qualities which elsewhere appear only in different persons, the wholeness of His moral nature, the wealth of His personality, produce an extraordinary effect. Start with the dogma that Jesus is God, and difficulties spring up at every point. But start with the Person presented there in those parallel biographies, and you quickly perceive that you are face to face with a unique Man. And as you try to understand and interpret Him, you see that His uniqueness consists just in this : that He is so implicated with God that His character and words come as a revelation of God, and yet He is so implicated with man that His life and death furnish the offering which man presents to God. The doctrine of His Divinity, or the doctrine of the two natures combined in His person, or the doctrine of the Atonement which He made for sin, will result from the study of His life and character ; but it makes all the difference in the world, whether you start with the dogmas and seek by them to interpret the person, or start with the person and see how the dogmas grow naturally out of it. The critical way of handling the Bible has brought us back to its essential authority, and opened up again the living streams which were choked. If I had kept silence in 1888 the truth would have made its way, and I should have escaped the censure and hostility which seemed for a time to threaten the usefulness of my ministry, as it actually did sadden and embitter my life. But on the other hand, I should have missed the rare joy of helping those who, by reading my book, found faith, and I should have gone through my work with a secret feeling of cowardice. It is not necessary to defy public opinion simply for the moral strength which comes from battling against it ; but it is fatal to shrink from braving public opinion by the utterance of truth, on the plea that truth will ultimately prevail, and is too strong to need your feeble aid.

But in the second place, the publication of this assailed book turned the current of my whole life and altered the character of my work. It opened to me the way of literature. When I wrote my Roman History I felt the fascination of literary work, and I turned from it reluctantly to undertake the work of the ministry. But now I had been led to the discovery by quite unexpected events, that literary work may be useful in the ministry, and even that it may become a ministry both wider and deeper than mere speaking to limited audiences. I used to wonder as a young man when I saw the effect produced by Baldwin Brown's books, *The Higher Life,* etc., whether I could ever find my way into a ministry of that kind. Now, without choosing it, I found myself thrust along that very line. From 1888 until now I have never been without requests, more or less urgent, from publishers, to undertake specific work. Book after book has been written ; sometimes the sale has been very limited, sometimes it has been comparatively large. I have never written anything which has commanded general attention or a sensational circulation. But the books have gone out and found readers, and they have brought back to me marvellous evidences that this was a form of ministry which God accepted. Some of the books

I may mention in the following pages, but at present I cannot help dwelling on the remarkable way in which I was led into this channel of influence. My hands were so full with the claims of my Church and growing mission, and I had to be so constantly travelling all over the country to preach, or to speak, or to lecture, that in all probability I should have given up writing as impossible, but for the effect which was produced by *Inspiration and the Bible*. This experience showed me that the *litera scripta* reaches where the spoken word cannot. I found, for example, at once, that my audience was as much in America and Australia as in England, and that while those who may be helped in a limited population like Hampstead may be few, if you may gather your auditors from the whole English-speaking world, you may have an audience which will always demand your most strenuous and devoted labours. In a word, I turned to literature, at the continued request of publishers, knowing that they would not ask for books unless readers desired them, as a new means of discharging my ministry. And while for ten or fifteen years the pulpit work and the press work went on concurrently, for the last fifteen years the work of the books has, so far as I can judge, greatly surpassed the work of the pulpit. The acknowledgment of help from my own Church is small compared with the acknowledgments from that wider audience. Seldom does a week pass but some grateful letter comes from a reader far away. And often when I am discouraged by the apparent failure of my work close at hand, for some days running will come thanks for books of mine ; sometimes for a book which has become generally known, but often for a book which has seemed to fall still-born from the press.

Directly *Inspiration and the Bible* had run into a second edition, the publisher asked me to write a companion volume. *Revelation and the Bible* was the result. The book was not published until 1892, but it arose out of the necessity of trying to show what is actually *revealed* in the Bible, when we are compelled to admit that the writing of the books as such is not guaranteed against mistakes. The book was, as might be expected, slighted by the denominational paper, and not approved by any general recognition. But one letter from an unknown correspondent was a call to me to continue the work, whether it met with approbation or not. I often wish I might meet this correspondent, male or female, for the letter, anonymous as it was, had a decisive effect upon me.

SCARBOROUGH,
July 20, 1895.

DEAR SIR,—

I have just finished reading your *Revelation and the Bible* and feel moved, though only an obscure and unknown person, to write and thank you for what has been to me an exceedingly interesting and helpful book. From childhood on to middle age I have been privately seeking for some light on the many difficulties which the Bible presents to those unfortunates who can only be regarded as relatives of poor doubting Thomas. Why some people should be permitted serene, unquestioning acceptance of any amount of orthodox views about religion, and why others, born of religious parents, should be tortured and torn, from almost as long as they can remember, with a continued "how and why?" about everything, is one of the inexplicable things of life. However, being of that make, I have gone through life on the look-out for help, and feel that your book has given me more than anything I have ever read or heard, and I bless the day, now some time ago, when I saw it on the bookstall of Folkestone station. . . . You do not know what a comfort it is when men like you *speak out* on matters of Biblical research, and put modern views in language which the ordinary reader can understand. Though I venture to hold theological views which are not yours, or what I imagine yours to be (being on the great mystery of the Atonement more a follower of Robertson of Brighton than of Dr. Dale), yet I heartily and thankfully accept you as a guide in Biblical study. I hope that you may have many years of health, and above everything else of good sight—

(what a prophetic touch !)—

for the sake of all those who look to you for help and instruction.
Believe me, sincerely yours,
A READER.

But the book had another result. Among my friends at New College had been a thoughtful and interesting man named Horsburgh. The son of a rigidly orthodox clergyman, who regarded Seeley's *Ecce Homo* as the work of infidelity, he had turned in severe revolt from Christian faith. At College he urged with great skill all the arguments of Mill and Spencer against religion. My intimacy with him—I went to stay with him in his father's vicarage, and understood the reason of his unbelief—had no effect in convincing him. He was not a strong man, and died in the middle of life ; but not long before his death he wrote and told me that he had read *Revelation and the Bible*. " If," he said, " I had known that book in my early manhood, it would have saved me from the course I took." I always look with a deep gratitude on this book, which was used to bring my friend to the faith before he passed beyond.

These and similar experiences entailed on me a lifelong task. The indications were sufficiently clear. I must continue to write, so long as I could gain the attention of readers, and I must consecrate my books to the main object. I must try to bring the results of Biblical scholarship to confirm the faith, and enable those to recover their footing, who had necessarily broken with a discredited dogma, but had not yet discovered the positive truth. My own spiritual life became a quest to find the sure foundation, when the apparent foundation of Biblical infallibility had given way.

It will be seen, as this narrative proceeds, how I tried to keep true to the task which was laid upon me. It will also be seen how I was hindered and hampered by circumstances which were beyond my control, unseen forces working against me, failure of health, and, above all, failure of sight.

Looking back on those first ten years at Hampstead, I see that outside the constant loyalty and support of Lyndhurst Road, which, as far as the great bulk of the Church went, never flagged, the most salutary local influence was " the Fraternal." I was very early invited to join a group of ministers who met once a month for breakfast at the houses of the members in rotation. After the social hour, the morning was given to the study, or at least the discussion, of a chosen passage of scripture. In those days Newman Hall, Edward White, and Joshua Harrison made this society one of unusual value. Newman Hall, with his long experience as a popular preacher, kind, brotherly, appreciative, his house filled with the sketches and memorials of his tours, and his mind stocked with anecdotes from his experiences, was the most charming of hosts. Edward White, the persecuted champion of a heresy, that of Conditional Immortality, expounded in his work *Life in Christ,* was pugnacious and trenchant, the wittiest man, on the whole, I have ever met. His comments on the passage always revealed wide knowledge and much reading, but were memorable for their flashes of originality and caustic humour. Joshua Harrison was the embodiment of the devotion, the dignity, the orthodoxy of the generation that was passing away. These were the giants who had been in former days, and they moved, not ungraciously, among us, the pigmies of the later time. In this congenial and delightful society I was regarded as *l'enfant terrible*. My friend, Frederick Hastings, the secretary of the Fraternal still, recalls the grave headshakes and the genuine alarm of the seniors over the young man, who freely canvassed the most cherished doctrines of the Church, and habitually shocked them by treating the Bible on the same lines as he treated ordinary literature. It is with profound gratitude that I remember those noble and saintly men. Their courtesy to me, their patient defence of the old positions against the new, and, above all, the sense they gave me of the dignity and value of the ministerial office, made me their debtors for life. Alas, I am now myself the senior in this Fraternal ; and though the company now, drawn from Congregationalists, Baptists, and Presbyterians, is far more scholarly, and not less earnest than it was then, I have the infirmity of the head boys in a school, who cannot help feeling that the school has declined, because they occupy the places of those heroes, those Paladins, those Admirable Crichtons, to whom they used to look up with awe from the distances of the lower forms.

It is a remarkable instance of vitality in a voluntary association of this kind. For close upon half a century a group of fifteen ministers, originally drawn together by a local connection, constantly changing in personnel, has met without intermission month by month, to study the Bible and to enjoy the strength of fraternal intercourse. In my early days I used to contrast this little company with the New College dons and other Oxford residents, whose society I had enjoyed for some years before. I always felt how much warmth of manner, cordiality, does for the happiness of life. But a warmth, which came from a genuine faith in Christ and a common desire to do His work in the world, was a very favourable exchange for the polish and the varied interests of an Oxford common-room. As time went on I found this fraternal intercourse a very substantial element in my life. I learnt more from the two hours' conversation than from a long morning in my study. I felt increasingly the discipline that comes from fellowship. Our differences never trouble us ; our denominational peculiarities are the subject of banter and occasional wit ; but the bond which holds us together is in a very perceptible way the Person of Christ. We love one another, it is true, but it is because we love Him. When one after another retires, or is withdrawn by death, the place is filled, and the Fraternal goes on as before, because Christ remains. The old members are not forgotten ; their words, as well as their names, are in the minutes ; they are frequently recalled with gratitude or amusement, but the Body of Christ is felt to be continuous and real.

If any one doubts the Presence of Christ with His own to-day, it would be a telling, if not a conclusive, argument to visit this company of ministers, to hear the cheerful conversation, the animated discussion of current events at the table, and then to see them turn to the Bible and draw out its varied meaning, Jesus Himself often manifestly drawing near. Especially would this evidence of His presence be plain on those occasions when, stirred by the study of the Word and drawn close together by the interchange of thought, we recognize our need, and the Present Supply of it, by kneeling all together for a few fervent united petitions before we separate to face our several duties for the day.

In the study and struggle for progress, and for Theological Reform, it is a society like that which feeds the life and keeps the ardent spirits from leaving the King's Highway.

CHAPTER VI

AT THE MIDPOINT OF THE WAY

1890

Now in the centre of life's arch I stand,
And view its curve descending from this day;
How brief the road from birth's mysterious strand!
How brief its passage till it close in grey!
Yet by this bridge went all the immortal band,
And the world's Saviour did not reach half-way.

H. W. NEVINSON.

I WAS one of the first victims of influenza when that scourge of God came to our shores. In January 1890 I was stricken while preaching at Crouch End, and some weeks passed before I could do my work properly again. I did not know it, but a thorn in the flesh had come into my life to stay. Time after time for ten years, and at longer intervals for ten years more, I was laid aside, and convalescence was followed by a nervous prostration, which deprived me of all the physical *élan* which is necessary for effective preaching. This was the first pull of "the bridle of Theagas," which warned me that I was never to accomplish in this life what I hoped. But in that same year encouragements and aids were sent in accordance with a principle of God's dealings with us, which is, in my experience, invariable. The principle seems to be to hold us in a narrow road, always to send severe trials, lest life should be too bright, but always to send unexpected blessings, lest it should be too dark. That *via media* of life is designed.

Never elated while one soul's distressed,
Never dejected while one soul is blessed.

That was Pope's philosophy, but it is a law of the Divine government.

Accordingly in that year of physical depression I received an access of spiritual help. This came through my acquaintance with Mr. Reader Harris, to whom I was introduced by my friends the Carus-Wilsons. He was a Queen's Counsel who practised at the Parliamentary Bar. Raised up from illness by the prayer of faith, he became a spiritual leader to others. Through want of theological training he was betrayed into statements about the eradication of sin from the human heart which laid him open to a suspicion of teaching "sinless perfection." But he was a most remarkable and inspiring man, whose character and work I have never seen properly commemorated. He had a distinguished bearing and an easy delivery, which, added to a singular sweetness of temper and genuine warmth of heart, made him, next to Henry Drummond, the most attractive man I ever knew. He was irresistible. On one occasion a lady urged him to come to a dance. "But," he said, "I never like to go where I cannot do as I please." "But you may," she said. "May I say just what comes into my mind?" he asked. "Of course you may," she replied quite delighted. He went to the dance and charmed every one by his manner and friendliness. Then he stepped forward among the dancers and suddenly said : "Our kind hostess has given me leave to say what I please." Every one was startled, but interested. And then in the most winning way he preached Christ to them, and urged them all to seek a full salvation in Him. No one was upset, and he least of all. On another occasion a vicar invited him to speak to the people from the lectern. The vicar had a good voice, and sang well in private. A hymn was given out by the vicar in the pulpit, and Reader Harris saw that the congregation would be at once hypnotized by the place, and the custom of decorous conventionality. He looked up to the vicar and said : " Can you sing this hymn, vicar? " The vicar, frowning, nodded, implying that it was all right. " The vicar will sing the hymn as a solo," said Reader Harris. And, strange to say, the vicar did.

On another occasion he told me that he was pleading in a case before the House of Lords. There was no reference in his speech to anything but the case. And yet, to his astonishment, when the Court rose, a reporter came to him and asked him about his own soul. Conviction of sin and a desire for deliverance from it had reached his heart while the Queen's Counsel spoke. One day an agnostic came to Reader Harris's chambers when he was hard at work, and wished to state his doubts and difficulties to him. " Quit sinning and you'll cease doubting," was the one reply he gave. " But," he began, " my difficulty is ——" " I know," said Harris, " but quit sinning and you'll cease doubting." The man got angry and went away. Nevertheless the word had gone home. The agnostic came to him some time after, an agnostic no more. The shrewd thrust had turned him to the truth. In surrendering sin he found Christ and lost doubt.

Reader Harris, driving in a hansom, would open the lid and talk to the driver about his soul, and always without giving any offence. He had caught the Spirit of Christ, and it made him infinitely attractive and convincing.

I got him to speak to my people on several occasions, and in intercourse with him myself I made a discovery which brought singular blessing into my life. It was a very simple discovery, and in words it sounds almost a truism, but it is quite revolutionary in its effect. I found that faith in Christ means not only a deliverance from the ultimate results of sin, but also a deliverance from the actual power of sin. Forgiven for His sake, because He bore our sins in His own body on the tree, we may be " saved by His life " ; held in the strong invisible arms, so that sin cannot have dominion over us. This was a glad, a radiant, discovery in that year of weakness.

But two other refreshments came in that year, an interesting visit to Scotland, and another tour in Norway, which sent me back with a new inspiration. At the end of April I was sent by the Congregational Union as its representative to the sister Union of Scotland, meeting in Edinburgh. Congregationalism in Scotland is very small, and but for the famous names of Dr. Alexander and John Pulsford, both of whom I had heard in Edinburgh fifteen years before, it occupied a very small place in public attention. It was this which made the generous action of the Presbyterian leaders the more striking. At a public dinner in the Free Church Assembly Hall, Principal Cairnes, Principal Rainy, Dr. Alexander Whyte, and Dr. Walter Smith came and spoke. Mr. McFarlane, the great missionary of New Guinea, was present, and interested every one in his account of the Papuan languages, which betrayed in their richness of accidence, syntax, and vocabulary, the former greatness of the degraded peoples of New Guinea. But to me the meeting with the great Presbyterian leaders was, at that time, even more interesting. Cairnes, known as " You go first " Cairnes, because of the habitual humility that made the phrase frequent on his lips, was a striking figure. The shock of white hair surmounted a face of great strength and tenderness. Rainy was the consummate ecclesiastical statesman : then and afterwards I was amazed at the real humility, and warmth of heart, which could be combined with that kind of force. Dr. Whyte gave a singular impression of authority. Afterwards I learnt to sit at his feet, as the interpreter of William Law and St. Teresa, and the best exponent of John Henry Newman. I knew his brilliant colleague, Hugh Black, and had pleasant interchanges of thought, not only by meeting him, but sometimes also by correspondence ; but that first contact with a great practical Mystic marked, though I did not know it then, an epoch in my life. Walter Smith I had admired since my schooldays, when the anonymous *Olrig Grange* took me captive. In my first visit to Edinburgh I had hastened to his church to hear him preach, and was amazed to find the poet, whose sharp wit and easy verse had conjured up a very different figure to my mind, a heavy preacher of the Scotch type. But it was a joy to meet him on the social side, and to hear his kindly humours and shrewd judgments on life at close quarters. It is not always that poets and writers seem personally as great as their books. I had early bitter disappointments in meeting George Eliot and Robert Browning. But in those four great Scotsmen I had an experience, not to be forgotten, of finding great writers greater than their writings. No other Church, in my experience (I have been privileged to meet the best in all the Churches, except the Roman Catholic), has succeeded in securing such great men, such vital personalities, as the Free Church of Scotland. I pass no judgment on Presbyterianism as a Church system, but of Presbyterians I unhesitatingly say this, the greatest men I have known are included in their ranks. Of a different, but hardly an inferior, interest, was a very humble minister whom I saw in those meetings of the Scottish Congregational Union. His name was Morison, and he was lame. I noticed the intense avidity with which he drank in all that was said. In conversation with him I found the reason. His work lay in a remote island of the Hebrides, which contained two hundred and sixty inhabitants. He was the sole minister, and

the friend of all. At that time there was much talk
of the " lapsed masses " in London. I remember, in
speaking of his remote island, which was three and
a half days' journey from Edinburgh, his remark :
" There are no laapsed maasses therre." Only once
in three years could he afford to make the journey
to the Union Meetings. He was then drinking in his
supplies of thought and inspiration for his lonely work.
I went back from Edinburgh feeling grateful that I
had been allowed to help that solitary worker on the
outposts of the British Isles. When just twenty years
later I was speaking at the World's Missionary Conference in Edinburgh, and the delegates were assembled
from all lands, men of all languages and colours, my
mind went back to Mr. Morison, and I realized that
the " cup of cold water given to a disciple in His
name " was Christ's description, not of the least, but
possibly of the greatest service we can render.

I have a great and unaccountable love for the
Scotch. Every time I have been among them I have
felt at home. Johnson's antipathy to them alienates
me from him, who otherwise would be my chief
literary hero. I account for his prejudice by the fact
that he judged them from his knowledge of Boswell.
But Boswell is not a typical Scot, and Johnson ought
to have known it. And even so Boswell wrote the
greatest biography in the English language. It is a
curious irony that the great Johnson really owes his
fame to the despised Scotchman !

Many of the best members and workers in my
church at Lyndhurst Road have been Scotch people.
And if the Anglican Church has to seek Scotsmen
to fill its two archbishoprics, it is small wonder that
we, as Congregationalists, owe to the same source our
greatest missionaries, Moffat, Livingstone, Chalmers,
Gilmour, and our greatest theologians, Fairbairn, Duff,
Forsyth, and I may add, Garvie.

The mountains and the moors, and above all the

intricate and haunting beauties of the Western High-
lands, the indented coast, the kyles and nesses, the
cloud-capped islands in the sunset, the romantic legends
of the clans, and the great names dominating the
country, Burns, Scott, Raeburn—they are a host not
to be enumerated—give to Britain North of the Tweed
a romance and a charm which the Southrons miss.
Myself an Englishman all through, with no drop, so
far as I know, of Scotch, Irish, or Welsh blood in
my veins, I am better able than the Scotch themselves
to express what the country and the Church owe to
them.

But from Scotland it is an easy transition to Norway.
That year my friends took with them their little
girls, Gwendolen and Melicent, with their governess ; the
three were settled at Hop, near Bergen, and we returned
to them for a fortnight at the end, after a few weeks'
tour. We landed at Stavanger, and made our way
by Sand, Suledalsvand, and Bratlandsdal, to Røldal,
where we spent a Sunday. The glorious river that
rolls through the rocky valley became henceforth a
companion and allegory of my life. The Norwegian
elv is unlike any other rivers I have seen, so short in
its course, so splendid in its brief achievement. The
one short hour of glorious life endows it with a
charm which the vast stream of the Mississippi, or the
sacred Ganges, winding through featureless plains, lacks.
It comes racing down, now in broad reaches where
the great volume slides translucently clear, revealing,
its rocks and pebbles in the channel many feet below ;
now entering a narrow gorge, where it breaks over
gigantic boulders in curtains of pulsing spray, or shoots
back in eager waves which run foaming and dancing
up the stream. At times the body of water appears
liquid emerald, under a tossing and wreathed coverlet
like delicate white lace ; now the eye catches what
might be a mould of solid beryl silently dissolving ;
and now, after an impetuous plunge over a rocky

barrier, the stream enters a cauldron, the sides of which it
has hollowed out, and is churned into a snowy yeast, which,
as it drives, recoils, and swirls, assumes a faint tinge
of dainty pink. All the time a loud, musical murmur
—the violinist Ole Buhl declared he caught all his
music from those rushing waters of his native land—
too softened to be called a roar, but too multitudinous
to admit a milder term, expresses the tranquil and
continuous exultation of the ever-rushing waters. The
reverberation among the precipitous rocks which stand
on either bank, and the birches which cling miraculously
to their sides, sounds the praise of that Spirit of Beauty,
which here takes on the form, the colour, the magic
of motion, and the sustained roar of music, to express
as clearly as is possible the very essence of our human
life. Such a stream, issuing out of the inaccessible
mountains, passing under rainbow arches, so swift, so
brief, so unfathomable, so untamable, so glorious also
as it debouches into the infinite sea, is Life.

At Røldal the village priest, Ringdal, came to see
us, and brought his wife and children : he was too
ill to preach that day, but he was a consoling companion
to a somewhat jaded London minister. Our imperfect Norsk did not prevent a perfect understanding.
He ministered to the scattered country folks in the
midst of grandeur and loveliness, which seemed to
make preaching unnecessary ; it was my lot to
minister in London to a multitude burdened with heavy
cares, and but faintly conscious of Nature's convincing
godliness. In the evening the clouds came down low
on the lake (*vand*), but a strange underlight turned
all into silver like a picture of Jan van der Capelle.
The wonder of Norway is that grandeur and delicate
beauty are closely wedded. If the precipitous mountain
wall, four thousand feet high, descends into the fjord
with a frowning and beetling austerity, the line where it
meets the water will be marked by a continuous golden
band of seaweed. If the mountains with their lipping

glaciers seem too forbidding, they will be suddenly clad in rainbows. If the little *gaard* is too rough and cheerless, the roof, as there at Røldal, will be a piece of the flower-carpeted hillside, red with sorrel, blue with delicate harebells, blended with a skill that no artist can reproduce.

My dear companion had a wonderful gift of clothing in verses those passing impressions of Norwegian travel—

> The purple mountains reach the sky,
> And stern in lurid gloom defy
>   The fury of the rain.
> The torrent roars and flings aside
> The white robes of his strength and pride,
>   And rushes to the plain.

> With sudden smile the light breaks through
> In glancing shaft and rainbow hue,
>   And burns where mists have spun ;
> Its magic touch the gloom has stirred ;
> And here it turns a flying bird
>   To silver in the sun.

Going up from Røldal to Breifonds we passed a wet day in laughing over the quaint advertisements of Norwegian hotels, done into English for " the honoured traveller at best." That shy, courteous, single-hearted Norway has, I fear, now passed away under the invasion of English and Germans. Such gems as the following can no longer be found—

" This first-class hotel is beautifully situate at the very bottom of the fjord and accommodates transient as well as permanent boarders."
" The River Driva is here pressed in a narrow chink with mighty giant kettles. One must be cautious, as the mountain is polished."
" Occasion for shooting and fishing. Bird-dogs on sale or to be let. The hotel will look out for horses."
" The hotel is surrounded with piniferous and foliferous weeds."

The closing fortnight at Hop, spent in a small house with the dear people who could only speak Norsk, was for me a memorable time. Continuous rain fell. It was possible to bathe in the lake only from a boat under a macintosh. Now and then the sun would conquer for half an hour, and the glory of the deep forests, the red roofs, and the bare glistening rocks would be revealed. But in that happy and enforced inactivity came a new vision of my life, and a consecration of whatever powers God had given me to the work of the ministry.

The year 1891 was for me eventful in two ways. The first International Council of Congregationalists introduced me to Americans, and led incidentally to my visit to the United States ; and an attempt to get me to Westminster Chapel was the only serious temptation to leave Lyndhurst Road which has come to me all these years. The year was also marked by the illness of my friend Mr. Oakes, which led to a very beautiful holiday in North Wales.

The Congregational Council was held in the new Weigh House Chapel, Duke Street, which had just been completed. Representatives of Congregationalism, three hundred in number, assembled from America, Australia, Sweden, and Japan. Dr. Dale, though his health was even then manifestly breaking down, made a great and worthy President. Dr. Waldenstrom gave a wonderful account of the origin and growth of Congregationalism in his country. In twelve years seven hundred and seven Churches had been formed in Sweden, and there were one hundred thousand members. The movement had come not from contact with English Congregationalists, but simply from the study of the New Testament. What happened in England towards the close of the sixteenth century, almost exactly repeated itself in Sweden three hundred years later. That was perhaps the most significant point of a memorable assembly. The tenth and closing day a large number of the delegates travelled to Scrooby, just beyond Doncaster, whence came Brewster, Bradford, Clyfden, and Robinson, who established the principles of Congregationalism on English, and then on American, soil. We met in Scrooby Church, and some of the American delegates spoke on the event which was the real starting-point of their great State, the landing of the Pilgrim Fathers on Plymouth Rock.

The American delegates, however, caused some disappointment at the time. With the exception of Professor Stearns, whose premature death shortly after evoked general sorrow, they were singularly antiquated in their theology. Dr. Goodwin preached the sermon in the City Temple. It might have come from his namesake in the seventeenth century. The ideas which were moving us in England, the scholarly understanding of the Bible, the larger views of God, the brighter hope for men, had apparently not yet penetrated the American Churches. Even Dr. Parker, who was nothing if not orthodox, when he entered the pulpit on the following Sunday, in his characteristic way sniffed round, and explained to his attached people that he perceived a smell of sulphur. I learnt before long to know that the impression made by our American friends had to be corrected in a fuller knowledge of the other side, where Munger, Newman Smyth, Amory Bradford, Washington Gladden, and many others were maintaining American Congregationalism in its honourable reputation for enlightened conservatism and spiritual progress among the Churches of America.

That Pan-Congregational Congress of 1891 had the effect of turning thought to the origin and principles of the denomination in which I was born. When two years later we celebrated the Tercentenary of the Congregationalist martyrs, Greenwood, Barrowe, and Penry, we became more than commonly alive to the positive value of the truths which called these Churches into existence. Dr. Dale was a Congregationalist High Churchman. For him there was no separatist meaning in the principle, but rather the largest Catholicity. He was not deprecating the Church, but exalting its transcendental claims, when he advocated the polity, the ministry, the sacraments of his Church.

My friend, Dr. Hatch, in his *Organization of the Early Christian Church*, one of the few Bampton Lectures that rank with the original work and scholarship of Continental theologians, showed unmistakably that the Churches at the beginning were Congregational. Later on the Cambridge Scholar, J. F. A. Hort, in his *Christian Ecclesia*, showed by an even closer study of the New Testament writings the same fact. Harnack has, later, in his *Expansion of Christianity*, pointed out how the brotherliness and mutual service of the Church were greater in that first century, when the primitive Congregationalism was not yet over-ridden, than at any subsequent period. Thus, when I was asked to contribute to a volume, *Our Churches and why we belong to them*, I was able to give a very clear and definite answer to the question submitted. Congregationalism was the order of the Apostolic Church, and the only order as yet known in the Apostolic writings. Its principle, therefore, it is fair to assume, was only lost under the stress of alien forces, but never in theory surrendered. The attempt in the vigorous early days of the Reformation to recover that principle was a proof of the fearless logic which was developed, when men turned back, after ages of dogmatism, to the primitive documents of the faith, and inquired what the intrinsic principle of the Church was. The actual new birth of those who believe in Christ, the close fellowship of those who are regenerate ; the immediate presence of Christ the Head, to guide, to teach, to correct and inspire wherever even two or three of His own were gathered in His name : this was Congregationalism, which must be retained, whatever development the organization of the Church may undergo. Its retention at the heart of the Church is the condition of health and of free expansion. As my own mind had embraced more and more contentedly the ideal which I had received from my father—he himself had written in his early days a book on *The True Theory of a Church*, showing from his own study of the question just what John Robinson

found in the seventeenth and Professor Hort in the nineteenth century—and as my practical work at Lyndhurst
Road afforded a more secure test of the value of the
principles, I had become a Congregationalist in the
succession of Dr. Dale. I understood, and I understand
by it, those fundamental principles of the Church's life
which are revealed in the New Testament. I count
it a high privilege and duty to spend my life in the
defence of those principles. If the Church of England
should succeed in crushing them for a time, that would
be no gain, for they would certainly revive ; her wisdom
lies in finding room for them in her organization. Meanwhile, as a Congregationalist, I feel myself to be Catholic,
recognizing Christ's Church in its diverse forms. If
I may use the language of Philosophy, I recognize what
Leibnitz called the monad as the constituent of the sum-
total of being which is made up of monads : and the
individual Church is the monad, the One Holy Catholic
Church is the whole.

The mention of Lyndhurst Road, my own dearly loved
Church, in which I had tested my Congregationalism,
leads me to refer, not without a shudder, to the one
occasion on which I was tempted to leave it. Mr. de
Sélincourt, as a boy, had come to London from France
to start in business. Invited one day by a member of
Westminster Chapel to go with her to the service, he
had heard the saintly Samuel Martin and been converted.
From that moment he was devoted to Westminster. When
Samuel Martin died, Henry Simon carried on the great
work, not unsuccessfully, but when Simon left, Mr. de
Sélincourt clung the more tenaciously to the imperilled
sanctuary. He made up his mind to persuade me to
step into that consecrated pulpit. He was a man of
much charm and persuasiveness. He used to come up
to " consult " me about the Church. He would appear
before breakfast, and would not go until we had prayed
over the question which was nearest to his heart. Gradually he revealed his purpose. Speaking for the Church—

and in effect he was the Church in the evil days on which Westminster had fallen—he made me the most handsome offers. I should have a free hand to carry out all my dreams for London, and for the world ; ample resources would be at command ; I might have one or more assistants.

The proposal was to me extraordinarily alluring. There was the great central church, close to the Houses of Parliament and to Buckingham Palace. There was the great tradition which had been created by Samuel Martin, whose beautiful face I had seen, and whose beautiful voice I had heard, speaking from the words, " For My sake," at the opening of my father's Church, Queen Street, Wolverhampton. I should escape the suburbanity, the weakness of which I had already discovered, and be in London itself.

I could profit by the twelve years at Hampstead and leave my mistakes behind. I should have beside me a man of ample means, prepared to help me in the schemes with which my head at that time teemed. I could not take counsel with my own Church, but only with my own heart. But my never-failing counsellor went through the struggle with me. Her shrewd wisdom saw both the claims which Lyndhurst Road had upon me, and the weaknesses of the proposed arrangements at Westminster. After our summer holiday I returned with my mind made up. Dr. Campbell Morgan has done at Westminster, in recent years, more than I could even have done. But never, even now, do I pass Buckingham Palace, or even Victoria Street, without a question : " Did I after all miss a great opportunity? " Was it a certain timidity or cowardice which prevented me from launching out just there at the mid-point of my life on a work which might have touched London in a way that a suburban ministry cannot? The next ten years at Lyndhurst Road, with ever-increasing numbers and resources, and ever-widening opportunities in the country, and, as I shall show in the next chapter, beyond the

country, were perhaps the best answer. And afterwards
I came to see how dangerous a foundation I should have
had in the support, sincere and loyal as it was, of the
man who urged me to go. In looking back I am
increasingly impressed with the conviction that a life
committed absolutely to God is led by a way that it
knows not, a way that proves to be His way.

That summer my friend, John Oakes, was recovering
very slowly from a severe attack of influenza, and we
had to surrender Norway and find invigoration at St.
Anne's and enchantment at Penmaenmawr. It was a
salutary experience, for Norway had stolen our hearts
from our own land. The North Sea, put between us
and home, silencing even correspondence, the complete
change of the unsophisticated life, the unapproachable
grandeur, the variety of fjords and fjelds, of delicious
steamer days, and still more delicious days of driving
by carriole or *stolkjar*, halting for *middags,* arriving for
aftens, and finding everywhere honesty, kindness, intelligence, had made us feel that no holiday on our own shores
could be more than a make-believe. But the austere
width of the sand dunes and the arching sky, with the
sweeping winds of St. Anne's, brought health to our
invalid and inspiration to our hearts. And then North
Wales opened to us a variety of beauty and of interest
which proved a welcome help in the momentous decision
which that year I had to take. Newman Hall was
staying at Penmaenmawr. We climbed together through
the Green Gorge to the Druids' Circle, and he told me
how he had first met Gladstone on that mountain. The
Bishop of London was also there, and I met him in my
walks on Moel Lys. An extract from my journal on
September 18th shows what effect the exquisite scenery,
the amazing sunsets, and the purple-golden hills were
producing—

To-day I am thirty-six : the solemn feeling of entering on another
year, now past the midmost point of human life and henceforth
moving as it were on the downward slope. None of us was feeling

well, thus with the sense of our frailty and mortality I feel again the quick pulsation of the flying years. We drove to Conway; the clouds cleared and sunshine covered the land : enjoyed the quaint old castellated town, and still more the drive back over the mountains covered with purple and gold, coming down the pass to Dwygyfylchi. Before bedtime we had some prayer together for the consecration of this new year of my life. I long unutterably to grasp more firmly the Divine truths, and to live more constantly as a witness for Him whom I profess to serve. At sunset the east was exquisitely tinted, salmon colour ; then in the west, above a long bank of dark leaden clouds flashed the splendour, changing into red-gold, all up the sky.

Again, on the day that we found light upon the Westminster problem, we had a glorious excursion up the Conway River. Nothing in Norway or in Italy is more charming than the reach from Bettws-y-Coed to Conway Castle : all the history of England, and all the glory of creation are in miniature there. From Llanrwst, with its graceful old bridge and the ring-ouzels fishing in the river, we drove up to Llyn Grafnant, the lonely lake, where we had a slight meal in a cottage and were charmed with the simplicity of the poor people. Returning, we inspected Gwyder Castle, originally built by Sir John Wynn to be a resting-place for kings on the way to Ireland. Spanish leather, Gobelin tapestry, the furniture of Tudor times, the carefully planned gardens, planted with the rarest trees, and above all the lovely situation by the river and under the hills, make the place a haunt of memories, an epitome of the great story of England for the last four hundred years. Another entry in the journal that evening may be quoted, because it is a witness of the Spirit's presence and effectual working at a momentous point in life.

Days of such deep and tender friendship, such varied interest and beauty, such unclouded serenity and joy, must necessarily be rare in life ; but they give me some apprehension of that possible life which, we fondly believe, the Father of Spirits has in store for those who love Him.

I always love that inscription on a sundial, *horas non numero nisi serenas*. I should like to live in that spirit.

The sunny hours of life are all worth recording ; the gloomy hours have their value, and are indeed absolutely necessary, but they are seldom worth recording. In reviewing my journals I feel a shame at each morbid and depressed entry ; but wherever I have dwelt on the happy experiences, the favourable interpositions of God, the beautiful realizations of the meaning of things, I feel that I touch the real life, the only lasting life.

That beautiful spirit whom I was permitted to know so intimately and so long had a life of suffering. She was a martyr to neuralgia, and she suffered from a congenital defect of the heart, which made her always an invalid. Loving Nature passionately, and eager to climb mountains and roam through the lanes, she could never walk more than for half an hour at a time, and she could know the things she loved only by driving, or by the swift and unlimited excursions of her mind. It was a treat to drive with her down a lane ; not a flower escaped her eye or remained unnamed, not a bird flitted but she saw and welcomed it. It was an even greater treat to be with her in a coble on her beloved Yorkshire coast. She was quite fearless ; when the spray drenched her, when the boat heeled over and the water came pouring in, or even when " the green water " was above the mast, she only exulted in the joy of the elements. At Filey the people on the beach would watch with astonishment the delicate lady returning from the boisterous sea after a sail with her trusted old fisherman Sayers, and stepping to the pony carriage to be carried up the cliff. But the spirit, so physically hampered and tormented, was always bright, hopeful, witty. Her times of deep depression were hidden, the times of disabling pain were borne bravely, and smiles and merriment came directly the grim fingers of torture were relaxed. From her I learnt the possibility of keeping troubles and anxieties to myself, and of showing to the world a cheerful front. When Sir Walter Scott's Journal came out, she eagerly read it, for he was one of her heroes, and the passage she liked best was the one in which he told his own practice ; he felt the positive wickedness of inflicting on those he loved his own gloom of spirit. And it is a curious fact that the habit of cultivating happiness and making those around us happy, brings to our own hearts a more abiding joy than joy itself (if the paradox may be pardoned) does. We start as innocent hypocrites, and soon are the *dramatis personæ* that we intended only to play. One of her letters at the end of this year may be quoted as an illustration of her temper at a time when her right hand had been for long almost disabled by weakness.

December 6, 1891.

I must, dearest and kindest, write a wee in ink, because to-day and yesterday my hand has felt much less cumbersome, if weak. And I want you to see that at a pinch, and on some days, it hasn't lost what little cunning it ever possessed. It is to me too a great relief to find that the power is still there if often enfeebled. Not that I ever, I think, let the arm worry me, but its disability lasts a long time, and sometimes it seems as if it must be permanent : such days as to-day prove that this is not so, and you will take the comfort of it, won't you? We are in the midst of violent gales, " whose sound is like the sea" in storm. The birds are wind-blown all about the sky, and quite late this morning I saw a benighted sparrow, a ball of grey-brown fluff, his head under his wings, quite tired out with the wild doings of the storm. He looked up for a moment in a pathetic puzzle, and said, "Can you explain these things, madam?" quite plainly, but I told him that I too was much flustered by these violent doings, and couldn't sleep o' nights. I thought there was a slight contempt in his resignation, as he tucked in his head again, as if he muttered, "So big and so ignorant." But what *can* these continual gales mean? Perhaps in London you don't have them. And if so this may account for your School Board Election and other things ; your nest is not stirred up enough, you are all too comfortable. I forgot to tell you another cause for my indignation, the German Emperor's speech! How shocking! None but a maniac or an Augustus could use such language—and the times cannot hold an Augustus. Nay, I think it threatens the acts of a Nero. Did you read it? And did your heart grow hot within you? Poor egotist! It must end in disaster. You would have enjoyed yesterday's sky. The west held sunset colours all day, a band of clear gold twice as high as the hills which never lost their dawn—purple, a violet so warm and glowing that the upper clouds seemed flushed with it, and the immediate gold turned saffron.

I suppose it betokened the terrible night, but as I lay in the quiet afternoon I quite hugged my spirit in a joy at its loveliness and upliftingness. Did I tell you that Mr. L. (the minister of Square Church) is beginning his holy raid too ? He has seen the two most prominent offenders, and I think they will be, must be, erased. But he feels very sad. One of them is such a fine, open-hearted man, and he very frankly told Mr. L. that one of his sermons was the primary cause ; the Christian life he described was all too high for him to live. If that was Christianity, then he wasn't a Christian, and so could take the Sacrament no longer. He is, though now well off, from the poorest class, and he feels that for him the true Christian life would be to go back among those people and try to raise and help them. That he is not prepared to do, but he can help being a fraud, he says, and will do so. All this (Mr. L. said) with a sad frankness that made him see the fine elements of his character. I fear that when the tie is broken, his conscience may more easily put on its nightcap, but perhaps not.

This morning these words of Mrs. Browning were almost completely realized—

> Cloud walls of the morning grey,
>   Faced with amber column,
> Crowned with crimson cupola
>   From a sunset solemn.
> May-mists for the casements fetch,
>   Pale and glimmering,
> With a sunbeam hid in each,
>   And a smell of Spring.

CHAPTER VII

AMERICA

1892–1893

ON February 8, 1892, a letter arrived from Yale inviting me to undertake the Lyman-Beecher lectures on preaching for the following year. Dr. Dale had recommended me to the College authorities for the work, and such was my respect for him and his judgment that I felt bound to accept the invitation. But it was a serious step : I had before me Dr. Dale's own Yale Lectures, and the more recent volume of Phillips Brooks, a deliverance so fresh and original that I felt myself wholly unfit to come in so great a succession. Also I was committed to the publication of *Revelation and the Bible*, which appeared in October and went into a second edition in December. And to be asked to lecture on preaching was sufficiently alarming, because, though I was impelled to preach by the Spirit, I suffered then, as I still do, from the most distressing sense of inadequacy. Preaching was never to me the delight that it is to most preachers. I remember talking to Dr. Cave of Hackney College, and experiencing an unspeakable amazement when he told me that he " revelled in it." That was to me unintelligible. I saw, too, how Newman Hall found it a recreation and refreshment ; it did him good physically, and like John Wesley he could at any time, indoors or out, get up and deliver an effective sermon. My difficulty was not want of words or of subjects ; speaking in a debate or on a platform was a pleasure ; but preaching was different. I always knew that if the sermon was to be of any good it must come direct from God, that it must be not mine but His. The anguish of doing it was that sometimes I felt it was mine ; my own preparation, or my own prejudices, had got in, and prevented His voice from being heard. When His voice was heard and I was duly subordinated the humiliation was intense. Once after preaching in Halifax my dear friend wrote to tell me, with great satisfaction, that my sermons had given the people at the Square Church " much pleasure." I replied in an agony, which she, I dare say very properly, rebuked, telling me that I ought to be very glad if I could give pleasure to good people. But I felt with the prophet Ezekiel, that it was a reproach to be " unto them as a very lovely song of one that hath a pleasant voice, and can play well on an instrument, for they hear thy words, but do them not " (Ezek. xxxiii. 32). Often when Lyndhurst Road was thronged, with seats down the aisles, and people up the pulpit stairs and in the organ loft, I had the sickening sensation : " I must be speaking *my* word, and not God's, for God's word is not popular." I found in the language of the prophets, especially Ezekiel and Jeremiah, exactly the sensations that I had myself in preaching. I always had to set my face like a flint, and to speak " whether they would hear or whether they would forbear." Hardly ever did I go to my pulpit without the wish that I might be excused, and permitted to leave the ministry ; hardly ever did I leave it without a strong wish to run away, that I might not face what I felt to be the criticism, the contempt, or the hostility of my hearers.

To lecture, therefore, on preaching seemed to be an impossible task. And yet, on reflection, I found in the difficulties of my own experience a reason why that task must be faced. I was committed, therefore, early in 1892 to cross the Atlantic in the spring of 1893, to lecture on preaching in the Divinity School of Yale University.

Luther said that he had noticed that whenever he was called to some work of exceptional importance he was beforehand prostrated with illness or sorrow, which he accepted as a discipline necessary to humble him and to throw him wholly on God. I have observed the same fact in my own life. I remember no piece of work, unusually important, which I had not to approach through a valley of humiliation. In the summer of this year I had an experience which to me was more severe than any illness. Perhaps I ought to record it, because it is clear, as I look back, in its place as part of God's mysterious ways. In August we went to Norway, my friends, their two little girls and I. It was more glorious than ever, but filled with episodes which bordered on tragedy. The arrival at Stavanger in the purple morning, the rugged outline of mountains against a saffron sky and the translucent air, brought the peace and the uplift which had often come before, and the quiet sail within the *skjaere* up to Bergen was a long delight. But at Bergen we lodged in a pension kept by Fru Cadd, recommended to us by our Norwegian friends the Waages. My bedroom was in the roof, and after midnight I heard strange and alarming sounds next door. I rushed out, and on the dark stairs found some of the boarders anxiously attending to the proprietress, who had been taken ill, and, as I afterwards learnt, a pious sea captain had been fetched to pray with her. I returned to bed and fell asleep. But I suddenly woke with a sound like the rush of wings in my ears. I started up, but fell asleep again. In the morning I learned that at that moment when I heard the sound the soul of the woman had taken flight.

We sailed on to the Nordfjord, and finally came to Loen. An interpreter on board took us to Kvamme's hotel, and with his help on Sunday we gathered the country people together (there was no church service that Sunday) and prayed with them. When, after visits to the incomparable Loenvand and Oldenvand, where we

heard the fall of a terrific avalanche, which sounded as
if the whole mountain wall had given way, we left by
the steamer *Alden* in the early morning for Nordfjordseid,
the hotel people all came to the little quay, moved to
tears, and waving handkerchiefs until the bend of the
fjord hid them from view. We had been with them
only four days, but they had given us their hearts, and
we had found again the depths of the Norwegian character, not unlike the fjords themselves, with the water
below unfathomable, and the frowning precipices above,
smitten with the sun, wreathed in the cloud and draped
in the rainbow.

The approach to Volden was a memorable vision.
As we drove over the pass, 1,640 feet high, we caught
sight of Birkedal—a lake lying between huge mountains
lit by the afternoon sun, the shadow of the one range
thrown across the water to the slope on the other side,
a mystery of purple and gold, through which the waters
of the lake glistened, the rich birch woods on the lower
reaches and the snows above. It was like coming to
the promised land. We went on to the Hjorund Fjord ;
the jagged Tinderne had formed our western horizon
for some days, all very solitary, and seldom visited in
those days, and came by the steamer at midnight in
floods of rain to Øie. In the morning we started in
two *stolkjære*, my friend and his two children in one,
his wife and I in the other, to drive up the Norangsdal.
The grand and beautiful Slogan rose like an altar in
the sunlight above the rain-clouds. My companion and
I, who were in a car with a stupid *skyds-pige*, instead
of the usual intelligent boy, were descending a very
rough road. She held the cords which served as reins,
and, fascinated by the glory of the Slogan, she turned
for a last look. I saw a large stone on the left of
the road, and said " Take care "—but it was too late.
The left wheel went over the stone and the frail vehicle
was upset. We were both flung out, the luggage breaking
loose and rolling on us down the mountain-side, which

at that point, though dangerous with boulders, was not very steep. I was not hurt, except for a sprained thumb. But my beloved friend, always so fragile that one feared even the most ordinary strains of life, lay on the ground with blue lips almost unconscious. She was in agony, and thought her thigh was broken. Her husband, who was in the car just behind, was by her side in a moment. With difficulty we lifted her to a *stolkjære*, and drove to the nearest house, a small station or inn, at Fibelstad-haugen, two miles away. The only available room was up a narrow and winding stair. Our dear sufferer was patient, and even by now smiling, but quite helpless. The nearest doctor was miles off at Hellesylt. We dispatched a messenger, who came back with the news that he was away on his long rounds, and could not come for two days. But a young medical student from Christiania came up and gave us his counsel. He was confident that nothing was fractured. It was only the stound and the bruises, which would make it necessary to be still for a time. Never was fee given to a qualified doctor more thankfully than to that student ; I prayed fervently for his professional success. The recovery was gradual. But the joy seemed to have passed from Norway. The accident felt like a shadow on the past and on the rest of the tour. " The only resource is prayer," is the entry. Much sooner than we expected, the brave sufferer was able to go on to Hellesylt on the Geiranger. But we were far away from the base, and the long rides caused her pain and sometimes brought on a collapse. At last we reached Fjorde, where a coasting steamer would take us down to Bergen. But in changing steamers at Askevaald my friend John slipped backwards on the rainy pier, and staggered to the saloon in agony with a bruised back. On that voyage I had two semi-cripples to convoy home. The only comment on that tour was : " Thankful indeed to be safely back again."

This was the preparation for the duty of next year.

The first of January 1893 was a Sunday, the happiest beginning of a year. It was a happy day, as an entry in my journal shows. "Got up for the early Prayer Meeting at 7.30 in keen cold, but the morning was lovely, and the bright promise of the year bowed my heart with gratitude to God. The services were happy —not very large attendance—but God was with us, and He hears our vow to make the year a glad offering to Him. In the morning we gave as the year's motto : 'If ye have love one to another.' The evening lecture was entitled, 'Excuses good and bad.' Saw the ponds on the heath covered with skaters like emmets moving rapidly over a sheet of note-paper."

I had in the early year to contribute an essay on the Atonement to a volume called *Faith and Criticism*, which my friend Dr. Adeney was issuing, as a very modest Free Church companion to the famous *Lux Mundi*. My essay was tentative, and I have myself advanced on it very much since, but one thing makes me thankful now : I did not, in impatience, throw up the Atonement, as many did then, because the explanation was inadequate. As a man nears the "dark portal at the limit of his human state," he praises God for the restraining hand which has kept him in the rough seas of life and tumult of thought from making shipwreck of the Faith.

The lectures for Yale were getting written, and Mr. Fisher Unwin had been asked to publish them so soon as they were delivered. The subject had come to me with great force. My studies in Inspiration and Revelation had shown me that in the Bible the Word of God never means the Bible itself, nor any written book, but only the divine communications which come to men, prophets, saints, or humble men of heart, who are willing to hear, and that therefore the Word of God in the fullest sense is the equivalent of our Lord Jesus Christ, the Prophet, Priest, and King of our faith. That the Word of God, in this sense, uttered itself throughout the Bible, could not be doubted, but did the Word of

God cease to utter itself when the Canon of Scripture was completed? The Canon of Scripture never was definitively completed, because when the Council of Trent for the first time laid down authoritatively the contents of the Canon, it included the Apocrypha. Granted that the Word of God, in Christ, was complete, was there any reason to think, especially when the Holy Spirit was given through faith in Christ, that no fresh and immediate and authentic word would ever come to Christian men again? The Catholic Church maintained that fresh revelation had come through the Apostolic deposit, and had found expression through the Councils, and latterly through the utterances of an infallible Pope. This view, plausible as it seemed, was discredited by the substance of the things thus added to the teaching of Christ and His Apostles. But if the Word of God in Christ was held firmly as the standard, the test, the ultimate reference for the later utterances which should come through prophets, everything would point to the belief that God meant to speak continuously and widely and particularly through His servants. The prophets in the New Testament showed that this was the primitive view, and as they slowly faded away and were replaced by bishops, priests, and deacons, if there was a gain in order, there was a loss in the more important matter of freshness, progress, expansion. I was much impressed with a remark of Schultze : " A religion which is growing has prophets, a religion completed has scribes." Could it be, I began to think, that the intention of God all along had been, by the gift of the Holy Spirit, to send His Word regularly by those whom He called to be the pastors and teachers of His people?

I knew well that ministers did not take this view of their calling : my father once in a sermon, which I recalled, definitely repudiated the idea that the minister is a prophet, receiving any direct communication from God. But the conviction remained immovable in my mind : *that* was the intention of the Ministry. The Holy

Spirit meant to speak through every true preacher the
Word of God, not necessarily new revelations of truth,
but such timely and forcible messages as were given by
the true prophets of Israel. If this be so, the minister,
once sure of his vocation to the ministry, must surrender
himself to God, and submit all his faculties and labour
assiduously in order to receive the Word of God and
to deliver it.

That was the argument of my lectures. I was told
by a friend of mine, a young clergyman, that Bishop
Westcott, on reading my book, declared that it presented
a forgotten truth concerning the ministry. Again and
again I have met ministers who, in reading the book,
formed a view of their ministry which greatly influenced
their lives. But my plea was in the main refused by my
generation, though I still hope it may be heard by a
generation to come. I wrote out of my heart ; I said
as plainly as I could in public lectures what I had
myself experienced. The book, at first called *Verbum
Dei*, and then republished as the *Word of God*, was,
like Richard Jefferies's *Story of my Heart,* the somewhat
reluctant revelation of my inner life. Perhaps I was
all unworthy to utter the truth ; and when in that same
year a volume of my sermons, *The Lyndhurst Road
Pulpit,* saw the light, readers may have felt that the
results of my view were too inadequate. But the truth
I uttered must stand, even if I failed to illustrate it in
my own unworthy ministry.

In April I crossed the Atlantic in the *Umbria,*
which had just been refitted after a disastrous voyage.
I had with me Mr. Duncan Basden, one of my elders,
and his cousin Frederick Law, who were going to
America on business ; also Mr. Curtis, who was a
member of Lyndhurst Road. We were therefore quite
a little church, and were able to observe the times of
the home services, making allowance for the added forty
minutes daily. At that time there was more freedom
on a liner than there is now. I was able to range

throughout the ship unquestioned. This gave me
golden opportunities, especially in the steerage, where
a thousand emigrants were peculiarly open to a
message of love from Christ. Some young Welshmen,
emigrating from the tinplate works which were then
closing down, formed a most attractive choir. They
sang and I preached. On Sunday the captain asked
me to speak in the saloon, but the deck services were
far more spontaneous and effective. Mr. Senior, the
Daily News correspondent, sent to the Chicago
Exhibition, was on board, and we had some talks
together. He sent a very vivid description of one of
those deck services to his paper. There were also
many Swedes going out to the West. I remember
sitting down by one of them, and explaining to him
the message of Christ to the soul ; he took it home at
once with great joy. One or other of my friends came
with me even into the fo'c'sle, where the sailors gave
us a hearty welcome. The stokers' fo'c'sle was not
quite so friendly, but they suffered me to speak a few
words to them. There was a Miss Burstall on board,
sent out by the Gilchrist Trustees to inspect American
schools ; with her I had some long and interesting
conversations. I had an opportunity also with S. Correiro
da Graca, the Brazilian representative at Chicago. I
gave him a New Testament, and he was very pleased.
The gospels and testaments I had brought with me
were an introduction to many conversations, though it
was very touching when I had given some to the young
Irishmen, who formed a large section of the emigrants,
to have them bring the Gospel back to me, implying
that they dare not read it. There, I knew, was the
root of all Ireland's troubles. There was only one
person in that vast company on board, about 1,500
souls, who resented my efforts. His face haunts me
still. He was evidently in the advanced stages of
consumption, and his expression was unsatisfied, and
to me unspeakably sad. I had some conversation with

him, and tried to show him the joy and peace of
believing. He had nothing to urge against what I
said. But on the last occasion he said to me : " I
wish you had not talked to me." I think the claim
of Christ disturbed his mind, and, like the people of
Gadara, he said to Christ : " Depart out of my
coasts." Long, long ago he must have passed away,
but I am not without hope that the seed dropped would
bear fruit before he went.

The voyage was boisterous for the season of the year,
and many of the saloon passengers kept their berths
all the time ; but for me it was a week of happy
activity. I stilled my home-sickness and my anxiety
for the loved folk at home by finding a world of human
relations in the ship's company.

I had a little more than three weeks in America,
and they were very crowded. My lectures at Yale were
given three days each week, and in the intervals I was
able to go off to New York or Boston, and every
moment was occupied. The charm of American friendliness and hospitality completely captured me, and I
have always felt since that there is no country in which
an English visitor is made to feel so proud of England
and of his birthrights. From the day of landing to
the day of departure, when my stateroom was filled
with fruits and flowers by unknown friends, I was, as
it were, personally escorted and paid for, and everywhere I was made to feel absolutely at home. My
lectures in the Divinity School at Yale were very
kindly received, and the University people rallied round
me and entertained me, with the result that at the close
the parting from that bright, warm-hearted company
was quite sorrowful. Both at Yale and Harvard I
found all the charm of our own university life : the
culture, the varied interests, the striking intellectual
gifts, but a freedom, a naturalness, a vivacity, which
in Oxford at least are quite unknown among the dons.
One friend I met who left a lasting impression : Mr.

Weir, the Professor of Art, was greatly interested in my lectures, and asked me to his house, where his two beautiful girls played the guitar together. But his object was to illustrate to me the way in which the Word of God may have come to the Prophets—on this I had not touched in my lecture on the Prophets—he said that for five years he used to receive communications in the following way : he *saw* the words written before his eyes, and he copied them down without difficulty ; he had printed these communications in a book which he gave me. That book, he said, was not his at all, except in the sense that he wrote it from dictation. It is a remarkable book, presenting religious truths in a fresh and striking way. Here was a work very similar to the Prophetic literature, and the manner of its production showed why the prophet was called a seer, and why his oracles are described as visions. It was all very interesting, and I found that Yale had taught me more than I could teach it.

Dr. Munger was at that time leading thought into broader channels, and I greatly enjoyed my times with him and his young wife. In that charming household I caught the spirit of New England Puritanism. Mrs. Munger in my presence always addressed her husband as " Mr. Munger " ; it was a relic of the old times of shamefast reverence between man and wife. Professor Fisher was charming in another way : his stories, especially about negroes, were inimitable. Professor Stevens, whose books are studied by all theologians, Professor Curtis, and Professor Porter, were, in their own way, equally attractive. Between them the Yale people gave me one of the happiest experiences of my life. My visit to Boston from Friday to Tuesday was almost equally delightful. Professor Ashley, who had been one of my Nonconformist Union at Oxford, entertained me at Cambridge, and showed me Harvard and the sights of Boston. At an assembly I met Oliver Wendell Holmes, the

smallest man that ever carried so large a heart and
so bright a wit. Perched on a chair in the midst of
an admiring group, he read us his *Dorothy Q*. He
was very pleased when I told him how often we sang
his hymn " Lord of all being throned afar." Professor
Henry Drummond happened to be at Harvard that
week, and I came under the spell of his personality
for the first time. I have in my *Great Issues* depicted
him as an ideal Christian. He was among those
students gathered from many colleges for a conference :
a light, a challenge, an enigma, a reflection of his
Master. On the Sunday I preached for Dr. Gordon
in the New South Church. I realized there how a
prominent Congregational minister ranked with bishops.
He had been a close friend of Phillips Brooks, who
had just passed away. Trinity Church, that strange
freak in ecclesiastical architecture, is adjacent to the
New South. The bishop and the minister had worked
side by side as brothers. I went to the bishop's empty
house, and realized what a vast personal force had
been withdrawn from Boston and from America by his
death.

I was much amused by the description given by a
Boston paper of my pulpit work in the famous church.
I was, said the writer, just what would have resulted
if Matthew Arnold had become a Salvation Army
captain. The American Press is very piquant and
personal, and yet I am apt to think that the description
was just. I am conscious in myself of such a combination. On the one hand my sympathy is entirely
with the taste, the almost fastidious taste, of Oxford—
and Matthew Arnold was its embodiment—and on the
other hand I have desired nothing better in life than
to be an insistent preacher of Christ, without conventional
restraints, in season and out of season. I think I went
to Boston to get myself photographed in a phrase.

Dr. Amory Bradford, of Montclair, New Jersey, came
to Newhaven for one week of my lectures, in order to

carry me back with him to preach at his church. Of all Americans I have known, he was the most lovable. I was entertained in his beautiful house, and thoughtlessly put my boots outside my door, instead of blacking them myself, for which I had brought the brushes. My belief is that this cultured, loving, and beloved man rose early and blacked my boots for me. Certainly the " help " would not have done it for any price. It was just like him. My first acquaintance with him was made years before, when he called on me at Dunedin ; the maid left him in the hall, and I came down to be greeted : " I am not a beggar, nor a pastor seeking a church, but——" It was Amory Bradford, whom no one ever met without loving. It was a joy to preach in his church and to be among his devoted people. Of all positions I saw in America, I should choose that which he held. His influence spread like sunshine all through the Eastern States.

New York attracted me even in that first visit. The long line of buildings seen across the Hudson from Montclair, at a distance of ten miles, was then, and is now still more, one of the finest aspects of a city in the world.

Even then I was struck with the sumptuous offices in Broadway, and the habit of bestowing artistic skill and design on the high places of commerce, which distinguished medieval Italy, Genoa, Perugia, Pisa. At that time the highest building—the cathedral of the city, as it seemed from a distance—was the *World* newspaper office. I was shot up its fourteen stories in a few seconds, and surveyed the curious mathematical preciseness of the New York avenues and streets. I spoke in Broadway Tabernacle, of which my friend Dr. Stimson was the pastor, and after the service the people, some of them the most prominent in New York, filed past me and shook hands. One gentleman, greatly to my surprise, in reference as I afterwards saw to my sermon, jerked his thumb into my waistcoat on the left side, and observed : " Guess that came from *there*." New York is a fine example for other cities of the United States to follow, though it must be a despair to find such a site elsewhere : its two rivers, and the long strip of Manhattan, Brooklyn Bridge, and the glories of the Hudson, leave an impression that the city is destined some day to lead the world. In my last visit to New York, in 1913, I stood on Brooklyn Bridge in the winter sunset. The vast symmetrical piles, the Municipal Buildings and the Woolworth building, shooting up in the form of a vast church, to the height of fifty-four stories, stood outlined against the ruddy sky. Then the myriads of windows were lighted up, and the lines of lights ran along the roofs and domes (as they seem) of the huge piles. For vastness and splendour of effect I have seen nothing in earthly cities to surpass that sight.

When my work was done I left the country with a lasting love for it and its wonderful people. And yet, when the *Etruria* swung round from the wharf into the river, and we were facing home, my eyes filled with tears of joy. I had missed an English April, which could never be replaced ; my people and my friends had acquired a new preciousness by having the Atlantic roll between us. All the voyage home my heart was singing—

> Why this delight to leave a kindly shore,
> This rapture as the prow turns to the sea,
> This welcome to the great Atlantic roar,
>   This tearful glee ?
>
> Why are all faces lovely on the ship,
> All voices music, billows fairer far
> Than fields and spacious cities, as we slip
>   Across the bar ?
>
> Why do the mists seem angels ministrant,
> Why does the day seem favourable for flight,
> While with an eager breath the engines pant
>   Throughout the night ?

Why do we dare, as if in urgent haste,
To dock each day of minutes that it needs?
It is because the ship has *homeward* faced,
          And *homeward* speeds.

Blow, happy wind, and whistle in the shroud ;
Roll, happy wave, and fling your crest in foam ;
Gleam, tranquil star, between the bars of cloud ;
          I travel home.

Rush, mighty waters, fretted by the wind,
Heave the great ship in arms of quivering love,
Fall in long tracks of passionate white behind,
          Homeward I move.

Smile to the sky, O sea, now storms have ceased ;
Smile to the waters, clear ethereal dome ;
Hail, white-winged bird with welcome from the East ;
          We're nearing home !

What rises dark against the dusky sky,
Those hills that break the purple waves in spray?
It is my land, we in the port shall lie
          At break of day !

On the Sunday, by the captain's request, I preached
in the saloon on the Fruits of the Spirit. In the
afternoon I tried a service on the deck, but the temper
of people coming from America is strangely different
from the temper of emigrants who are starting for a
new country. It was difficult to gain their attention.
But I made a friend of the fourth officer, whose name
was Barr. He took me all over the ship, even down
into the hold where the long shaft of the screw was
revolving. He told me wonderful stories of the sea ;
how, for instance, once as an apprentice he was on a
ship when a man fell from the mast, and the roughest
of the crew came to him, as to one better educated, and
said : " Will you, sir, offer a prayer? " He had also
been under Captain Cook, the Commodore of the Cunard
Line. Cook was evidently a fine seaman and a good
captain. He would not talk to passengers, and was

absolutely imperturbable, whatever happened. One day Barr knocked at his cabin while he was shaving. No answer. Knocked again and again. The door half opened : " Is the ship on fire? " asked the captain. " No, sir." Then the door was banged to again.

A lady passenger watched for a chance of speaking to the captain, and thought it had come when he stepped out with a sextant or quadrant and a glass. The clouds came over, and she said pleasantly : " I see, captain, the clouds have prevented you from making your observation." " They have not prevented you, madam, from making yours," was the only reply. Once a passenger rushed into the smoke-room exultant, saying he had met the captain on the companion-ladder, and he had spoken to him. " What did the captain say? " was the question from all sides. The passenger's countenance fell, but at last he was obliged to repeat the captain's words, which were : " D——n you, sir, get out of the way ! " The bos'n came to Captain Cook on one voyage and said : " I'm going to leave, sir, I have a place on shore." " You're a fool ! " was the captain's reply, " you will do no such thing." And such was the captain's authority that the bos'n stayed.

One day we had a gale. Tremendous seas chased us astern, and once or twice broke in force on the deck. I was on the top deck, forty feet above the level of the sea, and incautiously went to the windward side of the deck-house for a moment. Immediately a wave dashed over, and a river of water would have swept me off my feet if I had not clung to a collapsible boat. The ship rolled a good deal for some days ; but when things were calmer I found extraordinary interest again from conversations with the people. There was on board a very charming man, Sir Alfred Moloney, the Governor of Honduras. He exhibited his wonderful collection of butterflies, and walked about a great deal with a lady who seemed undesirable. I had formed an impression that the genial Irishman was a man of the world, and nothing more. But one day, as we talked, he asked me into his cabin, which was a large stateroom on deck ; he surprised me by showing me an address which the people had presented to him in grateful acknowledgment of his good government, and especially for his efforts to combat yellow fever. Then he told me that his wife, who was everything to him, had died of the fever, and as if for her he had turned all his attention to overcoming the plague. I said a few words, to which he replied in a way implying that he had a deep and strong Christian faith, and lived in the hope of reunion with his wife. That experience led me to a conviction, which has grown stronger year by year, that the Christian faith is in the hearts of my countrymen, though they try rather to conceal than to show it.

In seven days I was home again, rejoicing in the warm welcome, first at Southwood, and then at Lyndhurst Road.

The few days of rest in Halifax before returning to work were, I think, the happiest I ever spent. My best friend was radiantly glad to see me back ; the English May was inexpressibly beautiful. The trees like lamps of lucid green, lit by the sun, the soft sweep of the Yorkshire moors and hills, the feeling : this is England ; the happy talks and reading together ; the sense of the protecting care that had been over me, and of a difficult task accomplished ; the hope (not yet disappointed) that *Verbum Dei* was a message of lasting import, filled me with unutterable gratitude and joy. " One more day of this large and conscious happiness hitherto not known in life " is the entry on the eve of returning to work.

I dare to believe that the life beyond will be of this kind, and the brief experiences of achievement and contentment here are granted to us as foretastes. Arriving in that haven of the Father's house, we shall feel that the stormy seas are passed, and the blessed society of comprehension and love has been reached. The task of life, attempted and finished, will be seen in its true light, and glorified by the Grace of God, which considers our intentions rather than our achievements, the tenor of our endeavour rather than the sum of the attainments.

'Tis not what we do exalts us, but what we would do.

At any rate, on that first return from America I formed a clear idea of what heaven might be. Even the country between Liverpool and Manchester, which ordinarily looks flat and uninteresting enough, seemed to eyes which had dwelt on the American landscape like a carefully kept and ordered garden, and all the people I met I longed to greet and to congratulate on the fact that they lived in the Island of the Blessed. It is well to be absent from England for a season, in order to desire her afresh, and to return with the spirit of a lover.

There was one immediate result of my visit to Yale. The University presently forwarded to me a diploma conferring on me the degree of Doctor of Divinity. This was embarrassing. I had always shrunk from titles and insignia of all sorts. It seemed to me that character and achievements are the only real tests by which men should be judged, and the highest title of all was the plain name, which for those reasons has come to be used as distinctive and sufficient. What title of nobility sounds so illustrious as plain John Bright? If I might have had my ambition gratified— but of course it could not be—I should have asked that my name, without any titles, might have been re- membered like those of Baxter, Howe, Dale. But before I could even consider whether to admit the title I was dubbed Doctor by the Press, and every corre- spondent, and every announcement, seized on the designation. It was amazing to me to find how the

world values, and therefore confers, an appellation of
this sort. I did not like to repudiate it, and request
that I might retain the plain name, Mr. Horton, which
had been enough for my father, and my grandfather
before me, lest I should seem to cast a slight on my
friends at Yale, who had treated me with only too
much kindness and honour. I consulted my friend,
Dr. Courtney, who as an old Fellow of my own College,
and at that time a frequent attendant at Lyndhurst
Road, whether, as an Oxford man, I should bear the
title of D.D., which might suggest that it had been
conferred on me by Oxford. He was of opinion that
the high repute of Yale made its Divinity Degrees of
equal value with those of Oxford. I followed his
counsel, and acquiesced in the uncongenial name. I
entreated my own people still to call me only " Mr.,"
and for some years they complied with my request.
But a new generation rose up, and the practice of the
outside world forced the Church into conformity with
it. I submit with as good a grace as I can. And it
is a pleasure to me as bearing one of its degrees,
honoris causa, to receive the notices and literature of
Yale. However distasteful the title D.D. is to me, it
at least constantly recalls to me those kindly, cultivated,
earnest people, who made my visit to the States so
delightful, and joins Yale with Oxford, America with
Great Britain, in all my thoughts and prayers, and
all my hopes for the future of the world.

In August we had a beautiful holiday in Scotland
at the mouth of the Clyde. My assistant, the Rev.
Basil Martin, published that month an account of me
in a magazine called *The Young Man* that greatly
angered my nearest friends. His candour was to me
not unpleasant, and his criticism seemed to me true.
My dear friend gave me one of those high and inspiring
talks which had been now for these long years my
greatest help, and I learnt more from the episode than
I could from eulogies. I became aware of some of

my most serious defects, and the rebuff came as a
most salutary counterblast to the praise and recognition
that had been showered on me in America. I have
come to regard it as a fixed law in God's discipline
of His children, that the *memento mori* shall be
whispered in the ear of the triumphator, and that,
whenever a success seems likely to turn our light heads,
some swift humiliation shall come to our deliverance.
It may be hard to love one's critics as much as one's
eulogists, but it is not hard to be grateful to them,
and to recognize in them true friends.

CHAPTER VIII

A SECOND DECADE

1890–1900

I HAD now been ten years at Lyndhurst Road, when in January 1894 the Church lost Mrs. Curwen, who had from the first been a mother in Israel. "We shall prosper," her dying husband had said to me. I thought he was referring to his own approaching entry into the heavenly country. "No," she said, "he means that the Church will prosper ; he is always thinking of it." It seemed like the blessing of a patriarch and apostle. And for ten years his widow had laboured to promote the good will in the nascent Church. She had drawn people together, cared for the poor, and organized the children into a missionary band. I was allowed to enter the room where she lay dead. The smiling peace upon her face was so heavenly that it seemed as if a light were shining in the dim January atmosphere, though the sun had gone. "Let us have this photographed," I said. But it could not be done. The picture had to live in our memories only. And there it has lived, and will. Hitherto members of her family have remained in the Church, and devoted their best powers to its life and work. I could wish that the name should never be separated from Lyndhurst Road. Not the least beautiful trait of that ideal character was the courage with which she faced new views and new methods. The changed way of regarding the Bible she tried with all diligence to understand and accept. And my own unconventional ways and proposals, though they shocked her, were treated with unfailing courtesy and consideration.

The tenth anniversary of my ordination was a serious occasion.

Robertson of Brighton, in Letter CLXI, speaks of a preacher who had lost his concise, sinewy, masculine style and degenerated into verbiage. " He has lost his power which was once the greatest I ever knew. The sentimental people of his congregation attribute it to increase in spirituality, but it is in truth a falling off in energy of grasp. I heard four sermons from him with scarcely four thoughts and much absolutely false logic. But how can a man preach for ten years without exhausting himself, or else pandering to popularity? Talk, talk, talk, for ever, and no retreat to fructifying silence ! "

It is a searching question. But I had refused Westminster, and was committed to enter another decade in the old place, and facing the same congregation. Unless the principle that I had advocated in *Verbum Dei* was correct, nothing but failure could be anticipated. Well I know that I had not any of those commanding and popular gifts which enabled Dr. Allon or Dr. Parker to continue in one place decade after decade. And I had been compelled by study and loyalty to truth to shake what seemed to many the very foundation of Christianity, viz. the verbal infallibility of the Bible. Evidently I had before me a task of reconstruction. I must labour to show that the real foundation of Christianity was not shaken by admitting the manifest facts of the Christian literature ; I must try to bring out the true foundation—" other foundation can no man lay than that is laid, Jesus Christ."

On January 18th I reviewed my ten years and made some forecast of the future. The notes of that address are before me : " I look back over these years with unspeakable gratitude. It appears to me that God has shown me nothing but favour. Not the least of His mercies have been my trials, my disappointments, the criticisms and attacks directed against me, and my unmistakable failures. Ten years ago I had just left Oxford with some misgiving. I had chosen the path, which, humanly speaking, seemed a mistake. Now, when I return to Oxford for a few days' work " (this was one of many visits to Mansfield for a fortnight or three weeks, to preach in the College Chapel and work among the Nonconformists), " I am in no doubt but that the path was the right one. On the occasion of my ordination I gave a statement of my views, which were summed up in two words, Jesus Christ. You were considerate and wise enough to demand nothing more specific. Now after ten years I am less than ever inclined to regret that definition of my ministry. He is simply infinite. I see why the records are imperfect : that we may seek and find *Him*. I suppose I often repeat myself, but that is not because the theme is exhaustible. If I say something about Him this week, next week the same thing said seems to mean more.

" Many have come and gone in these ten years—how rich we were then, and how we miss them ! On the other hand, this building has become hallowed by the presence of glorified spirits. In how many ways it is a sacred building now !

" As to the future, the swiftness of these ten years foreshortens the coming years. I used to dread life ; now it seems so rapid, a forced march across a plain to hills which are ever in sight, that there is no time to make much ado. I venture very solemnly to renew my ordination vows. And may I ask you again to enter with me into this one endless task of preaching Christ, who of God is made unto us wisdom, righteousness, sanctification, and redemption? "

So soon as *Verbum Dei* was published I set to work to present to the people Jesus, as He appeared in His earthly life. It occurred to me to take the earliest, briefest, and most picturesque of the gospels, and to expound it Sunday by Sunday, in order that the person of Jesus, as others saw Him, might be made plain. Thinking of the mosaics in St. Mark's at Venice, I called these pictures " The Cartoons of St. Mark." When the sermons were finished the book was published, although my best friend and adviser was apprehensive that I was publishing too fast. Her mind was, however, satisfied when she saw the reception given to the book. Even the *British Weekly* spoke with approbation of it, while testimonies came in for many years, showing that this clear-cut presentation of the very person of Jesus had struck people with awe, gratitude, and love.

But I felt the need of stating the whole doctrine of the Church in a connected form, in broad outline, relieved from the pettiness of mere texts and verbal arguments. I therefore followed the presentation of Jesus with a series of studies of the *Apostolicum*. I took each article of the Creed in turn, and attempted to present it, not with the scholastic minuteness of Pearson, but with the broad effects of what I believed the apostolic preaching had been. On one occasion, after completing the task, I said to the congregation which filled every part of the church : " Now with a better understanding and a fuller conviction of the faith once for all delivered to the saints, I ask you all to stand and to repeat with me the Apostles' Creed." It was a thrilling moment, and a most impressive sight, as those eleven or twelve hundred people recited the familiar words, not with the apathetic decorum of a church service, but with the freshness and eagerness of the early believers. I remember one member took exception to the proceeding ; as a Nonconformist he protested against creeds. It is a rather singular fact that his son sought ordination in the Church of England, and long after his wife followed her son into the same Church. An extravagant Noncomformity leads to reaction, but the joyful acceptance of all that is good and salutary in other Churches has a quickening and elevating effect. Those addresses on the Creed were published in a volume in 1895.

This year, 1894, was one of much physical weakness and consequent depression of spirit. Troubles, too, of an exceptional kind dimmed the prospect. But I have always found that in dark times gleams of exceptional light come, so that in retrospect the gloomy periods are like those landscapes of Copley Fielding or David Cox, in which the beautiful effect is produced by a bright ray of sunlight piercing the masses of rolling cloud. Thus in that May I find an entry like this : " Woke in the early morning with the golden sunlight in my room—never seen there before—and the most exquisite song of a bird (a nightingale, I wonder)— slow deliberate melody in short sweet bursts. ' Low in my heart he sings his carol to wake and to woo me ' was in my head, and a complete verse which, on fully waking, I could not recall."

The sorrow of the year was that my friends in Halifax, owing to business reverses, had to leave Southwood, which they had made the most beautiful of homes, and where the fancy of the children had turned the orchard into the garden of the Hesperides, and a little stream into the fountain of Arethusa. But their gifted and wonderful mother was to effect a more wonderful transformation. To economize, an old dilapidated house, known as Wood Hall, in the Sowerby Valley, was taken. It had some traditional association with Lawrence Sterne, and the actual owner was a clergyman living in Ireland. I well remember her taking me for the first time to this ruined abode. It was reputed to be haunted ; when I ran upstairs to see the bedchambers, she was left in the dimness of the hall, and she heard a voice saying, " You shall not come here." Everything seemed desolate and uncanny. But by the force of her own genius she transformed Wood

Hall, and made it in a few years better, I should imagine, than it had been in the whole course of the four hundred years during which it had stood. The large reception-rooms, with their windows opening out into the grounds, became beautiful. The dark, mullion-windowed bedrooms were turned into chambers of peace. One especially, the guest-chamber, she adorned with a quotation from the *Pilgrim's Progress* : " They brought him to a large chamber with window opening to the sunrise, and the name of that chamber was Peace." Even the room with a great beam, to which the ghost story was attached, became human and sunny, suitable to its lovely outlook. The garden was a wilderness, and in that early summer I offered my services to dig, and to rebuild walls, and experienced for the only time in my life for a few days the peculiar blessing of manual labour in the open air. It brought health, wholesome sleep, and happy dreams.

> O fortunatos nimium, sua si bona nôrint,
> Agricolas !

The ghost, however, was not laid, but rather evoked. Both my friend and the girls frequently saw the black form flitting through the rooms, or even in the garden, and sometimes they would feel an icy current of air accompanying the vision. Guests, too, would hear on the old stairs or gloomy landing loud talk and peals of laughter not accounted for by living inhabitants. For my own part I have not been gifted with second sight, and I was apt to treat these apparitions as fanciful. But looking out from the dining-room one day I saw a man's figure coming along the drive ; he was hidden by a clump of laurels ; indolently I watched for a second to see him appear again in the drive, but he did not. " What has become of that man? " I cried. And when I told Melcie what I had seen, she said : " That was the Blackie," the name they gave to the ghost.

But the sweet lives lived in the old house gradually drove away the uncanny atmosphere, and it became the most restful and inspiring abode in the world. The valley, marred by mills, with the stream of the Calder, defiled by dyes, was, in spite of man's desecration, perfectly beautiful. It lies between the rocks on the Skircoat Moor, the most picturesque object I know in any English town, and Norland Moor, which crowns the opposing line of hills—the moor often purple with heather, and in the springtime carolled over by larks, that were to me an annual renewal and inspiration. Nor were human interests wanting. My friend, cut off a little from the life of the town by the long steep hill, gathered round her the farmers and other labouring people in the valley. She had them in the dining-room on Sunday evenings and gave them of her best in spiritual guidance and uplift. There was a man named Tankard, who farmed a few acres, and might have done well, but he was defiled and ruined with drink. He would sell a cow, and with the sovereigns in his pocket would go to the public-house, dropping them about, and never recovering sobriety till they were all drunk or lost. This wreck of a man came under her influence, and a startling change took place. He was clothed and in his right mind. He proved to be a man of fine countenance, which had been up to then marred by his debauchery, and of strong intellect which had been ruined. He was like a prodigal son returning to his father. Alas! there was a relapse, and Tankard vanished in the darkness of his irrecoverable doom. But the loving effort to save both him and others brought a beautiful light into the days of loss and anxiety. She idealized the valley, and in reference to the vision of it, seen in the descent from the rocks, dotted with the lights from Sowerby to Copley, she called it "The Valley of Stars," and a story bearing that name was written for a periodical, though unfortunately not afterwards republished.

That summer we could not go far afield, but spent some health-giving weeks in the Isle of Man, reading Hall Caine's books on the spot, and marvelling at the imagination which enlarged and glorified the island. When *The Bondman* came out I thought we had discovered an English Victor Hugo. Though that impression was not established, there was much interest to be found in *The Deemster*, and the other Manx books, read in the midst of the scenes which produced them. Also we had long known and loved that other Manx genius, T. E. Brown, whose *Fo'c'sle Yarns* had made him a friend before the posthumous edition of his works gave him an assured place among the minor poets of the nineteenth century.

But the person who stands out most distinctly in that Isle of Man holiday is not Hall Caine, or T. E. Brown, or Farrar, whose *Eric* was placed in King William's College, near to Port St. Mary where we stayed, but a Castletown working-man, whose name was Stowell. We used to go by preference to the little Primitive Methodist Chapel, for we had learnt to love the Primitive Methodists among the fishermen at Filey. Our first Sunday the services were taken by the most plain and unpretentious man that I had ever seen in a pulpit. His face was marked with lines of thought and care. His voice was untunable, and his diction merely that of the street. But we were at once brought into an atmosphere of reality. In the morning he spoke on knowing God, and tears of deep feeling welled in our eyes as he showed how he had come to know God, not from books, but in the workshop ; not by arguments, but by the stern discipline of a workman's life. We were eager to go again in the evening ; he spoke on the words, " to live is Christ." It was all drawn from experience. He taught me a twofold lesson, that effective preaching must have practical points of contact with the lives of the hearers, and must be wrought out in the life of the preacher. Through fulfilling these conditions these two addresses, badly delivered, and without pretence of form or construction, were better than any sermons I had been able to preach. I knew that in God's sight they were on a higher level.

During my Oxford days I heard most of the great Anglican preachers : Liddon, Lightfoot, Bishop Magee, Bishop Alexander ; and since then I have listened to most of the preachers held in repute among Free Churchmen. But I cannot say that any of them affected me as that carpenter did.

I think it was this year (it may have been a year or two later) that Mrs. Ormiston Chant undertook her crusade against the immoralities of the London music halls. I determined to preach on the subject, and prepared my notes. Then it occurred to me that I had never been in a music hall, and perhaps I ought to know what I was going to speak about. I got a friend to accompany me, and we determined to go round to the three halls to which exception had been taken. We first went to the Empire. I was surprised to find the audience very similar to a congregation in Church. In the balcony opposite me I saw a clergyman in his clerical dress. The performance, perfectly decorous and incredibly stupid, dragged on till the interval. Then we went round the promenade, and certainly saw a number of abandoned girls, and far more abandoned men in evening dress, but no patent impropriety. We were to have gone on to the Pavilion, but the concluding piece on the programme bore a somewhat suggestive title, " The Court of Love," and I thought that perhaps the worst was kept for the last, and I should get a wrong impression if I did not sit it out. But " The Court of Love " was as harmless as the previous part of the programme. It was deplorable that human beings should find pleasure in things so banal, brainless, and insipid. But as I left the hall I saw that I was on the wrong tack. My notes had to be entirely recast. These London entertainments were not deliberately vicious, they did not aim at exciting dangerous passions. Their fault was negative rather than positive. They did not venture to treat the public as composed of rational beings with intelligence, good feeling, and a certain measure of idealism. Whether because the purveyors of the entertainment were out of touch with the people's life, or because performers of high character could not be secured, the entertainment missed the mark ; it excited curiosity, wonder, and occasionally mirth. But it never ventured to play upon the nobler side of men, or to give them that genuine joy which comes when they are lifted above themselves and incited to nobler life or more exalted ambition.

My fortieth year (1895) was crowded with work, but it was made singularly happy by the study of the Teaching of Jesus. I had seen the necessity of finding the sure foundation, when the foundation of Biblical infallibility was surrendered, and with that in view I had tried to bring out the self-evident and convincing authority of the Person of Jesus in the original Gospel records, and I had tried to show the whole Creed of Christendom growing out of that one unique Person. But now I turned all my attention to His words, the actual truths which He had uttered during His momentous life. Helped by Wendt and Beyschlag—Wendt's *Lehre Jesu* was for my life an epoch-making book—I tried to review and to present to my people all that Jesus taught. It was Wendt, I think, who first made me see that the apparently casual teaching of the Master presupposes a consistent structure of thought and belief, which can with sufficient clearness be outlined, and that the whole conception, the circle of ideas, presented in the Teaching, is so overwhelmingly great and satisfying, that on that alone might well be rested the attribution of Divinity which the Church had given to His Person. That is to say, I saw Christ taking His place as the Son of God and the Saviour of the World, not on the ground of an ecclesiastical dogma, nor yet on the ground of an infallible Book, but simply and solely on the ground of the words which fell from His lips. " Never man spake like this man." " The words which I speak unto you, they are spirit and life." He was the Word of God incarnate, and for that reason such words were uttered by Him.

It is impossible to describe the effect which this discovery had on my own inner life, and on my work as a minister. I felt that my feet were on a rock, that my message was assured, and that I now knew distinctly what I believed. In September the results of this study were published in a small book, which was called *The Teaching of Jesus*. I had no idea how it would strike the world, I only knew how it had struck me. But I dedicated any profits which might come from the sale to the London Missionary Society. I felt it impossible to appropriate a penny. His teaching commanded that all should be given to make the teaching known. I fear the profits were small, not more than £50 or £60. But I was allowed to see one edition after another demanded, and evidences came in from many sides that what had been to me a great discovery was coming as a great discovery to my readers.

I was particularly touched by the action of Mr. James Clarke, the publisher. He had published several of my books, but this one was brought out by Isbister. But Mr. Clarke bought a hundred copies of the *Teaching of Jesus* and distributed them through the country. I did not take it as a compliment to me the writer, but as a tribute to Jesus, whose words were thus brought before a hundred readers.

I had also a singular joy in connection with this book. My dear friend, Mrs. Oakes, with the view of helping her husband in the difficulties which were gathering about him, wrote a book of short stories, which was this year published by Mr. Dent, under the title of *The Ringby Lass*. It was an exquisite little volume, rich with humour and pathos, and the genuine love of her native county, which was one of the writer's most distinguishing characteristics. The dainty book was received with extraordinary favour, and it was evident that if only she had the strength of body she might write books that would live. On Friday, September 27th, I had the joy of seeing my *Teaching of Jesus* and my friend's *Ringby Lass* reviewed in neighbouring columns of the *Daily Chronicle*. It was always a proud moment for me to be put beside her in any sense. She had carefully read all my proofs and made many happy suggestions. I, alas ! could not help her in her imaginative work, which was quite beyond my range. But we were side by side that day in our literary productions.

That summer we spent in Wensley Dale. We had rooms in a little farmhouse in the one street of Thornton Rust. The village had no shop, and only one quaint little chapel in which " Passon " Hunter ministered, a Calvinist, who expounded with learning the five points of Calvinism, and during the week, clad in a smock, did his ordinary work as a farmer. The hymn-book used was Gadsby's, and it would be hard to find anything more amusing. It seemed incredible that this quaint survival should be an actual fact in the end of the nineteenth century. Here we sang about ourselves as " worms " sailing over life's troubled sea, and offered the pious prayer : " Permit Thy worm to bow." And best of all there was a hymn, entitled Linsey Woolsey, which after quoting the prohibition in Deuteronomy, not to mingle wool with linen, started off bravely—

> Everything we do we sin in,
> Chosen Jews must not use
> Woollen mixed with linen.

But the quaint survival in this corner of the Dales was only an agreeable touch of humour in a time of rich human interest. There was a man in the village who drove us over to Bishop's Dale, and then to Swale Dale by the Butter Tubs, and all up and down Wensley Dale. We got deeply interested in him because he was taking a downward course, and drinking, in spite of the fact that there was no public-house in the village. We longed to save him. And in deference to our wishes he came to the chapel. We went praying for him with all our might. And that evening " Passon " Hunter was lifted entirely above himself. He seemed to shake off the torpor which had settled on him from moving in the same narrow ruts for many years, and from the general indifference of the villagers, and he preached as a dying man to dying men. That was one of the occasions when I learnt how much the hearers do for a preacher. If they pray and expect and believe, their minister rises above himself and gives to them the Word of God, in spite, as it were, of himself. Our poor friend was as deeply impressed as we were, and I always cherish the hope that he got his feet upon the rock.

In Thornton Rust we were living in the days of Queen Elizabeth. A funeral—a very rare event—took place while we were there. When the cortège started for the church at Askrigg, some miles away, a bell was rung. It was a very ancient bell, which had been handed down for many generations. Shortly afterwards I happened to read Archbishop Grindall's report to Queen Elizabeth three centuries before. Among the pagan practices which he wished to exterminate from his diocese was " the ringing of a bell at funerals," which was indeed the old superstition of pre-Christian times, that as the soul left the body it was necessary to scare the demons, which otherwise might snatch it away. At the village of Bentham, between Thornton and Hawes, a horn was blown every evening to recall the labourers from the surrounding forest. The man who blew the horn was named Horner. I asked if his father blew it.—Yes. And his father?—Yes. And his——?—No, they did not remember. In Wensley Dale you feel the link with ancient times absolutely unbroken and unstrained. By lonely Senner Water, you seem to meet the tall archers who went to fight at Flodden. Bolton Castle, where

Mary Queen of Scots was imprisoned, seems quite modern. And the ruins of Gervaulx Abbey, and many another chantry and church, produce the vivid impression that the past was greater than the present.

It was in those happy holiday times, among the farmers, and the cows that yield the Wensley cheeses, that my friend was inspired to write her book, *Joan Seaton*. Parsifal-Dian is Thornton Rust, and the characters in the book are based on the people we met. Mr. Stansfield, the Member for Halifax, loved and commended the book as a true picture of his native dales, and Professor Wright considered that the Yorkshire dialect is preserved there in its purest form. It was an intense delight to me when Mr. Dent published *Joan Seaton* in Everyman's Library. I love to think that, when I and my books are forgotten, as the ephemeral outcome of a pastoral work, which of all works, except the actor's, is most confined to the lifetime of the worker, her books, as the work of art, and inspired with a rich and true imagination, will live and be read.

But again I felt the need of supplementing the insistence on the Person and Word of our Lord by presenting the whole counsel of God. It was an idea which I first gained from Dr. Dale, that a minister should avoid the temptation of teaching only what is palatable to himself, and neglecting the sides of truth which do not make to him a special appeal. Dale at the beginning of each year jotted down the doctrines which he felt it necessary to bring before his people. In that way he made his ministry that full-bodied and complete work which has left a permanent mark upon the Church. To be *teres atque rotundus* was always my ideal of personal character, and a similar ideal for my ministry took possession of me. Though now the Person and Teaching of Jesus seemed to me the whole doctrine of Christianity, I wanted to present the completeness of Christian truth, always preserving the centrality of Jesus. Dr. Dale had himself issued a book called

Christian Doctrine ; and taking his book as my text-book, I tried to expound and connect all the doctrines of the Church in a series of sermons. It was not necessary to publish these sermons, because they were sermons on a book already written by a far better and greater writer ; but the notes remain by me as the groundwork of a book which I should like to write before I die. Great changes have occurred in the relation of the Christian doctrines. What once seemed central is now on the periphery. What once seemed sure is more than doubtful. But the mould (τύπος) of the doctrine remains. The truth is molten afresh and poured again into the mould ; but the great body of reality presented in the revelation of Christ is eternal and essentially immutable.

But though I did not think it necessary to print my sermons on doctrine, I wrote a book this year which had, for the writer at least, an uncommon value. My friend, H. C. Beeching, now Dean of Norwich, was bringing out a series of Leaders of Religion. He asked me to undertake John Howe. Little did I think what a service he was rendering to me. I felt it my duty to read, not only all that had been written on John Howe, but all that John Howe had written. *The Living Temple* was but a part, I found, of the work which had come down to us from the hand of the great Nonconformist. I steeped myself in his thought ; I think I caught his spirit. To live for days and weeks with one strong and elevated character is an advantage which does not come to every one. Nor should I, in my crowded life, have come into this close contact with Howe but for the demand to write his biography. I do not remember how the book was received. I dare say there were many faults in it, but its effect on me was lasting. Unworthy as I feel to rank myself among those first great Nonconformists, I gained an ideal of Nonconformity from John Howe which I can never lose. He was of opinion that Nonconformity was a matter *unius ætatis*, that the reasons for it, arising out of the reaction of the Restoration Government, would be removed, and the Nonconformists would be allowed to return to an enlarged and enlightened Church of England. As he sighed at last for " the all-reconciling country," so he hoped for a Church on earth in which these divisions and antagonisms would become unnecessary. Ever since my study of Howe, for a quarter of a century, striving, as I have done, to consolidate the Free Churches and to conserve the truth for which they stand, I have always cherished the hope that some favourable gale of the Spirit would bring the Churches together again. We are ships, belonging to one navy, scattered by a storm. In the mists that fall on us, we mistake one another for foes, and forgetting the common enemy, congratulate ourselves if we sink or damage an alienated consort. In my desk has lain for years a proposal by which, I hoped, the Church of England and the Free Churches of this country might be drawn together again. Once my friend Dr. Headlam asked me to present that proposal to a rural meeting of clergy at South Mimms ; at Welwyn, of which Headlam was vicar, Young wrote his *Night Thoughts* ; there I was led to feel that my plans were but day-dreams. My plan may be futile, but my hope and desire remain unchanged. I should like, if I had room, to put down my view of the Church of England, and also my ideals for the Free Churches ; I venture to prophesy that a unity will one day be found, and that the scandal of Protestant Christianity will cease. That scandal is not that we differ and find the expression of our religious life in different forms or organizations, but that, differing, we can ever fall into the absurdity of regarding ourselves as rivals and antagonists when we all avow the same allegiance to Christ, and all desire above everything that He should reign as supreme on the earth.

In this year, as for years before and since, I was constantly preaching and speaking in all parts of the country. Hardly a week passed without one or more journeys. I had an effective colleague, Andrew Hamilton, who had been the senior student of Mansfield College ; and in his hands I happily left the Kentish Town Mission, but my own pastoral work at Lyndhurst Road had to be done. The membership was now over a thousand, and the organization had grown to a size and complexity which really demanded more time and strength than I could give.

It is therefore with a sense of surprise that I, with my present limited powers of reading, look down the list of the books read in that year. Mr. Fletcher, the editor of the *Daily Chronicle*, had enlisted me as a reviewer for his paper, which accounts for some of the miscellaneous books read ; but I think the list is fairly typical of those busy years of my mid-life. For a literary man, or one with any leisure, it would seem absurdly small ; but for one who had the charge of a great Church, and the claims from all parts of the country competing with the study, it seems to show that at least I tried to avoid the charge, which is sometimes brought against the ministry, of mental sloth.

Thirteen of the following books were read for reviewing, the rest for my own study or recreation—

1. Stanley Weyman, "My Lady Rotha." Weyman was my school-fellow at Shrewsbury, and I watched his success with much satisfaction.
2. R. L. Stevenson, "The Ebb Tide."
3. Miss Rossetti, "A Shadow of Dante."
4. C. Silvester Horne, "Story of the London Missionary Society."
5. Pearson, "National Life and Character."
6. Godet, "Introduction to the New Testament."
7. Dr. Denney, "Studies in Theology."
8. Principal Drummond, "Via, Vita, Veritas" : a book which gave me a rich hope for modern Unitarians.
9. Prince Galitzin, "La voix d'un Croyant."
10. Dean Farrar, "Daniel," in the "Expositor's Bible."
11. Blatchford, "Merrie England" : a heart-stirring book.
12. Pater, "Greek Studies."

13. "As Others saw Him" : that wonderful picture of Jesus drawn by a modern Jew, as I afterwards learnt from my friend Simon.
14. Scott Matheson, "The Church and Social Problems."
15. Philip, "Missionary Researches in South Africa."
16. Professor J. G. Romanes, "Thoughts on Religion."
17. Bernard Snell, "Loss and Gain."
18. R. L. Stevenson, "Through the Cevennes."
19. Quiller-Couch, "Story of Troy Town."
20. "Sonnets of the Century."
21. Coulson Kernahan, "God and the Ant" : a booklet which was a great book.
22. Miss Benson, "Subject to Vanity."
23. Dr. Stalker, "Trial and Death of Jesus."
24. Sheering, "Protestant Missions in India."
25. E. J. Dillon, "The Sceptics of the Old Testament."
26. Dumas, "The Three Musketeers."
27. Miss Frazer, "Stevenson's Samoa."
28. Craig Houston, "The Daughter of Leontius."
29. Herron, "The New Redemption."
30. Professor Adeney, "Canticles and Lamentations."
31. Ullmann, "The Sinlessness of Jesus."
32. William Canton, "The Lost Epic."
33. W. J. Dawson, "The Redemption of Edward Strahan."
34. Dr. Dale, "Christian Doctrine."
35. Björnsen, "Synnôvé Solbakken."
36. R. L. Stevenson, "The Merry Men."
37. Loti, "Pêcheur d'Islande."
38. Miss Harraden, "Ships that Pass in the Night."
39. Buckley, "The Moral Teachings of Science."
40. Hausrath, "The Time of the Apostles."
41. Harnack, "Dogmengeschichte," 3 vols.
42. George Smith, "Life of Henry Martyn."
43. F. A. Atkins, "Aspiration and Achievement."
44. R. E. Welsh, "In Relief of Doubt."
45. Tolstoi, "Anna Karenina."
46. Browning, "The Ring and the Book."
47. Stanley Weyman, "The Man in Black."
48. Ward, "Chaucer."
49. "Twenty Years in Khama's Country."
50. Beyschlag, "New Testament Theology," vol. ii.
51. Kidd, "Religion and Morality."
52. Miss Phelps, "A Singular Life."
53. Andrew Murray, "The Holiest of All."
54. Backhouse, "Church History."
55. William Law, "Serious Call to a Devout Life."

56. H. G. Wells, "The Wonderful Visit" : the book which at once set Mr. Wells among the great imaginative writers. I wrote an article in *Good Words* upon it, and doubt if it has, in its way, ever been surpassed for insight and wit.
57. Cobb, "Origines Judaicæ."
58. R. L. Stevenson, "The Vailima Letters."
59. W. J. Dawson, "London."
60. William Watson's Poems.
61. Rendel Harris, "Union with God."
62. Miss Stoddart, "Life of John Stuart Blackie" : Miss Stoddart was a member of my Church, and Professor Blackie had been a good friend of mine.
63. B. M., "Ezekiel and other Poems."
64. Andrew Bonar's Memoirs.

Now, when for many years I have been able to read only under severe restriction, and even then with difficulty, I look back with a sigh on the happy days when I could read as much and as variously as other duties allowed. The enumeration of the books read in 1895 makes me thankful that while my sight remained unimpaired I used my eyes to study as closely and as earnestly as I could. Often do I wonder at the courage of Prescott, who, blinded in the college campus at Harvard, yet succeeded in writing the two historical masterpieces with which his name is ever connected. When I think how my own work has been hindered by defective sight, I pay a tribute of veneration to the heroic blind—Prescott, Fawcett, George Matheson—who have "endured as seeing."

CHAPTER IX

IN THE TROUGH OF THE WAVES

1895-1900

THE closing five years of the nineteenth century had for me personally something of the tinge of a *fin de siècle* ; for repeated attacks of illness, with long periods of dubious convalescence, frustrated my plans and seemed to lower the tone of my work. Lord Rosebery's brief administration at the beginning of this period was said to have been ruined by the Premier's subjection to the same scourge that I suffered from. I had a strong fellow-feeling for him, and I learned to make allowance for men in prominent positions bearing great responsibilities. Influenza may be a more dangerous dilution of working-energy than the persistent assaults of the most vigorous opponents.

The year 1896, however, started with a happy feeling of peace and hope. And I approached the first Sunday, and the year's motto, " Redeeming the time," with two resolutions made in God's strength : (1) To work this year with a new devotion and concentration for the salvation of my own Church members, and to build the Church up in Christ ; (2) To avoid the glooms and declensions at the sight of failure and disappointment— by Prayer.

In discharge of the first resolution I began a much more systematic and laborious visitation of the members of the Church. In my early days I had visited the neighbourhood rather than my congregation : I had used the plea of inviting men to the Monthly Lecture in order to call on the publicans and as many of their customers as I could reach. The publicans were singularly responsive. One of them became a regular attendant at the church until he left the neighbourhood : once he embarrassed me by asking me as his friend and minister to secure for him a spirit licence, but he took my refusal in good part. Later, new members came in so rapidly that all my visiting time was occupied in seeing them. But now I saw the need of visiting the members and trying to know the homes and the families personally. I took districts and announced my intended visits on Sunday. Often I have visited for four or five hours at a time, until I was quite spent, and my tongue could no more. For twenty years I have kept up this practice, and a word may be said about it. From Richard Baxter at Kidderminster, and from my older contemporary Macfadyen of Manchester, I learnt the meaning and value of pastoral visitation, and came to regard it as a primary duty. For some unexplained reason this part of a minister's work is always laborious and uncongenial, and a thousand excuses are at hand for surrendering it. But, facing it *invitâ Minervâ*, week by week for many years, I have come to regard it as the indispensable foundation of successful Church work. I have known preachers of rare gifts who could dispense with it ; indeed, the odd thing is that the most apparently successful preachers do dispense with it ; and yet I remain convinced that the effect of preaching is never the same as that of laborious and self-sacrificing visitation. It leaves something wanting. The crowd which can always be drawn by a remarkable speaker is delusive ; the results produced on mere " audiences " are ephemeral. Preaching is best used when it is only subsidiary to the consolidation and building up of the Church. My experience has been that the best sermons are the results of talks in visitation, and further, that more are brought to Christ by that " fishing for men," or going out to find the lost sheep, than by the appeals of the pulpit. As I approach the period of forty years spent in one Church,

I am sure that this ministry could not have been, and it would long ago have lost its savour and power, but for the persistent and systematic effort to keep in touch with the people and to know them in their homes.

The resolution to deal with my personal difficulties by prayer leads me to set down some of the experiences which made prayer a power—an increasing power—in my life. During that year I heard an incident, wholly forgotten, of my childhood : when I was ten years old, a Miss Rogers, faintly remembered, mentioned in my home that she suffered from neuralgia ; the child (it was I) asked her if she had prayed to God, and there and then knelt down and prayed for her. How strange a light shed on the past, revealing what memory does not retain, that prayer was an instinct before it was a habit, a practice before it was a principle. Another incident, which I do remember, is of a more questionable quality. Convinced, as a child, that God could do what He would, I put a farthing in the dressing-table drawer, and in all good faith knelt down and asked him to change it into a half sovereign. I remember vividly the eager expectation with which I opened the drawer, and then, not a shadow of scepticism, but a certain sense of shame, as if I had tempted God. During schooldays the answers to prayer were very common. I prayed when I could not do my lessons, and did them. I prayed for my examinations, and every success seemed to me an answer to prayer. Once, in later life, an old schoolfellow told me how in the darkened room, which we shared, he was on his bed, and heard me come in and throw myself on my knees and ask for something aloud, supposing myself to be alone. He would not speak or move, and only years after said how it had impressed him. In Oxford days, when the chill mists of doubt often folded me in, and the inquiry into the possibility of prayer was met by the negative attitude of Mill and Huxley and Tyndal, I had one experience after another of the truth; however it was to be explained, that the prayer of faith was heard and answered. One instance stands out in my memory because it greatly influenced my life. In my Union time I felt it my duty to invite the Committee to breakfast. They were men at other Colleges, whom I did not know intimately ; it was a formal affair. It was then the universal custom— an odd survival from Elizabethan times—to bring up after breakfast tankards of college ale. To omit this would have seemed bad form ; and for Oxford in those days " form " came before both virtue and religion. I was greatly exercised, for I had, on principle, refused to keep wine in my rooms, and the custom of having beer at breakfast was to me revolting. And yet I wanted to show the usual civilities to my guests. The night before the party I knelt in my room and entreated God to guide me. While I waited on Him I opened my Bible, and my eye fell on a text in Isaiah, which up to that night I had never heard or seen : " Woe unto them that rise up early in the morning, that they may follow strong drink " (Isa. v. 11). I could not at first believe my eyes ; it was as if I had seen it written : " You shall not have beer for breakfast." The question was at once settled. In the morning my scout, on asking me for final orders, said : " Beer, as usual, I suppose, sir." Without hesitation, and with an emphasis which surprised him, I said, " No." God is very gracious to those who make any venture for Him. All through the breakfast I dreaded the look of surprise, and possible contempt, on the young faces, when the beer should *not* be brought in. But, strange to say, before the marmalade was disposed of, one of my guests rose and said, " Very sorry, I am due at a lecture ! " Then a second, and then a third, made a similar apology ; and so it came to pass that they all departed before the beer could have come in. I had the comfort of holding to my principle without failing in courtesy to my guests. Another stand for temperance was even more successful. I was glad to row in my College boat, but I declined the beer and port wine, which were at that time considered essential to training. "No," I said, "I will leave the boat, but I will not take drink!" I was strengthened by a firm assurance that I was obeying the commandment of God. Strange to say, five of the eight men followed my example. The Common-room butler, with the licence of an old servant, looked in at our meals and said derisively: "Toast and water! you'll be bumped—no boat can go up on toast and water!" It was that year that our boat rose from the bottom of the river and started on its career which at last put it at the head.

The habit of asking God, and depending on His guidance and help in the most ordinary circumstances, grew upon me. It was by finding the answers in daily details that I gradually learned to depend on prayer for the larger issues. Once in Norway, it must have been in this very year 1896, I had a startling illustration of the little things being in God's hands. We had rowed three miles up the Esse Fjord from Balholm, and then wandered among the birch woods and the broken boulders which covered the low spur of the mountains. When we returned we found an overshoe was missing, and for our delicate traveller those overshoes were absolutely necessary for wet steamer decks, and irreplaceable without many days' delay. Where the lost shoe was on that trackless mountain-side none but God knew. But in the afternoon I pulled up the fjord again, and through the three miles' row I asked God to show me what He alone knew. When I landed on the beach, and went clambering up the rocks, and without knowing how or why, plunged my hand down into a chink between them, there was the shoe! Nothing could be easier for an outsider than to ascribe the recovery to chance. Nor would it be worth while to quote the incident as a proof of the power of prayer. But to me it was an unmistakable evidence of the truth, so often verified in the important duties and difficulties of life: God is at hand, and hears, and answers. He does not often work miracles, but His answers to prayer form a continuously miraculous life.

In the periods of illness and slow convalescence, I fell into the practice of writing down prayers, and making lists of persons for whom I wished to pray. I always attached the dates to those entries. In the course of years these became a storehouse of arguments for the reality and value of prayer. I discovered that the answers to prayer are not, as a rule, sudden and startling, but gradual. If by night you watch the stars you never see them move, but if you mark their position, and look again in an hour or two, you see how the whole starry frame has glided over from west to east ; so it is with these answers to prayer ; only when time is allowed, and you turn back on the records of the past, do you stand in awe before the demonstration that your prayer, so helpless and imperfect, going up into the silent heavens, has yet been allowed to work and to achieve unexpected results. This practice, which grew out of my times of weakness, led me to the discovery that the times of weakness themselves were part, and not the least fruitful part, of the plan. I found again and again Samuel Rutherford's secret : " Whenever I am in the cellar of affliction, I put out my hand and find the King's wine."

But more important than these definite answers was the experience enjoyed by making the hours of prayer regular and dutiful, and by learning to regard the times of prayer as the essential parts of the day's work. I was impressed by the saying of a minister who, in looking back over his life, said that his main regret was that he had spent too much time in work and too little in prayer ; and I tried, imperfectly I know, to forestall that regret. *Bene orasse est bene laborasse* became a fixed maxim of life.

In 1896, in order to preserve health, I began to ride a bicycle ; and the young men of the Church

presented me with a beautiful Beeston Humber. Soon
after I got it I set out to Mill Hill, where I had
to speak. So easily did the machine run, and so un-
practised was I in riding, that suddenly on the Hendon
Road it shot off at a tangent, and plunged into a deep
ditch which at that time ran inconsiderately between
the road and the path. The delicate cycle was jammed
and the clumsy rider was thrown off after receiving
a stounding blow from the handlebar. When I rose,
I found that I could only with pain—and the machine
could not even with pain—proceed. Ignominiously I had
to return and break my engagement. Here was a
bitter chagrin ; I had begun to ride in order to increase
my efficiency in work, and the first result was to disable
me. I earnestly prayed that I might be able to go
on ; and keeping silence about the accident, and
dispatching the machine to the shop, I preached and
visited as if nothing had happened. A slight pleurisy
was caused by the blow, but in a few weeks the effects
wore off. When the bicycle was similarly restored I
began the practice of riding out on Saturday afternoons
with any of my young people who cared to come. It
was a great success. We rode out a few miles and
had tea together ; and I rode back hard, to be in time
for the Saturday evening prayer-meeting. In this way
I got to know the young men and maidens of my
Church : they were an untold joy to me, and many a
fruitful enterprise in the Church sprang out of those
councils on wheels. I remember with joy the long
spins in summer, or the wintry skies glowing in the
west as we reached our destination. All who used
to ride with me remain in memory as a pleasant
company, engaged in a Pilgrim's Progress, and yet to
arrive at nightfall in the heavenly home. It was one
of the saddest effects of my sight failing in 1904 that
these pleasant rides had to be abandoned, and the
machine which had given me so much pleasure was
passed on to a better, though not a happier, rider.

In these mid years of life it was very difficult to get regular exercise. Visiting tired, without refreshing, the body ; and travelling by train was then and always a kind of purgatory to me. Occasionally I went with my young men to the river for a row from Richmond to Teddington or farther ; but it came to be too common to do all the exercise in the holidays and make the work times almost unbroken, and for this I had to suffer.

That year also brought some interesting holiday times. In April I had a delightful experience of Wordsworth's country. Dr. Andrews and his family were among my kindest friends in the Church, and they had a house at Brathay. Perched on the hill above the stream it looked out towards Wetherlam and the Langdale Pikes ; behind, it was an easy excursion over the fells to Loughrigg, and round the Jubilee Path above Grasmere, to Dove Cottage and Rydal Mount. Those Lake days, in congenial society, offered nutriment to mind and body. There was a glorious day in which we traced the Duddon from source to mouth, and the series of sonnets became thenceforth a part of mine, as of Wordsworth's life. Another day, in rain and wind, we got to Tarn Hawes, and round by Esthwaite. To Wordsworth's school-house at Hawkshead was an easy walk. Canon Rawnsley's *Literary Associations of the Lake District*, together with Wordsworth's poems, made the whole country enchanted ground. Again, in the summer of 1897 I was in the district. My dearest friend and her family were at Patterdale during the Queen's Diamond Jubilee. I was climbing Sunday Crag, Place Fell, and Helvellyn every day ; and on the night of the Jubilee we rowed far up Ullswater, and saw the beacon fires lighted on the encircling mountains. Take it for all in all, I think our English Lakes make the most perfect combination of enjoyments that the earth affords. I never feel that Wordsworth invested them with their charm ; rather I think of the connection between him and the country as that of child and parent. He was ordained priest and interpreter of the Nature which elected him.

But the same year gave me some of the grandest mountain climbs that I ever had in Norway. The Lakes are better than Norway because they are English. But an impartial visitor to this planet, without the bias which comes from being born in England, might give the preference to Norway. That, however, is not my business. All I know is that Norway, with Knut Kvikne, and when I might have with me that kindling and inspiring presence that made a home for me anywhere, gave me the most thrilling moments of Nature-joy that I have ever had.

From Balholm, the Kjipen is seen at the end of the Esse Fjord ; the name means rowlock, for that is what it looks like at the distance of many miles—a slight notch in the snow ridge. One day in July Knut and I started off to reach it. Three-quarters of an hour's row to the end of the fjord ; by noon at the saeter, from which the summit seemed quite near. Three hours more of zigzagging up the seeming precipices and we stood on the summit. The rowlock on close view proved to be a chasm of 500 feet. Coming down was a delightful experience. Knut had taken up sacking, and making a rude toboggan, we shot down a thousand feet in a few seconds. The whole expedition took about nine hours, and Knut was the perfection of kindness and courtesy. To him the mountains were a church in which he praised God, and his talk was altogether human, wholesome, entertaining. Two days later he took me and a small party from the hotel up Totum, the long precipitous ridge which forms the eastern wall of the Esse Fjord. It was clear and warm ; we crossed the fjord to Tjugum, and ascended through the sweet birch woods, lovely with foxglove and fragrant with juniper, the soft grey bilberries and the multebær waiting to refresh us by the way. The fjord beneath was green or purple, and the mountains assumed all colours in turn. At the top was a stream, of which we could drink. We looked down on Fjærlands and the Vettli Fjord. And from one marvellous point on the ridge was a view which a wise Baedeker would mark with a double star. You look down an almost precipitous ravine in the mountain-side, and there, 3,700 feet below, is the green fjord sparkling in the sun. The descent in the hot afternoon was one prolonged kaleidoscope of shifting colours—the light remained broad—everything seemed transparent. Back under the nine hours, I had a swim in the fjord, and retiring to rest entered in my journal : "A day too perfect to describe, yielding every delight that earth affords."

There was another mountain experience not to be passed over. On August 9th was to be an eclipse of the sun. Professor (afterwards Sir William) Ramsay was staying at the hotel ; and we decided, under Knut's guidance, to climb Monkeggen, on the western side of the fjord, to see the sunrise. A party of fourteen started at 10.30 p.m. For four hours and a half we climbed in darkness or the glimmering twilight. Once two moving objects on a near horizon were pointed out to us as bears. By three o'clock in the morning we were on the crisp snow cornice of the summit. The sky was overcast, and when daylight came everything suddenly became sombre ; an awful, ghastly darkness stole over the scene. Strange to say, forgetting the eclipse, we thought a terrific storm was approaching, and the word was given to descend. Only, when in an hour or so the light returned, and we were going down, did we realize that *that* had been the eclipse. As the morning came the view was glorious ; a dense canopy of white cloud lay over the Sogn Fjord, and we looked down upon it, like a sea breaking on the mountain-sides, an occasional rift revealing the sea-level far below. At a saeter we found bowls of fresh milk ;

leaving the kroner to pay for it, we drank our fill, the most delicious draught I ever had. We were back for breakfast at eight o'clock.

One other scene stands out in memory. We stayed at Lofthus on the Hardanger and made friends with the pastor, Olaf Olafsen. From the steamer you see behind the village a valley which is closed in by a waterfall, breaking, as it seems, over the edge of the mountain. One day I set out alone for the fall. After climbing up for two hours I struck a ravine which ran laterally down to the valley. And there, in an awful solitude, I heard a roar of waters. Pressing on, I came in sight of the river plunging over the cliff into the ravine, and running on to form the waterfall, called Bjornebykset, visible from the fjord. The sight of that river from the high tableland falling over the mountain-rim into the gorge filled me with an inexplicable awe. I almost trembled as I climbed up to the top and walked a little way along the banks of that high stream approaching its plunge. Those mountain climbs and mountain visions have been a joy and inspiration all my life ; and unlike the less striking aspects of Nature, they remain vividly in the memory. If I were spared to see a blind and inactive old age, I could climb those great mountains and breathe the upper air almost with the same rapture in memory as I felt at the time. I never climbed anything, to say I had done it, nor did I ever brand an alpenstock with imposing names. But in every country I have visited it has been my ambition to get to the heights, and the rarefied air of the summits gives me the best suggestion on the physical side of what the life beyond will be : celestial mountains, ridges, and mountain-horns, not beautiful only at a distance in the transformations of the morning and the evening, but a dwelling-place of the aspiring spirit, the crowning summits of earth's laborious climb.

On the boat returning to England we met Cecil

Boyle, and had some fascinating talks with that eager, lithe athlete. In the Boer War he fell. He gave up everything—home, business, and all the delights of a successful life—to help his country. In the *Fortnightly* appeared an article he had written about his service under French, and it was prefaced by a brief account of his own death. I am always glad I met him, because in him I saw what in the Great War has been seen on a far larger scale, but with no finer lustre—the gallantry of our race, the culture, the courtesy, the courage, the self-sacrifice which our boys learn at their schools and in their English homes. I see him leaning against the bulwark, graceful and strong, showing little of the great soul that was in him. Ever since I have been apt to think that young Englishmen are greater than they seem ; it is an instinct with them to depreciate their achievements, and in dread of cant they prefer to be thought flippant, self-seeking, mercenary, anything but the quiet heroes that they are. Doubtless other races have their heroes ; but ours I know, and to know them is to aspire, and to pray to be worthy of our England.

I now received a good many requests from different publishers to write for them. William Canton, who managed Isbisters, induced me to put together some articles I had written for his magazines on " The Art of Living Together." The small book attracted the attention of some literary judges, and led Mr. Dent to approach me with a request that I should edit for him a series of Saintly Lives. He was very enthusiastic about it, and got me to promise a Life of Tennyson in the series myself. Another request appealed to me very strongly, viz., to write a Life of Oliver Cromwell. This was a task which brought its own rich reward : it required not only the careful reading of Carlyle, but the sober judgments passed upon the Protector by S. R. Gardiner in his history and in *Cromwell's Place in History*. Other books had to be read. And the study of the man became not so much historical as religious ; it was " a study in personal religion." The book appeared in the spring of 1897, just as I was slowly recovering from a long period of disablement ; its reception was very kindly ; soon it came out in a small and cheap edition, and now after twenty years there are still a few sales. This careful study of a remarkable personality led me to lecture on the subject in many places ; it also brought into my own life something of Cromwell's spirit ; I became possessed of the idea that a certain fearlessness and resolution, if only it is dependent on the Divine Will, forms the first condition of accomplishing anything in the world. I conceived of all my tasks of brain or will as a kind of charge at Marston Moor or Naseby, after long prayer, and with heart uplifted to God. It was an undesigned preparation for the stormy and nerve-torturing experiences through which I was destined to pass.

While Oliver was yet in hand, a new firm of publishers, Service and Paton, asked me to write a book on the *Women of the Old Testament*. I got it off my hands by the autumn of 1897, but much to my sorrow, my dear lady did not much approve of my undertaking it. No doubt it was out of the line of my deliberate work, and came only as a parergon in a year of exceptional weakness. For many weeks in the spring of that year I was battling to recover strength after an attack of my enemy. First I was in Brighton, then I went north. Sunday after Sunday had to be given up, and at last, when I returned, it seemed to myself as if I had been permanently weakened. It was therefore an inexpressible joy to receive a letter from Josephine Butler commenting on the book. From earliest days I had heard her name from my father as that of a heroine who was bearing the cross for her sex, and once or twice I had the privilege of speaking to her ; it can be readily understood, therefore, how priceless this letter was to me, and I take joy even now in inserting it here.

EWART PARK, WOOLER,
NORTHUMBERLAND,
March 10, 1898.

MY DEAR SIR,

I have been reading with great pleasure your book *Women of the Old Testament*, which was sent to me by your publishers. I must thank you for the generous spirit in which you judge and speak of women, and for the light which you have thrown around the character and circumstances of those of whom you write. I am especially glad of your chapter on the sorceress of Endor, a woman whom I have always felt an admiration of. But I am glad of your condemnation of her " Art."

Since I was left a widow eight years ago, I have been persecuted, in a manner, by spiritualists, of the educated and philosophical kind, as well as some of the more vulgar. I do not know what their motive is, but they seem to have desired to draw me into their views, and have used trickery even in order to get my name to appear as favourable to their ideas. Having had since my youth some near and personal knowledge of Him who is the source of all truth, I have never felt the slightest attraction towards these dreamers. But their persistence has given me an opportunity of observing the effect on their own characters and careers of the researches in which they delight. In some cases I have observed a gradual deterioration of intellect, a certain feebleness of mind and loss of the power of healthy work. But the most serious thing of all to my mind is the obvious and proved connection of spiritualism with the grossest sensuality. While pretending to soar into the unseen, and to hold spiritual converse with departed saints, they fall into the very slime of impurity, often of an abnormal and horrible kind, and it is terrible that they are unconscious that they have thus fallen. I had lately a letter from a man of whom I had once reason to hope much good, in which he echoes the words of St. John the Divine, in his Epistles, about Love ; and in the same pages he does not disguise from me that he has been interpreting that word love into the gratification of base animal passion. He imagines that I shall accept and approve of his letter and position. Have you had occasion to observe this strange connection ?

It seems to me the time has come for theologians, moralists, and thoughtful and learned men to look very seriously into this " sign of the times." Christ said there should come many deceivers in the latter times. " But be not deceived," He says ; " behold, I have told you beforehand."

I sometimes regret that the magnificent story of Judith was deemed too little inspired to be ranked in the Canonical Scriptures. I do not know who that Council or Committee were who sat and decided which books of the Hebrew Scriptures were to be chosen and which rejected.[1] I am sure there was no woman on that Council, they were all men.

I regret that the horrible story of Potiphar's wife was allowed, as inspired, while the story of Susannah and the Elders was rejected. But it was natural that the latter should be pronounced apocryphal by a committee of men, some of them probably pious old fellows who could not believe that Elders could ever be so immoral. But it is a pity. The woman temptress is made public for the edification of men, but the man tempter is hushed up.

Now I know something of the world. For thirty years I have worked more or less in that inferno of human woe and wrong to which few can descend. I have dear sons; and I feel as tenderly towards men as towards women ; but I mourn the little justice done to the woman who errs even in this nineteenth century of Christianity. And I think that Potiphar's wife, and similar portraits, have tended to strengthen in men the widespread feeling that the woman, when not really chaste, is the temptress always, the snake, the pythoness, the enemy of every pure man, the *aggressor* from whose approaches we must *protect* the dear young man on every hand, by warnings based on Solomon's curses of the "strange woman," and by legislation which treats *her* as a mere chattel or slave, and which is supposed to further the purity of men.

Few things are more offensive to me than a good moral man who approves and delights in this cruel, illegal, and unChristlike treatment of women. Such are some of our bishops and clergy. I had rather claim brotherhood and work with a deeply "fallen" sinful man who has compassion on fallen woman. I knew a young man, a student at Trinity College, Cambridge, who when it came to his turn to read the lesson in Trinity Chapel, and the chapter happened to be that recording the horror of Potiphar's wife, turned over and took another chapter. When called to account by his tutor, and asked why he did not read the right chapter, he replied : " Because it is very bad for the men to hear it." He was partly right. It is not the noble character of Joseph on which they dwell chiefly. But the presentation of a woman possessed by the demon of lust, the impure woman temptress, fixes itself on the young man's mind, and makes him inwardly swear at the first poor fallen girl he meets in the street, who was probably *first* the victim of some man.

I know from the tone of your writings that you will pardon me for

---

[1] Mrs. Butler did not know that the book was not Hebrew, but Greek, and that accounted for its place in the Apocrypha.

the expression of these thoughts. I send you a humble treatise of my own, in which you may care to read some thoughts of a mother (chiefly about Hagar).

Believe me, dear sir,

Yours truly and gratefully,

JOSEPHINE E. BUTLER.

Certainly it was worth writing the book, if only to elicit this letter from that pure and noble woman-heart that has now ceased to beat. For myself I was vowed to the cause of woman from the time when in boyhood I was in playful seriousness dubbed Knight by one who was always unflinching in the love of her own sex, and unfailing in her inspiring influence on me. Without any sentimental interest in women, and with a dislike, amounting at times to nausea, to sex problems, I was from those earliest days filled with an unutterable compassion for women who have been betrayed by men. " The Bridge of Sighs " moved me as no other poem did. When, therefore, women brought the question of their franchise into the field of practical politics my mind had been for long made up. I was convinced that the wrongs from which women suffered— wrongs which were the more terrible because many men from use and wont were utterly unable to recognize them, and therefore quite apathetic in remedying them— would never be successfully righted until women were allowed to take their part in shaping the laws and directing the policy of the State. When W. T. Stead shocked the world by his *Maiden Tribute of Modern Babylon*, I disliked the sensational method of the journalist, but I loved the heart of the man. If I have seldom spoken in public upon these questions of sexual vice, it has not been because I have not studied the problem, and thought and prayed over it, but only because I dreaded the morbid excitement, and the dangerous exaggerations, into which the advocates of purity fall ; and I early came to the conclusion that I personally could best serve that, and other similar causes,

I 2

by steadily preaching the Gospel of Christ, and doing what was in my power to deal with individuals. In later years I have worked on the National Council for Promoting Public Morality, and my acquaintance with Mr. Marchant, its devoted and enthusiastic secretary, has shown me how, and by what silent and unobserved methods, the cause of purity may best be served.

In October 1897 I was called on to preach the sermon for the Congregational Union at its meetings in Birmingham. Dr. Berry was the chairman that year, and delivered a remarkable address on " The Churches and the Kingdom." The previous evening I gave my sermon in Carr's Lane. The large building, illustrious by the great ministries of John Angell James and R. W. Dale, was thronged with an eager audience. It has been a sorrow to me that, whenever I have been called on to serve my own Denomination in a special way, some physical weakness has hampered my effort. That occasion was no exception to the rule. But my brethren in the ministry have always been singularly indulgent to me, and they seemed to preach the sermon for me. Mr. Slater, whom I had learnt to know and love during my mission at his church, Sherwell, Plymouth, uplifted me by the way in which he prayed before I spoke ; and then I expounded my theme, on the text : " As He is, so are we, in the world," that we are called on to represent Christ among men by living the life of the linked spheres, a life full of practical activities nurtured by the life in the spirit's secret cell. Poor as, I fear, the utterance was, the truth uttered was the result of my seventeen years' ministry. I told the assembly what I knew from experience, and explained such success as I had achieved by showing the secret which I should have preferred to keep to myself. It is surely one of the hardest features of the Christian's life, that none of us may live to himself. All the mysterious passages between the soul and God, too sacred, as they seem, even for private conversation

among friends, are given like St. Paul's transports to
the third heaven, only that others may have the benefit
of them. And I reflected that the greatest aids I had
received in my spiritual life had come from those who
opened the secret of their own experience with God in
order to help others. Thomas à Kempis, William Law,
Brother Lawrence, had been more to me than any
formal theologians. They had laid bare their hearts,
admitted all the world into the secret chamber where
their life was lived with God. And as I had received
help I was bound in my very limited way to give it.
It has not, I venture to believe, been egotism that has
led me to reveal the private and inner life that I have
lived, but merely a conviction that it was " God that
worked in me to will and to do of His good pleasure,"
and while I was unworthy, His doings were worthy
of praiseful proclamation.

The invitation to preach the Union Sermon was a
sign that I must expect further claims from the
Denomination. I am afraid I did not view the prospect
with satisfaction. Congregationalist as I was and am,
my sympathies were always with the Church as a
whole, rather than with any denomination of it, with
the country as a whole, rather than with the locality in
which I lived, and with mankind as a whole rather than
with my own nation. Thus I have always found it
irksome to enter into denominational management ;
ecclesiastical politics and personalities have been very
distasteful to me. Loving intercourse with ministerial
brethren in private, and rejoicing to listen to their
preaching more than in preaching myself, I have never
attended large assemblies of ministers and delegates
without some sense of shame and humiliation. The
platform speeches, with their ingenious play on the
passions of the assembly, the immoderate pleasure in
witticisms which to my mind have seemed out of place,
and the extraordinary impatience of purely religious
appeals, which are not supported by tricks of oratory

or laughable anecdotes, have made my attendance at these annual assemblies a thorn in the flesh, relieved only by the happy intercourse with friends in the houses that have offered me hospitality. But there could be no doubt concerning my duty : if I was called to serve the Churches in an honourable way, I must try to do so, and be grateful for the trust placed in me and the rich rewards of fraternal gratitude.

This, then, and an accidental occurrence which involved me for a time in controversy, most reluctantly undertaken, with Roman Catholics, plunged me into the two most toilsome and weary years of my life— 1898-1899.

CHAPTER X

CONGREGATIONALISM AND CATHOLICISM

1898–1899

IN April 1896 I had been elected as Chairman of the
London Congregational Union for the ensuing year, but
my health prevented me from undertaking the duties
until 1898. Andrew Mearns, whose *Bitter Cry of
Outcast London* had touched the heart of the country,
was the secretary of the Union, and he was very eager
to make my year of office serviceable. I set out with
two objects in view : the first, to draw the two hundred
and fifty Congregational Churches of London together,
so that they might feel and act as one ; the second,
to get the United Church to undertake extension in the
large and growing suburbs of the Metropolis. To
achieve the first purpose, I tried to visit all the Churches,
assembled in representative groups ; I showed these
assemblies the reason for thinking that the real Congregationalism would lead to the principle of " one city,
one Church " ; our isolation was not only a weakness,
but a proof that we were not loyal to our charter in
the New Testament. I urged that we should, in order
to realize our unity, engage the Albert Hall for a united
Church Meeting every year. Ten thousand members of
Congregational Churches, gathered together under the
headship of Christ, acting in faith and prayer for the
spiritual good of London, would, I contended, represent
the inner significance of the New Testament idea of the
Church for a great city. I did not at that time face
the larger question of the Unity of all Churches, and
the still grander possibility that would open up, if for

London there were but one united Church of Christ. All I urged was the more immediate object, the deliverance of the Congregational Churches from an exaggerated and perverted notion of independency. To achieve the second purpose, I asked for means to erect four new churches—at Herne Hill, Hither Green, Muswell Hill, and Harlesden. If the Congregational Churches would plant four new Churches in the outer ring of London each year, they would perhaps be doing their part in making spiritual provision for the expanding city.

At the April Annual Meeting in the City Temple I explained the ideal to a large assembly. On October 18th we held, what I hoped was to be, the first of the Annual Church Meetings for London. It was too ambitious to start in the Albert Hall, but we secured the beautiful new Queen's Hall, and to a large assembly I presented my appeal for the four new Churches. I remember Silvester Horne on that occasion thrilling the large audience with his impassioned plea for the larger Congregationalism. I came away from that meeting with deep thankfulness and a large hope. But, though the four Churches were started, and have since flourished, little of a lasting character was effected. I have often regretted that our religious newspapers are not in touch with the larger and higher thoughts of the Church. On that occasion it was indescribably sad to find the leading Free Church paper publishing an account of the meeting; not a glimmer of an idea had it of the object in view. All it saw was a public meeting, which must be entertained and roused by popular speakers. Its absolutely irrelevant question of criticism was: "Where was Dr. Parker?" Now every one knew that we could crowd the Queen's Hall, or any hall, to hear Dr. Parker: his dramatic genius could call together a crowd and dismiss it delighted. But what could he have done to promote the idea of a Congregational Church, whose own congregation at

the City Temple was not, in a true sense, a Congregational Church, and whose whole influence tended
to the very individualism which we sought to correct?
But the completeness of my own failure appeared when,
on my laying down office, a successor was appointed
who was so little likely to promote my idea of four
new Churches annually, as that he was known not even
to encourage extension in his own neighbourhood.
The work for the London Union had utterly worn me
out, and with no substantial result. In May I was
again prostrated with influenza, and when I went to
my friends at Blackpool to recover, we faced together
what was to us the greatest public loss that could occur.
On Ascension Day, May 19th, Mr. Gladstone died. I
remember how in the little sitting-room looking over
the western sea we read the account of the great
man's passing and the appreciations uttered in Parliament, even by his political opponents, until the tears
streamed down our cheeks, and we had to pass the paper
from hand to hand to find the reader that was not
overcome. It is not easy for the present generation
to realize how Liberals regarded Gladstone in the
closing quarter of the nineteenth century. He seemed
superhuman in his energy and eloquence, and we felt
an intensity of moral earnestness in his utterances which
made him the ideal Free Church leader.[1] It was
pathetic to realize the absolute devotion that Free
Churchmen gave to him, and the coolness with which
he regarded them. But his High Church principles
never stood in the way of Free Church appreciation and
gratitude ; and though Lord Morley in his Biography
does not bring out the fact, in private at any rate,
Gladstone was friendly and courteous to Free Churchmen to an unusual degree. I had met him in early

[1] The saint and poet dwell apart, but thou
    Wast holy in the furious press of men
    And choral in the central rush of life.
                                STEPHEN PHILLIPS.

days, and never forgot one of his gracious acts. In the seventies, when Gladstone's Government had just surrendered office, Oxford Liberals were founding the Palmerston Club ; we invited a number of the late Cabinet to a dinner at the Randolph Hotel. Gladstone came, and Sir William Harcourt, Childers, and Lord Coleridge. Lord Lymington was in the chair, and after the great men had spoken and Gladstone had explained the difference of parties in this way : " Conservatism is a contempt of the people tempered by fear, but Liberalism is a trust in the people, tempered by prudence," it fell to Milner (now Lord Milner, but then a young Fellow of New College) to move a vote of thanks to Mr. Gladstone and the others. I was to have moved another vote of thanks to some one or other, but midnight had come, and Lymington sent a waiter to my end of the board to ask if I minded my motion being passed over ; of course I was greatly relieved. But to my surprise, when the party broke up, Mr. Gladstone made his way down to me, shook me warmly by the hand and said : " I am very sorry that I had not the pleasure of hearing you speak."

Later on, when I was a Fellow of the College, I had another opportunity of meeting the great leader. The Warden of Keble (now Bishop Talbot of Winchester) sometimes invited me to his house to meet distinguished guests, as a " well-known Free Churchman " in the University. It was in that way I had the most agreeable *rencontre* with Shorthouse, the (at that time) famous author of *John Inglesant*. And to Mrs. Talbot's hospitality that evening I owed a conversation with her uncle, Mr. Gladstone. He was charmingly affable, asked me about New College, and about Free Churchmen in the University, and made me feel how rich a gift it is that great men can bestow on young men who are setting out in life.

And now in 1898 the great man passed. An epoch seemed to end. There passed with him something which has not returned—the old order of great Parliaments, the ringing cry of sympathy with suffering populations, and the imperious demand for the downfall of tyrants. Such a voice we have not heard again, nor are likely to hear ; and it must be forgiven me if I feel that when Browning and Tennyson were still writing, and Bright and Gladstone were still speaking, our country had marks of greatness upon it which she has yet in some future day to recover.

In August we had a holiday in Ireland, my first and last experiment in that kind. We went to the house of Mr. Carrol, the landlord of Wood Hall, Munduff, near Ashford, in co. Wicklow, which he kindly put at our disposal. The beautiful furniture, books, pictures, prints, threw a glamour over everything while we were indoors. But when we went out, visited the Devil's Glen, Glendalough, Glenmalure, and the exquisite Vale of Avoca, a feeling like despair was borne into our hearts. The land was neglected and deserted ; the few people we met seemed like aborigines dispossessed, haunting the ruins and the woods. I had never dreamed that a country could be so beautiful and so forlorn. And one experience of the courtesy of the peasants made me sigh for the day of Ireland's redemption. My friend and I, leaving the ladies to go back by carriage, went up Glenmalure to walk over the mountain to Glendalough. We never doubted we could get food at one of the scattered farms ; but all were closed or in ruins. At last we saw a shanty to which the men were returning from the fields. We asked if they could give us anything to eat : " Aye, surely," was the reply. A large family was at the bare board, but the father, a stage Irishman in appearance, but with the manners of a nobleman, drew half a loaf from a bucket and offered it to us on a cracked plate. Could we have a little milk? Half a cup was presented between us. " I hope we are not taking your dinner," I said. " No, surr, indade ; it's not dhinner we're having, but a tay like." Two faded and battered chairs were brought out from the ben of the cot, and we sat in front of the house among the pigs. On the strength of that crust we climbed the hill and came down into the vale of St. Kevan and the Seven Churches. " But how," I cried out in my heart, " have we allowed this beautiful country and these beautiful people to come to this pass? "

One of our party was Mr. Walter Keatinge, who was to marry Gwendolen, the elder daughter of my friends. He was an Irishman, and was inclined to twit me with my hope in Home Rule. When we had been north and spent some wonderful days around and on Slieve Donard—one day in a lonely climb on that crowning peak of the Mourne Mountains, I had an enchanting vision : the heavens seemed to stoop and roll down from the summit to meet me, and then to draw me up, and set my foot on the top, from which I saw Lough Neagh and all the tumbled beauty of Ulster—we came back to Greenore in order to sail up Carlingford Lough.

The steamer was to leave at two o'clock, as the card in the station and the hotel everywhere announced. We all had an early lunch, and at 1.45 went down to the quay. At the top of the steps a porter casually asked where we were going. " To the Carlingford Lough steamer," we said. " Well, thin, she's gone," was the cool reply. " Impossible," we cried, " she goes at two ! " " You can go down and see for yourselves," he replied. And from the quay we saw the steamer already a half-mile up the lough. I suppose I showed my annoyance, and Mr. Keatinge cruelly asked : " What do you think of Home Rule now? "

Well, I will not report my immediate answer. But that visit to Ireland filled me with an unspeakable love and compassion for the Irish people. Depleted as the country is, blighted by some fatal misunderstanding and ill-treatment, which even Gladstone's passionate chivalry could not correct, so loyal to the Church which to the

outsider seems rather to exploit than to bless her, so
courteous and friendly to strangers, so brilliant and
capable in her most distinguished sons—she makes an
irresistible appeal to the heart and conscience of England. If self-government can save her, all the world
will be the gainers. If it is too late—and even self-
government cannot restore the ancient nationality, or give
the virtues, the temper, the honesty, which are needed
for a true national life—at least we can and must
say that we have tried every other remedy and failed.
To win the heart of Ireland might well have seemed
to Gladstone the dearest ambition of his closing years,
and whoever may be fortunate enough to achieve what
he attempted will be reckoned among the greatest benefactors of the British Empire.

The glimpse I had of the working of the Roman
Church in Ireland did not tend to soothe an anxiety
which at this time overwhelmed my soul. In 1896 a
young cousin came to live with us while he studied for
his articles with a solicitor. He was a bright, charming,
affectionate boy, and my aunt loved him as his mother
did, and sought in every way to help and to save him.
He was good at football, and delighted in the gaieties
of London. Soon, to her intense dismay, for she was
a Protestant of the type that sees in Rome the Babylon
and the Scarlet Woman of Revelation, she found the
boy was being drawn to the Dominican Priory, and
in defiance of his parents and his aunt, he insisted on
entering the Roman Church. In that year Purcell's
Life of Cardinal Manning was published, and I spoke
about it to my young men, my cousin being present.
I referred to the lamentable picture of equivocation there
presented ; Manning being already admitted to Rome
when he was yet defending the Church of England,
and Manning's own judgment on the converts to Rome
before him, that their common characteristic was the
want of truth. Next morning my cousin, in conversation
with me, delivered a shock from which I could not

recover. Referring to my address, he said with perfect
simplicity : " But you may deceive in the interest of
Religion." In vain I argued with him. He had imbibed
this doctrine in his first contact with the Roman Catholic
Fathers.

This set me to read books of Roman Moral Theology,
and I found that the boy's impression, crudely as it
was expressed, was justified by the Roman casuists. The
indefeasible claims of truth, the uncompromising duty
to be true and to speak the truth, seem to me to be
the foundation of moral character, and one of the chief
reasons of our national influence in the world. And
here was a near relative of my own, in my own house,
surrendering the great fundamental principle at the touch
of Rome.

I began to speak to my people and to other meetings
upon this question. The addresses were published in a
small book called *England's Danger*, and had a wide
circulation. When the first of them, *Romanism and
National Decay*, was printed, I sent it to Lord Ripon,
the most distinguished convert to Rome since Newman,
and I asked him to say whether my statements were
justified. He replied very politely, but to my astonishment said, that such questions he left to his priests. A
great Englishman had handed his judgment over to Rome
in such a way that he would not pass an opinion on this
vital subject : Does the domination of Rome tend to
the ruin of a country? There seemed to me to be
one of the causes why the Roman Church fatally injures
a people ; it succeeds in silencing the thought of its
members, on the plea of forbidding private judgment
in religion, and imposing the faith of the Church on
the individual, it lulls the lay mind in a dogmatic slumber,
makes the reform of abuses and the progress of religious
faith impossible, except under the strict control of the
ecclesiastical mind.

I incurred at once the hostility of the Catholic Press,
and this opened my eyes to a new set of facts. The

Catholic papers had a totally different standard from that which has established itself elsewhere in England. A hectoring, insulting tone, which to refined English ears is intolerable, was apparently acceptable to the readers of those papers. I found it the most striking argument I could offer in a new edition of *England's Danger* to print what a leading Catholic paper had seen fit to say about me. This opened people's eyes ; they saw that the spirit of the Inquisition slumbered in the Catholic Church, and that, unable to use racks, thumbscrews, and the stake, the Catholic mind still felt that bludgeoning and assassination, so far as the law permitted, were the authorized way of maintaining the rights of the Church. A Catholic monthly even insinuated charges of immorality against me. Later on priests were set to write against me, and the literature produced was sent privately to the young women of my Church in order to shake their allegiance. It was all a most painful discovery of the ways and methods of Rome, even in England, where an overwhelming Protestant predominance puts a severe curb on methods employed elsewhere. And yet I look back with a great distaste on that period of controversy. I thought I was bound to enter into it, and I think I should have been cowardly to decline it. Whether people would listen or not, it seemed a duty to utter my conviction and to open men's eyes to the steady and insidious advance of Rome in the national life ; but I could not endure the atmosphere of calumny, the insulting letters, the subtle influences employed in the Press to hinder my work. And looking back upon the episode, I am inclined to think that a minister should avoid controversy, because the servant of Christ should not strive, but be gentle towards all, apt to teach, forbearing (2 Tim. ii. 24).

I see more clearly than I did then that the evils in the Roman system work out their sure result in the modern world, and make it virtually impossible that the Papacy can ever gain its old authority or draw into the Roman obedience more than a certain section of our population. I have even learnt to think that some minds are better for the strict supervision of directors and confessors, and many are held in the practice and faith of Christianity by the powerful hand of Rome, that would yield no allegiance to the authority of Truth or the decisions of Reason. And in later years I have come to cherish a hope that a fairer synthesis is awaiting the Church of Christ, in which the virtues of Catholicism will be blended with those of Protestantism, and a Church will appear, still built upon the Apostles and the Prophets, with Jesus Christ as the chief corner-stone, but capable of embracing the varieties of temperament, the habit of obedience to authority, the strivings of progressive thought, and the longing to discover a genuine unity for the human family. Whether that dream is to be realized or not, I pray increasingly, as my life's end appears in sight, that I may live and die in charity with all mankind, and may cordially love and appreciate all those who, under any form, acknowledge our Lord Jesus Christ as the supreme Head of men. I hope I do not value Truth less, because I desire Love more. But the conviction has grown on me that Love is the condition of seeing Truth herself. What I dreaded in an Inquisitor I have come to dread in myself. And even with Papists I have no controversy except to see how to love them, and with them to love all men.

In that October I published the *Commandments of Jesus*. It was a sequel to the *Teaching of Jesus*, and grew out of it ; for the definite commandments of the Master offered a rule of life, as His teaching gave a scheme of truth. It was a soothing and healing task to write the book, and some readers found it an aid in Christian life. "Thank you for giving us a book so full of heavenly thoughts," wrote one, and referred to three passages which I desire to copy out because the book is now out of print and the firm that published it has ceased to be. These passages, though the correspondent could not know it, are autobiographical—

Love is the Sleeping Beauty which lies under an age-long spell dormant in the heart of man. It is Jesus who has kissed the lips and awakened love. The latent forces in the Gospel for awakening love to God and to men appear to be inexhaustible. One will arise and work and seem to expend itself ; but as it subsides another shoots out for a new generation, and then another and another. Then an influence which had apparently died down awakes with new and irresistible attraction. . . . The mere delineation of God as Father, Son, and Holy Spirit appeals to the understanding and the heart as a motive to love, because the Gospel presents the Godhead as engaged in the task of saving man. " I love the Father," said the little boy on his deathbed to McCheyne, " who loved me and gave Jesus to die for me ; I love Jesus who shed His precious blood for me ; and I love the Holy Ghost who made me know the love of the Father and the love of the Son." The golden text of St. John, *God is Love*, puts into three words the sum of the Gospel of our Lord Jesus Christ. There is no metaphysical exposition of God ; it is not thought necessary to adduce theistic arguments ; but the being of God unfolds itself as essential love, as a process of love between Father and Son, and as Love in operation towards the world, both in creation, when the Spirit brooded on chaos, and in redemption when the same Spirit came to regenerate human hearts.

And again—

Just as the bays and inlets along the shore can, none of them nor all of them, contain the ocean, and yet may each be filled with the ocean, welcome the sparkling waters, the freshening brine, the authentic murmur and the secret treasures of the deep : so human souls, though none of them, nor all of them, can contain God, may each be filled with Him, betraying His presence, His eternal Godhead and power, and even obtaining some throbs and pulsations of His fathomless depths.

And yet once more—

Strive, agonize to enter. The agonizing comes from the extraordinary diversions and seductions of earthly things. To get the mind even interested in the heavenly issues, to get it concentrated on the claims of Christ, fairly to consider the competing attractions of the Father and of the world, that is where the difficulty occurs, and one has to make a steady effort to push in at the gate. And then along the narrow way it is always the alluring sights and sounds on either hand which imperil the journey. The straitness would not matter if we would only go steadily on. And the difficulty always is rather in imagination than in reality, and strikes the observer more than the pilgrim himself. The life lived by faith in the Son of God is not accurately described as an unremitting conflict. It is the voice of the tempter that says : "Always fast and vigil ? Always watch and pray ?" The saint's triumphal answer is : " While I breathe I pray."

There was comfort and help in dwelling on the *Commandments of Jesus*, but the year, with its labours and conflicts, quite wore me out. On January 1, 1899, I struggled through the New Year's Sermon and my Lecture on " Dale : Citizen, Saint, and Seer." But I was obliged to take a three months' holiday. My dear friends were willing to go with me, and we set off for Italy. On the platform at Victoria I had the comfort of receiving a letter from some Oxford clergy, headed by Canon Christopher, thanking me for my stand on behalf of Protestant principles. But I had just the feeling that R. L. Stevenson describes in *Ordered South*. I fully expected to return, and I had with me the best of friends, but I seemed going into a long and distant banishment.

On the journey we had some disturbing adventures. On the Cornici Express a thief got at my inner pocket and stole my pocket-book with £20 in it and my letter of indication. At Ventimiglia, coming out of the buffet, my dear lady had her purse taken, and an appeal to the chief of the police for redress suggested that he was in distraction or in collusion. But nothing could prevent the sense of relief and joy in reaching Italy. Lingering at Genoa and Pisa, we got to Rome by the end of the week. There was a Hôtel Belvedere in the Via Nazionale at that time, which was just opposite the Villa Aldobrandini ; the fragment of the wall of Servius Tullus was close at hand, and from our windows we could see the Palatine and the Capitoline. This was a great improvement on the hotels about the Pincian or the Corso, which afford no glimpse of ancient Rome, and only a sight of St. Peter's by climbing up the steps. Our friend Dr. Gray came to see us, and cautioned me against putting up my name in the porter's lodge, for fear that I might be molested by the spies of the Vatican who were everywhere. Mr. Joseph Hocking was in Rome preparing to write one of his books, and this kept me alive to the nature of the gigantic Power that I had ventured to criticize. But we were not disturbed, and the interest and air of Rome began very soon a healing process ; though immediate recovery was not possible ; I seemed worn out.

I remember a driver to whom we became really attached. He was a devoted believer in Victor Emmanuel and Garibaldi, and we called him V.E.G. The great, simple, honest Italian gave a peculiar flavour to our Roman visit. One day he had driven us out to Hadrian's Villa and Tivoli. Just as we reached the Villa the shaft of his poor vetturia broke ; I see his rueful countenance now as he demonstrated his shame in leaving us ten miles from the City to get back as we could. Tivoli we never reached, but the ruined Villa, the treasures of which fill the Roman Galleries, brought us into touch with England, for Hadrian had been there for a time. Also I remember the guide plucking some violets and holding a lighted match under them ; immediately they became etiolated and were pure white. I have tried to do that since, but always in vain.

On February 6th we heard of Dr. Berry's sudden death as he was taking a funeral ; the two great figures on the Esquiline, Castor and Pollux, as they are called, are always associated for me with that brave, bright, eloquent spirit, that wrought so well and passed so early. In the English cemetery, too, the *lacrymæ rerum* touched me deeply. Not long before, John Addington Symonds had been laid there, and I read the epitaph under the cypresses, beneath the pyramid of Cestius—

> Lead Thou me. God, law, reason, motion, life,
> All names for Thee alike are vain and hollow,
> Lead me, for I will follow without strife,
> Or if I strive, still must I blindly follow.

Keats, Shelley, Symonds—oh, those English names on that southern boundary of the Eternal City, overlooking the wild and desolate Campagna ! Among the monuments of Cæsars and Popes, and all that made Italy great, my own countrymen, dying in banishment, with hearts turned to England !

Then here are some faded crocuses which bring back a day at Albano, the Alba Longa, whence Romulus came to found Rome ; and from the hill the view across the Campagna, spanned by its broken aqueducts, threaded by the Via Appia, lined with tombs, the vast dome of St. Peter's rising above the seven hills of the City. We saw Nemi, the lake hidden among the woods, as Richard Wilson painted it, haunted with memories of Aricia, and the priest ever succeeded by his slayer, the starting-point of Frazer's *Golden Bough*. We drove to Marino and Frascata, and these crocuses were plucked from Cicero's Villa at Tusculum. That was always the joy of Rome to me : I slipped past the inanities and superstitions of the Middle Ages, and the vast vulgarities of Popes, and reached the solid strength of the Republic, through the golden age of Augustus. The tomb of Romulus in the Forum, the remains of the Cloaca Maxima in the Suburra, the church which is on the site of the Roman Senate House, the Rostra where Cicero and Scipio spoke, or the gigantic roofs of the mere transepts of the Basilica of Constantine—these make the atmosphere of the Eternal City—these and the soft air of the tufa-galleries of the Catacombs, and the blue line of the Sabine Hills, seen from Trastevere, where the fountain gushes out from the hilltop like a river, drawn by the aqueduct from those Sabine Hills. But the people who loiter in the Corso, or on the Pincian, and dally with the insidious lures of the Vatican, the Rome that Zola paints in his pitiless realism, the sordid monuments of spiritual tyranny, and of Princes of the Church living in a luxury like that of the decadent Cæsars—from these I would escape ; and the only comfort in leaving that city of memories and dreams is that all this vain pomp of the perverted and exploited religion of Galilee is left behind.

We went on to Naples, escaping from wintry cold into a glorious summer. Oh, those gleaming, wicked faces, bright colours, and finely caparisoned horses in the streets—that sense of ineradicable human wickedness, as if the Levantine rascals who founded that first Neapolis two thousand years ago had remained, unchanged by the adoption of one paganism for another, and by the civilization which swept over Italy, but could never penetrate the people who clustered under Vesuvius !

We drove out to Baiæ, the scene of Imperial luxury, and the murder of Agrippina, the Parthenope, where Virgil lived and sang. I saw Lucrinus, where the oysters were cultivated, and Avernus, which Virgil made the gate of the Kingdom of Dis. Our Neapolitan driver treated himself to a bottle of wine at my expense (though I would not pay), and was so drunk that I had to mount the box to get us safely back. I rated him in such Italian as I had, and sent him away with thunder clouds on his brow ; but next morning he was at the door wreathed in smiles, and eager for another fare.

Mr. Gutteridge, who had a business in Naples, and seemed loved and trusted by the whole population, came with us to Capri—most memorable of all Italian dreams. The blue grotto in the cliffs, into which the boat is heaved through a narrow entrance, and the water penetrated with light and quite blue—and the naked boys diving under the boat, also cærulean : and then Anacapri, and the precipice with the blue sea a thousand feet below, and the grim memories of Tiberius, who found refuge here from the sycophants and schemers of Rome, and indulged, so said the Roman scandal, in nameless vices. Still the women of Capri frighten their naughty children with the name of " Timbero." It is from Capri that the Bay, with Castellamare and Vesuvius, and Naples, and Ischia becomes so incomparably beautiful, that the memory is that of having been in Paradise.

I remember the concern of Mr. Gutteridge when on returning I took out my purse to make the necessary payments : " Put it up," he whispered ; " if you are seen to have money in the street you may be tracked and robbed."

Can nothing change the heart of Naples? Even the liquefied blood of St. Januarius, and the black madonna that is duly worshipped, cannot produce the mere ground-work of honesty and truth—

Il fingere e un defetto,
Ma chi non sa fingere non e perfetto.

Mr. Irving, the Presbyterian chaplain, was a man of genius, and to us was kindness itself ; but he had an honest Scotch loathing of the shameless mendicancy, importunity, and dishonesty of the people. He came with us to Pompeii : from the top tier of the old theatre, built on the hillside, I thought the view of Castellamare and the bay the most beautiful sight I had ever seen. But then we climbed, on horses, to the summit of Vesuvius, over the scoriæ and lava and cinder-ridges, the smoke puffing up at our feet. That last slope of the cone,, made of fine dust, in which the feet sank ; and the officious guides insisting on shoving and pulling ; then the crowning plateau ; and just as we reached the top a stone larger than a man's head shot up from the crater and dropped at our feet ; and the crater : the hideous, obscene, malodorous cauldron filled with smoke and shooting flames—this was the most repulsive sight I had ever seen. Here beauty and ugliness mingle : nothing more beautiful than Vesuvius seen from Naples ten miles away, with the lava streams red at nightfall ; nothing uglier than to be on Vesuvius and to gaze into the crater.

We went from Naples to Assisi and I fell under the spell of St. Francis. I tried to form an order of Brothers Minor when I came back ; but found, not without joy, that Jesus is a better name even than Francis. At the Carceri, and on Monte Subasio, and in the Franciscan

Monastery, a devout little Brother showing us the monuments, and the dignified prior explaining to us the Giotto frescoes ; or out at the Portiuncula, in the little church which Francis built, forgetting that it was overbuilt by the vast pretentious dome of later days, I caught the best of Medieval religion, and suffered, with Francis himself, in the usurpation of Rome, which exploited even the piety of the Little Brother to promote its own ambition.

In Siena we found a true Italian hotel, and enjoyed the medieval city, almost unconscious of the present, but that a sentimental Italian had fallen in love with Melcie in the train, and brought sonnets and passionate protestations to offer to the fair signora. We called him the Passionate Pilgrim. But no harm came of it. In the Duomo I heard an eloquent sermon, demonstrating that the intellect cannot grasp the things of faith. Why does Rome delight to depreciate the intellect? The intellect could at least rid the Roman Church of some of its flagrant superstitions. Over the Porta Romana at Siena is the Latin verse addressed to the Virgin—

O regina Patris summi dignata coronâ.

The intellect would at any rate rebuke the monstrous perversion which sets the crown of the Supreme Deity upon the brow of a mortal woman. Florence, Bologna, Padua, Venice, Verona, Milan, then Como and the Villa D'Este, and back by Lucerne. Each place has golden memories, for as health returned the fascination of Italy grew. A day in the arena at Padua with the Giotto frescoes gave me a Monthly Lecture on my return. Verona and St. Zeno, with the tomb of Juliet, and the pictures of Girolamo dai Libri, bound me in allegiance to the city on the rushing Adige, as, on the whole, the most interesting city in Italy, outside Rome, Florence, and Venice.

But at last the beautiful pilgrimage was over. I began my work again on April 8th, still far from strong.

My elders thought I had better decline the Chairmanship of the Congregational Union of England and Wales, which was proposed for me in May. And I began then, for the first time, the practice of taking Monday as a *dies non* ; that, more than anything else, enabled me to go on when my strength seemed so decidedly impaired.

During the rest of the year which closed the century I had to walk very cautiously. There was a glorious September passed at Castell, under Snowden, and in October at the Union Meetings in Bristol, my dear friend Arnold Thomas delivered what seemed to me the ideal address from the chair. He has always been too modest to claim the recognition he deserves ; but the friendship I have enjoyed with him, and his *fidus Achates*, Elkanah Armitage, has been for me my most treasured link with the generation of ministers that preceded my own.

In September my grandmother died, close upon a hundred. She had been the kindest friend of my childhood, and with youthful form and silver curls she had been present at my ordination. It seemed appropriate that she should go with the vanishing century. How could she face 1900?

There was some controversy at the turn of the century as to when the new century began. Some said that obviously 1900 years only ended on December 31, 1900. But I took the view, and I had the rare satisfaction of finding that for once I could accept Papal authority, that a century begins with the new numeral. The cinquecento began with 1500, and so on.

To me, therefore, 1900 sounded the bell of the coming era ; and I wrote a booklet entitled *The Awe of the New Century*. It was a too sanguine hope of a better day coming, in which Peace and Human Brotherhood would occupy a new earth and make it a new heaven. Yet I want to rewrite those pages for the days when the War is over. The hope is only deferred, and though that makes the heart sick, hope trembling lives. The new

century which has opened so disastrously, with the Boer
War leading on to the Great War with Germany, has
time yet to redeem itself. Before 2000 dawns my dream
will come true—

This is the awe of the new century ; not the awe of terror or even of
apprehension, but the awe of the ship rounding the point and entering
untraversed sunlit seas. It is the awe of wonder and anticipated surprise. Wordsworth tells us how once in boyhood he loosed a boat on
Coniston, and pulled out into the lake until he saw emerging over the
boundary hills the huge peak of Wetherlam. Overwhelmed with that
majestic vision, he turned hurriedly back, and sought his home : fui
days he went about haunted with "unknown modes of being." It is
that awe, solemn yet pleasurable, which is upon us, as out of the unknown future loom up large and kindly shapes, promises of better
things, for which the ages have been waiting. The heart beats high at
the thought that the pace of things in the nineteenth century hurried
towards a climax. It was a familiar thought that in that one century
there was more progress than there had been in the previous eighteen.
Yes, time slipped on, eager and quickened, to achieve some final step.
It is not the end, but the consummation that draws near. "That in
the dispensation of the fullness of times He might gather together in
one all things in Christ, both which are in heaven and which are on
earth, even in Him." Awe, and yet glory ; the thrill of the world's
hope. He has striven for the centuries, and they have slipped out of
His hand, hardly acknowledging Him, though they bore His name.
But in the dispensation of the fullness of times must come a century
which will bear His Name and also His Spirit, and He will see of the
travail of His soul and be satisfied. That century may be the twentieth.
"Blessed is he that waiteth, and cometh to the thousand three
hundred and five and thirty days." The mystic time may be upon us,
and the blessing may be hovering over our heads.

For myself the first decade of the new century brought
an accumulation of sorrows, in the midst of which the
heaviest tasks of my life had to be performed ; so
that in looking back over 1900-1910, I always marvel
how I was carried through. If in the following pages
I bring out with some emphasis this combination of
calamities and duties, it is because I wish to put to my
seal that God is gracious. Whether the troubles, following one upon another, for all those years, were chastise-

ment for my sins, or merely the sculptor's chisel at work on the statue, I have no doubt whatever but that all was rightly and lovingly ordered. If it seems to me that the duties were hampered by the troubles, I cannot help accepting this also as a Divine purpose—the thorn in the flesh, the messenger of Satan to buffet me, lest I should be exalted above measure.

CHAPTER XI

THE TURN OF THE CENTURY
1900

THE Boer War was a terrible blow to me, and made the work at Lyndhurst Road more difficult than it had ever been. For years I had given more and more thought to the possibilities of International Arbitration, and though never a Pacifist, I had spoken at meetings of the Peace Society. It was at one Peace Society meeting that I heard the most amazing misquotation that ever came to my notice : Mr. Handel Cossham, M.P. for Bristol, wound up his speech by saying, "And did not our Lord say, ' I came not to bring a sword, but Peace '? " This deliberate reversal of Scripture, to suit a foregone conclusion, was just the kind of thing which always revolted me in special crusades. And I recognized that war might well be one of those ineradicable vices of human nature which must be endured until Christ comes to establish a better order. But I was convinced that a European Court could be established, to which questions of international difference could be referred, and that a general recognition of such a tribunal would ultimately make war amongst civilized and Christian nations unthinkable. When the Boers poured through Lang's Nek, and the British Government had to meet them by force, I recognized that to advocate peace principles was no longer timely. Moreover, Milner was an old friend, and Fellow of my College, and I had at that time a confidence in his judgment which made me think that a war which he allowed must have been inevitable. But I was convinced that only the grossest mismanagement could have brought things to such a pass that war should be inevitable ; and I was stung with shame to think of a great Empire organizing its forces and drawing men from Australia and Canada, to reduce two small Republics, which did not number, all told, more than a couple of Welsh counties. For two years and a half I felt the shame of the situation ; and when at last, by sending out as many troops as our enemies had population, and by commanding the services of our greatest generals, we had reduced the Boers to submission, the only comfort I could find was in Sir Henry Campbell-Bannerman's magnanimous resolution to make our enemies friends by according them full rights of self-government. The justification of that bitterly criticized policy has been seen in 1915-1917, when a Boer General has stood by us, as the Premier of South Africa, and another of our quondam foes has victoriously ejected the Germans from East Africa.

For those two years and a half—before we saw how a great country could win, not so much by arms as by generosity—I suffered acutely, not only from the fundamental jarring of the war, but from the unreason, and violence, and passion, which a state of war creates in our population. It was ill to live in those years, and it was still more heartbreaking to think that this was the opening of the new, the twentieth century, when, as I hoped, the better day for the world was to dawn. In the autumn of 1900 I published a sonnet in *Good Words,* which, defective indeed as a poem, yet expresses the passionate conviction which has been the spring of my patriotism ever since I entered public life—a conviction derived from my father, and constantly fostered by that dear friend whose swift instincts and wise reasoning helped me to all my best conclusions. I felt with William Watson in his address to England—

They best honour thee
Who honour in thee only what is best.

As most people seemed to dread any shrinkage of material resources, territory, armed forces, I dreaded the loss of the great thoughts and noble principles which, as I conceived, had been the strength of England. And in those calamitous years the great thoughts were lost and the noble principles were laid aside as inapplicable.

> Is it degenerate to fall from wealth,
>   To live in straiter coasts, on scantier fare,
>   To put on homespun, and to house in bare
> Simplicity, the hardy nurse of health?
> Is it degenerate, if Power or Stealth
>   Pluck from the brow uncertain coronet,
> And unsubstantial pride of sword and gun,
>   And make of realm on which sun never set
> A realm of spirit needing not the sun?
> Nay, these are accidents, which never yet
>   Could hurt nobility. But one thing may
>   Brand on the brow the mark "Degenerate":
>   To lose the vision of the truly great,
> And lapse from effort on the starry way.

It was an unexpected relief that February to escape from London and to spend a month at Oxford ministering to the undergraduates in Mansfield Chapel. Oxford was much finer, more clear eyed, than the country at large in that sad time. In the Master's Lodge at Balliol, Mr. Cronwright Schreiner and Mr. J. A. Hobson were allowed to speak unmolested, and to put the case of the Boers. The war in that atmosphere worked as a regenerating principle. Undergraduates and dons volunteered for the front, and went, but they left behind a chastened and a magnanimous spirit. During that month I sometimes wished that I had never left the city of dreams, to contend with the grim realities and ignorant interests of London. It was but a passing phase, produced partly by the discovery that people who had been loyal friends and members of the Church were caught by the Chauvinistic spirit, and condoned the disgraceful orgies of Mafficking. I feared constantly lest those on whom I most relied should exhibit marks of the plague and fall beside me.

But during the sad time of disappointment, reliefs and encouragements were not wanting. In January 1900 I spoke for the Student Volunteer Missionary Movement in Exeter Hall, and ever since I have kept in as close touch as possible with that noble uprising of the young Christian manhood and womanhood of the world for the extension of the Kingdom of God. It has been my privilege to know John Mott, Robert Speer, Sherwood Eddy, on the other side of the Atlantic, as well as some of the leaders of the movement in this country, especially Robert Wilder. And it is to the Student Movement more than to anything else that I look, notwithstanding the terrible setback of the great European War, to fulfil the golden promise of the twentieth century. In the summer, too, I met in a great conference at the Alexandra Palace another fine American, the author of *In His Steps*. Mr. Sheldon, like Moody twenty-five years before, and like Dr. Clarke, the founder of the Christian Endeavour Society, touched the old country in a way that only one from a new world can.

This year, also, I had the delight of finding a most congenial friend in Canon Streatfeild, who came to be the vicar of Christ Church, the parish in which I live. Unfortunately, he only stayed two years, but the friendship has continued. His scholarly habits and literary work gave me at once a sense of kinship ; and I experienced, as so often before and since, that spiritual affinity is a much more powerful bond of union than ecclesiastical agreement. Another dear friend at this time was a member of my own Church. Jonathan Brierley, known in the Press as J. B., was a man to put you in good conceit with life and all the world. Disabled by ill-health, he produced volume after volume, all alive with brilliant thought, quotations gathered from the whole range of literature, and unflagging optimism.   He was always in his place on Sunday morning, entering into the service with a warmth and a response which brought to me inspiration and joy.   Sometimes he would give us, though at terrible cost to himself, a speech or a sermon.   It was like sparkling champagne, exhilarating and yet feeding.   Often I took heart in those weary middle years of my ministry, because I thought, if J. B. found help in my preaching, I could not be quite so useless and ineffective as I felt myself to be.

And Nature always had her healing and restoring influence on me.   I find an entry in my journal, June 28th.   "A gleam of light on my dark spirit from a white-throat and a redstart on the Heath :   God's messengers.   Took heart."   That June I got a brief holiday at Castell, to which we drove from Bettws (the most glorious road in this island) in the amazing glory of evening, Snowdon like transparent porphyry against the western sky.   What a boon to us is that glorious and storied corner of North Wales !   In August we spent some weeks at the most improbable place I ever entered, Pwllheli, and yet it proved to be a gate of the dawn.   Round the coast to the gardens and picture gallery of Glen-y-widdw, and beyond to Abersoch, Cardigan Bay, bounded eastward by the great Snowdon range, may call itself without presumption the Bay of Naples.   Its glories are milder, gentler, less emphatic, but on the other hand they are lovelier and more appealing.   That year I was president of the Chatauqua, which met at Barmouth, and I went over to preach and lecture to them.   One afternoon, looking from the mountain-top over the bay to Bardsley Island, I was overwhelmed for half an hour with a miserable anxiety about my dear friend ;   and on returning to Pwllheli I found that at that time they were in a poor boat on a rough sea, and in much fear if not in great danger.

One evening from the beach at Barmouth I saw the most resplendent sunset that I have ever seen in

England. The whole bay was liquid gold, and a rosy light made all the people on the shore seem like trans-figured spirits. The planets and Virgo gleamed out as the glory faded ; and I never lost the sense from that day to this that such would be the other world, which eye has not seen, just such a mellow and harmonious fulfilment of the aspirations that have possessed our hearts here : a waking into light, a discovery that " everything was worth while, leading to this."

And one other experience of Cardigan Bay came to me with a spiritual message. One hot August day the sea was very calm. But at two o'clock a gentle wind blew, and we started off in Captain Thomas's small yacht. At four, when we were well out in the bay, a dead calm succeeded. A haze gathered which hid the coast, and the red sun glowed through it on the oily waters. Hour after hour passed. We had nothing but a little afternoon-tea basket, and a loaf which the captain kept in his locker. No boat could come near us, for there was no wind. Steamers are not in that shallow part of the bay. Night fell, and there was nothing for it but to get a shake-down under the hatchways and try to sleep. We had a time of prayer, and with great composure waited for the breath of the Spirit. In the middle of the summer night, the hot air rising, a breeze blew from the eastern mountains : we woke from our doze to find the boat scudding through waves that slapped joyously at the prow. By one o'clock we made the beach above Borth, but the captain said he must wait for morning to make the estuary of the Dovey. We slept for a few hours, and then woke to see the Morning Star like a great lamp hung in the blushing east. We were hungry and overtired, but nothing could take from the glory of the morning and the beating up the river to Aberdovey. The incident always remained with me as a symbol of our de-pendence on the Spirit. We are helpless and cannot move ; we have nothing to do but to wait patiently for God. And then His wind blows and fills the sails, and we are carried by a power not our own to the haven where we would be, the Morning Star shining in the forehead of the day.

Once more that year Nature spoke in majesty to me. At the time of the Equinox I had to go to the Channel Islands to preach. We were due in Guernsey at six in the morning. But the gale had delayed us for four hours, and when I went up early on the deck, I saw a wonderful sight—we were plunging through great billows which seemed to let us down to the ocean-bed ; and there were the Casquets in the morning light, with the waves breaking high over the lighthouse. That glorious approach to the islands has endowed them with a splendour, and the kind hospitality of the friends who entertained me has warmed them with a glow of friendship that makes me extraordinarily attached to that piece of old Normandy, to which William the Conqueror added the neighbouring islands of Great Britain and Ireland !

But not only Nature had her consolations in a troubled time. I had my literary work to do, and in May I had the joy of preaching the Annual Sermon for the London Missionary Society : " God will have all men to be saved."

My pen this year turned in new directions. I wrote the Life of Tennyson as a Saintly Life. One correspondent wrote : " It contains in my judgment at least, the most lovable picture of the great poet which has ever yet been given. Such a worthy book will surely be soon in a second edition." But it was not to be. Appreciations came even from the other side of the world ; but the overruling hand discouraged me from leaving my ministerial for literary work, a course to which I was always tempted. Quite decisively I was told that my pen was given me only as an instrument for the proper work of my life, and not to win either fame or money. I accepted the admonition.

The other book of this year was a *Commentary on the Pastoral Epistles* for my friend Professor Adeney's *Century Bible*. This (published next year) not only proved of great use to me in its preparation, but was approved by reviewers and readers. I wished that I had worked earlier at commentaries, but I had been discouraged by my book on *Proverbs* in *The Expositor's Bible*, and had too hastily concluded that I had not the leisure or the scholarship for more exact exegetical work. I think now, that, apart from all thoughts of publication, a minister would be well employed in making careful and exact commentaries on the books of the Bible from the beginning to the end of his ministry.

Another task was offered to me by the opening century. The Free Churches arranged for a Simultaneous Mission all over the country. Falling in with the plan, I went to Nottingham early in December, and preached daily for a week. No striking results appeared, but I formed an attachment to Nottingham and its people which has made me go there to preach again and again. Nottingham in return sent me a family that has given me help and blessing at Lyndhurst Road for many years. I like to think of the many places in the country in which I have been privileged to exercise a regular though intermittent ministry. Though I have remained always at one Church, I think my ministry has been as extended as if I had, in the modern fashion, moved every five or ten years.

But that first year of the century (as I regarded it) had some sharp blows for me. In September my old school friend, Theodore Mander, who had become an active and useful man at Wolverhampton, died suddenly, and his wife asked me to go down and speak at the funeral. It was an extraordinary scene. Queen Street Chapel, which my father had built, was thronged with all the important people of the town.

As we drove out to the grave, all the streets were lined with people, just as they had been, I was told, a few months before, when my friend as Mayor had entertained Royalty at Wightwick Manor. At one time my friend had been engaged to my sister, and I had loved his family from boyhood. He was cut off in the prime of manhood and at the height of his public service.

But the year's end brought me a severer loss still. My father resigned his Church at Portishead, being nearly seventy-three, and took a house at Hendon, that he might spend his closing days near to me. In November he came to stay with me for three weeks, and was beautifully bright and tender. In December he went to his new house. On Saturday the 15th, stopping to speak to an old man in the road, after his genial fashion, he caught a chill. I saw him that day, and he insisted on getting up from his bed to find me an old address of his " On Winning Souls," which was his last bequest. On Monday I saw him again, full of interest in my Sunday and my work. But at ten that evening I was fetched over to Hendon. He had had an apoplectic stroke. But he seemed cheerful, and said good-night in a phrase of his own invention : " We'll go to the regions beyond." I remained watching all night, and at 6.20 in the morning he fell asleep.

I tried, the following Sunday morning, to tell my people what he had been to me. He was the most affectionate father and husband in the world. He was a warm-hearted, genial friend, with no guile in his nature. His long, faithful ministry in London, Reading, Wolverhampton, Bradford, and Portishead, was, like my own, often with much suffering and depression to himself, but (would that I could say like my own !) rich in fruit. In those closing weeks evidence poured in, and as I go over the country I constantly find it added to, that he was the means of bringing a great number of souls to Christ—the one thing worth living for.

When Queen Victoria died on January 27, 1901, the nineteenth century seemed finally to pass. For King Edward I felt a peculiar loyalty. I liked his tact and affability, and was persuaded that he set about to establish the peace of the world. His illness, too, and the postponement of the Coronation, gave me a feeling that God was speaking to him, and he heard. In February of the new year I had a mission in Halifax—a new century mission—and it was to me strangely encouraging. The town was dear to me from long association, and the attentive audiences night after night gave me hope of good results, but I was overwhelmed with gratitude afterwards to find that about a hundred came to their spiritual decision during the week.

I set to work also on a volume of sermons, published under the title of *The Trinity* in the Present Day Preachers Series ; and I found strength and hope in dwelling on the great truth of God, on which the Christian religion rests. Early in March I attended the Annual Meetings of the Free Church Council at Cardiff, and there began a pleasant custom which has continued for many years. Sir Joseph Compton Rickett asks a party of ministers to stay with him at a hotel for the three days. The consultations over meals, and the long causeries when the day's work is over, have contributed much, not only to the personal joy of his guests, but also to the work and policy of the Council itself. At that Council J. H. Jowett stirred the Assembly as no one had done for years ; and from that time I think dates the supremacy which he has long held in the Free Church pulpit of this country. I always had a peculiar interest in him because he came from the Square Church, Halifax, and owed much to Dr. Mellor ; but closer acquaintance made me value him, not more for his great gifts as a preacher than for his singular modesty and brotherliness. Few men I have met could have borne the overwhelming and dazzling success that he has enjoyed without a subtle deterioration of character. It is proof of a strenuous inward life and constant self-discipline when a popular preacher escapes ruin. " Lest I myself should be ἀδόκιμος" should be the motto inscribed on the study table of every preacher who begins to draw a crowd and to win popular applause. Frederick W. Robertson, the greatest preacher of the nineteenth century, dreaded nothing more than being a popular preacher, and therein lay his greatness. But whether he would have escaped, if he had lived to fifty, is a secret known only to God.

In that March I had one of the treats of my life. I went to Italy for three weeks with my friend Joseph King and Dr. Fairbairn. We were the happiest of comrades. We enjoyed Lucca ; in Rome we visited S. Clemente, and Dr. Fairbairn explained to the friar (I fear in vain) that the communion-table of the fourth-century church, at which the priest sat facing the audience, showed that in the Early Church the table was *not* an altar. We had an instructive time at St. Peter's. We paused at the oldest tomb in the church, that of the Pope who had sixteen children, and to prolong whose life three boys were bled. His motto is : " In mea innocentia ingressus sum." Another old tomb is that of Paul III ; at his feet are his mother, as Prudence, and his sister, the mistress of Alexander VI, as Truth.

> O where is Christ, the lowly Lord of ruth,
>   The world's transcendent love and radiant hope ?
> Is this His Church, His city, and His truth ?
>   Here is no Christ, but everywhere—a Pope.

Assisi did not appeal to Dr. Fairbairn as it did to me. He was intensely indignant with a friar at Portiuncula who offered him a card of prayer for the

conversion of England to Rome. But Assisi is sacred
in my memory.

> This line that soars against the Eastern sky
> Is Mont Subasio, the mount of prayer,
> For to the Carceri the saint would fly
> Assured of finding God and silence there.
> This is Assisi, to the hill it clings,
> City of massive walls and vanished men,
> Hoary with olives and with human kings,
> Charlemagne, Propertius, kings of sword and pen.
> But there is one who rules this countryside,
> Il Poverello, God's gay troubadour,
> The gentlest chastener of human pride,
> The tenderest friend of the forgotten poor—
> That is the Portiuncula, it stands,
> The centre of the hill-girt Umbrian plain,
> Type of the Temple fashioned without hands,
> The soul surrendering all, all things to gain.
> Ah, peace of God, dear heaven-descended peace,
> Thou didst on this high hill and town descend
> Eight centuries ago, nor wilt thou cease
> To brood upon Assisi, to the end.

Then we went to Ancona, but not, alas ! to Fano to
see the " dear Guardian Angel." At Rimini the doctor's
wrath was stirred again in the Malatesta Church, with
its unblushing Renaissance paganism, Sigismund and
his mistress Isotta, inscribing their initials everywhere
in place of the I H S. And then going round under
the walls we were stoned by the boys of the city,
and found ourselves in a quarter from which it was
hard to find a quick enough retreat. Then Ravenna
gave me a new aspect of Italy : the Baptistry with
the fifth-century mosaics, Christian not yet Catholic,
the twelve Apostles with equal crowns, Peter not yet
endowed with the keys, S. Apollinare with the great
life-size saints and virgins moving in procession along
the mosaic walls up to Christ, S. Maria in Porto Fuori,
with the water of the swamp rising through the floors,
but the same Christian mosaics ; and the mysterious
Pinetum on the sand-dunes, where Dante saw his

visions, and lastly, Dante's tomb ; yes, altogether I concluded that he who has not seen Ravenna has not seen Italy, the Italy of Theodosius and Justinian, the Italy of Dante.

Then we went to Ariosto's Ferrara, with its vast castle-palace, and pictures of Dosso Dossi and Garofalo. Then to Padua, and the Arena Chapel again ; and finally to Venice, the Hôtel Danielli. The days there were entrancing : the long row to Torcello, Dr. Fairbairn descanting on his hopes for his boys, a close examination of S. Marco, under the guidance of Dr. Robertson, whose book on the subject is a treasure. We had a peep at Verona, and then went to Munich, where we enjoyed the pictures and German life (how barbarous after Italy !) and Mozart's opera *Cosi fan tutti*.

When the three travellers parted at Holborn I for one was quite heartsick. Travelling with friends whose minds are stored and whose temper is equable must be ranked amongst the greatest pleasures of life.

When we came back in April there was a united meeting of the Baptist and Congregational Unions, and that was the one occasion on which I met Dr. Maclaren. I had a great admiration for him, and wrote the obituary notice in *The Times*. When he died in 1910 I was roused in the middle of the night by an express message from Printing House Square, to know if the name was spelt Maclaren or McLaren. How careful *The Times* is to be faultlessly accurate.

One little effort this summer brought the richest reward that ever comes to a minister. I went to preach at Walpole ; the chapel of 1646 still stands, a roof supported by a wooden column in the centre, and clumsy galleries closing round the small pulpit on three sides. It was a broilingly hot afternoon, and I laboured through my sermon on " Taste and see how gracious the Lord is " with an unusual sense of wooden inefficiency. In fact, when I left the place I felt ashamed to look the people in the face, and during the tea in a field I wandered round with a dear little maiden, whose artless talk restored my equanimity. (The little maiden remained my friend, and fourteen years after I married her, and she wrote to me from Egypt not long ago, sending me a photograph of herself and her baby.) But this was what I learnt afterwards : A young man from the village was present that afternoon, and the appeal went home to him. He surrendered to Christ, joined the Church, and gave himself to Christian work. That incident came as an unspeakable comfort to me in those sad years ; it showed that the preaching of the Gospel does not depend for its success on buoyant, physical fitness, but that sometimes when we go about our work with a sense of weakness bordering on despair, a strength other than ours carries the word to the heart of the hearers with transforming power.

In July I had my last visit but one to Norway. We had some strange experiences. After some lovely days at Balholm we came back to Voss, and drove over the splendid new road from Graven to Ulvik. Strange to say, my dear lady saw vividly on a rock by the way the letters HELA, the old Norsk god of death. The striking illusion received a curious comment ; following close behind us came a Canon H., who was coming to act as chaplain in Ulvik. He walked up the steep road, and at the top where the letters had appeared on the rock he fell down dead. Next morning, when I opened my door, the rude coffin lay in the passage, and the body was carried back to England by his son who had come with him.

We were going to Fosli, to stay with Ole Garen in his little hotel above the magnificent Voring Fos. He met the steamer at Vik with horses for the ladies. It was a wonderful ride by the lake : the valley seemed shut in, but at a turn it opened out, and at last we saw the house high up on the edge, apparently, of a precipice. The road ceased. There was but a track which passed along perilous edges and over rocky slabs, and finally zigzagged up the mountain-side, which looked from below almost precipitous. The girls were safe enough, and so, as we learnt afterwards, was our dear lady, on the sure-footed mountain pony that had known the way all its life. But to see her, so fragile, an invalid of years' standing, perched on the saddle, and daring the desperate ascent, brought my heart into my mouth ; and when at last we arrived in safety I was full of apprehension for the descent ten days later, when we must return. All night long the Voring Fos, just at hand, a considerable river rushing at a leap into a cauldron 900 feet below, thundered like a terrific storm. In the middle of the night Major Norris arrived ; he had come to woo and to win our dear Melcie. It was an ideal situation for such a romance. Nature here seemed almost too lonely and terrible to be beautiful. One day we went on ponies to see the reindeer on Bokolen, 5,000 feet high ; I alone, the least accustomed to horses, avoided a fall. After six days the gloom began to disperse. I grew more at rest about the descent, and by the time we actually descended from the mountain eyrie we were all thoroughly sorry to go.

But that Fosli experience was memorable ; it left a mark which I can never lose. Nature could be terrible as well as restoring. Even dear friends could not bring relief, when anxiety about them was a large part of the distress. Care, ennui, anxiety, can be worse in holidays, and in good health, and even in the grandest surroundings than in work, monotony, and sickness. But one resource never failed ; it was prayer. The words of the Bible acquired new meanings. The present help, the sufficient promises, the shining verities of Christ and His Gospel came to me as a new experience. On leaving Fosli I made a note : " I hope to cherish this example for the rest of my life

as an instance of what God can be, and is willing to
be, to one troubled soul." I have tried to do so, and
by the lesson then learnt I have been able to pass
through the real troubles since, as I passed through
then the imaginary terrors which foreboding, anxiety,
and the sterner aspects of Nature conjured up.

My dear friend, always fearless, and lifted above
presentiments and fears by a buoyant hope, wrote a
sonnet at Fosli which I always cherish—

> Here, with its silver moss and herbage crowned,
>   Here, where the white rocks stretch their feet in flowers,
> The world is mountain-high, with not a sound
>   Of worlds beneath, whose heavy-laden hours
> Yearn for the highland country and its voice,
>   Utterance of mighty rivers fed from snows,
> Of winds that in the sunlight cry "rejoice,"
>   Of creatures wild that every mountain knows.
> Stern are its bulwarks; in its chasms dread
>   Wander the echoes, hollow-voiced, austere;
> But Nature's gentlest graces overspread
>   With living green each lineament severe;
> And where the great Fos roars through night and day
> Upon its breast the tender rainbows play.

In October 1901 Lyndhurst Road Church came of
age. There was a strong wish to celebrate this event,
and the celebration brought me great and unexpected
joy. In spite of the baleful influence of the War, the
Church was still very flourishing. During the year
a hundred and twenty-six new members were enrolled.
The unfailing generosity of the people was shown by
contributing to the Twentieth Century Fund of the
Union (without any diminution of its ordinary subscriptions to its own and outside work) £7,451. And
now, to celebrate its own majority, it decided to raise
a fund of £2,000, and to present it to the branch
Church at Cricklewood, that Mr. McEvoy and his loyal
supporters might lay the foundation of a more suitable
building than the Lown Memorial Hall. But this
generosity to others did not prevent my devoted people

LYNDHURST ROAD CHURCH.

from giving to me a personal recognition. They furnished a little room in my house with a bookcase, in which they placed a complete set of Ruskin's works, bound in brown calf, with a desk and chair, and curtains and carpet, so that whenever I grew despondent I might enter the little shrine and see the inscription which told of the twenty-one years of work and of my people's love. On Monday, October 28th, I had the pleasure of meeting Bishop Tucker of Uganda, who gladdened my heart with the account of the progress of the Church in Central Africa. The following day we celebrated the twenty-first anniversary of our own Church in Hampstead. Dr. Fairbairn, who had opened the new church in 1884, came now and preached again, a very massive sermon, on " Faith is the substance of things hoped for." Afterwards Sir Henry Harben presided at a luncheon in the Town Hall, at which the pleasantest feature to me was a letter of congratulation from a working-man, who assured me that some working-men had valued my ministry and my advocacy of their cause. On that occasion, too, Sir William Robertson Nicoll gave me a frugal note of commendation. The evening meeting was one of the most striking ever held in the church. Mr. Asquith came and delivered an encouraging address. My old friend and tutor, Courtney, spoke charmingly of his connection with the Church in Hampstead. R. J. Campbell, who at that time regarded me as his chief friend in the Nonconformist ministry, came and said so. My dear old college chum, Nathaniel Micklem, blessed me with his presence. And Mr. McEvoy, the member of Lyndhurst Road who has, perhaps, conferred more distinction on it than any other, by his ministerial work at Cricklewood and throughout the country, gave one of his fine, scholarly, and saintly addresses, touching the depths of humility and the heights of faith.

My gratitude to God for this occasion I could not

express to others, but I think He knew and recognized by His Spirit.

Before the year ended I received the kind contributors to my " prophet's chamber " on two afternoons and evenings. My dear aunt welcomed them all with a stately courtesy and graciousness which no one was likely to forget. On December 29th a friend was at dinner, to whom she spoke, urging him to distribute religious literature amongst the men at Kentish Town. He, a little quizzically, asked her about her own faith. She rose up from her sofa ; her blind eyes seemed to shine, and her face glowed, as she uttered a beautiful confession of her Saviour who had been her Guide and Friend all through her life. Next morning, when I was just starting for Halifax, I was called from the breakfast-table to find her helpless on her bedroom hearthrug. I saw that it was a stroke. With that sudden access of strength which comes in an emergency, heavy as she was, I lifted her on to the bed, and fetched the doctor. She lingered for a fortnight, but the end had come. Ever since 1873 she had tried to take the place of a mother to me. It was not her fault that she could not sympathize with my theological development. With my work for Christ she always sympathized, and I know she never ceased to pray for me. On her devotion to Christ, and untiring labours for Him, the blessing of God rested. Her work for the free distribution of the Scriptures was taken on by our friend Mrs. Pridham, and has not fallen off. Her beloved nephew, for whom she had wrestled and prayed, not only withdrew from Rome, but by a vision of the wickedness of Paris was led to a new life, and used the money she left him to go to Cambridge ; and he is now a clergyman of the Church of England. And perhaps most wonderful of all : she had given up her beautiful property in Derbyshire to be a college for the training of industrial missionaries. During her life Dr. Grattan

Guinness used it in connection with his Harley House Mission. I was a trustee of the property, and the trust directed that, if for any reason the house and estate could not be used for missionary work, we should sell them, and divide the proceeds among certain missionary societies, of which the London Missionary Society was one. On Dr. Guinness's surrender of Cliff, we determined to sell it. Our one fear was that the Jesuits would purchase, under an assumed name, the beautiful estate. We knew that to my aunt that would have been deplorable. I cannot help believing that her prayers received a signal answer. We sold the estate, and distributed the money to the missionary societies ; but the purchasers were the Methodists who have used the premises as a college, with Mr. Chadwick at the head, for the training of evangelists. When I visited the familiar spot a few years ago, I was touched to the heart to find that the College had sent out that year as many foreign missionaries as would justify us in regarding it as a missionary institution. Thus Cliff continues to do the work which the noble and generous donor desired. My aunt lived in prayer, and though her pre-occupation in religious work prevented literary culture, she had a good brain as well as a loving heart. Her old-world courtesy gave a dignity to my home. And among material things the memorials from Cliff are my chief treasures.

CHAPTER XII

THE CHAIRMANSHIP OF THE CONGREGA-
TIONAL UNION

1908

When sorrows darken all the sky of life,
    And blinding showers of doubt and trouble fall,
When—flesh with soul and heart with head at strife—
    Uncertain ill and certain doom appal ;

When all the glamour and the light are gone,
    And scarce a vision of the prime remains,
But still the ship must labour darkly on,
    Shattered by shocks, and shivering in the strains,

Have mercy, Lord, and if Thou bidst me live,
    Reach from the lowering clouds Thy helping hand ;
Some strong resolve, though I am helpless, give ;
    Give faith, albeit I may not understand.

.   .   .   .   .   .

Be strong, O heart, for over this dark main
    Myriads of ships have kept the trackless track ;
They have arrived, although none comes again,
    For God and Fate forbid the voyage back.

Fair is the haven; light of setting suns
    Plays on the mole, and ripples on the bar,
Over the tide which homeward ever runs
    Glimmers and shines the constant evening star.

Although thou seest not, and thou canst not see,
    Because until thou reach it, it is hid,
In its good time that light shall fall on thee,
    And thou shalt hail it, as those others did.

Oh, it is well, my God ! And cut not short
    One storm, one cloud, one shock, one strain, one jar ;
Only assure me I shall gain the port,
    And with my opening eyes behold the Star !

THOSE lines express the mingled feelings of the
two difficult years, 1902-1903. The New Year, 1902,
opened with the strangest coincidence of a great sorrow
and a great joy : I went from the deathbed of my
dear aunt to Halifax, to marry Melicent Oakes to
Major Norris, R.E. In 1899 I had married Gwendolen
to Walter Keatinge. And thus the two children whom
I had loved from their birth were settled in homes of
their own. In my own childless and homeless life
these two, who always called me Uncle Robert, had
constantly kept alive within me the joy in childhood
and the sense of home. If, therefore, I was able to be
a father to the children in my Church, and to understand
the interests of a home life, I owed it chiefly to them.
It was a sacred joy to me to be allowed to baptize
and to marry both of them.

But this coincident joy and sorrow meant that I was
left alone at Chesils, and my dear friends were left
without children at Wood Hall. At that time business
difficulties and losses made it necessary for them to
leave the house which they had made beautiful and
dear. The works had to be given up. And the best
arrangement that could be made was that they, my
friends of thirty years' standing, should come and make
their home with me. This was not only an intense joy,
but also a great convenience, to me ; for my aunt's
furniture, silver, china, etc., had to be divided among
a dozen nephews and nieces, and I should have had
to refurnish the house. But now the beautiful furniture
and books of Wood Hall came to beautify Chesils ;
and better still, the beautiful spirit, that had made the
charm of Wood Hall, came—for all too short a time—
to make an atmosphere in my house. It would be
fruitless to attempt to describe the mingled feelings
of pain and joy which underlay this rearrangement.
If my friend's health and life might have been spared,
I should have entered on the happiest period of my
days. But it was not to be.

In May I was elected Chairman of the Congregational Union of England and Wales for 1903. I longed for strength to discharge the duties of the office, and more, to realize the possibilities of the opportunity ; but that was not vouchsafed. In November I had to preach at Haslemere, and I went down, aware that influenza was upon me. That afternoon Hugh Price Hughes, who had a little house there in which he tried to conserve the strength he needed for his great work in London, was present at my sermon and took me up with him to his house. By evening I was totally incapable of speaking, and he in his eager brotherly way went down to the town and spoke for me ; it was the last address, I think, he gave. My friend Joseph King took me to his house at Witley, and I was most tenderly nursed. On Monday, November 17th, Hugh Price Hughes died of apoplexy. This came as an appalling blow, for not only had he been showing me so great kindness just before, but we had for years, ever since I knew him at Oxford, been real friends. At the first Grindelwald Conference, where the idea of the Free Church Council came to birth, I was with him. I see him now on the platform as we started, with his ice axe, as if he meant to scale the heights of that lofty mountain of a United Church which he saw in his dreams. And when we two came back for our Sunday's work, the people met on the little Grindelwald platform, and sang " God be with you till we meet again." All through the journey we talked, he, with his infinite ingenuity and kindness, " picking my brains," to use his own phrase for the process. He had helped me at the opening of Lyndhurst Road, and again at the opening of Lyndhurst Hall. And in his paper, *The Methodist Times*, in many a too generous appreciation of me, he not only encouraged me to aspire but furthered my work.

And now in a moment he was gone ! There was a print in my room at Haslemere, of Albrecht Dürer's *Tod als Freund* ; I looked at it again and again, and in my weakness would have welcomed his friendly approach. I tried to recover strength, and on the first Sunday of December managed to preach ; but a reporter came into the vestry about the evening lecture, who told me that he had influenza. Next day I was down again with a relapse. For the rest of the month I tried to recover by going to Burnham, where I was greatly drawn to my kind host, George Sully, a man whose work for Sunday Schools and the Adult School made him beloved in all that West Country. In my miserable weakness I recall an experience on the seashore, which brought hope to me. I saw rising from the wintry sea a vast flight of dunlins ; they spread out like two great wings ; they wheeled in orderly evolutions, forming, breaking up, reforming. And as it chanced, the dead body of one of them was at my feet on the shingle, so that I seemed to know them and to take part in their rhythmical dance of the air. Nature never does deceive the heart that loves her.

I came back for the New Year 1903, and tried to preach, but it was no good. Sir Douglas Powell told me that I must go away to the Engadine, and I should recover and be ready for my task by the spring. But this seemed impossible. I had no heart to set off alone. My dear lady, very poorly and exhausted with the removal and the change, was willing to take me down to Sidmouth. In that healing air I seemed to make progress ; and there we met Mr. Rhodes, the minister of the Church, who preached to me hope and joy from the pulpit, and his wife, who ministered to us in other ways. The beauty and the love seemed enough to restore the weakest. But, alas ! my friend was seized with influenza, and I was overwhelmed with anxiety. Her husband was in the tightest place of his business arrangements and could not come. The waters seemed to roll over my head. I felt that I must do what Sir Douglas Powell advised, and see if the Alps would give me strength for the approaching duties. Another sorrow had come ; my prepared ground and they ask no more—except to talk about the way they did it for the rest of the day.

But whatever might be the remote effects of playing golf, I saw no prospect of being in an effective condition for my May Address, which I regarded with a kind of terror. In April I ventured to preach for the Somerset Union at Chard, and the birds singing in the spring lanes gave me hope. But I was sure that I could not go round and visit the Churches as a Chairman should. I therefore proposed to the Church that we should invite all the ministers to Hampstead in June for a Convention. We have often, before and since, had small conventions of ministers, entertaining from twenty to thirty for three days, and providing such spiritual refreshment as we could. But to ask all the two thousand or more Congregational ministers to Hampstead and to entertain them made a great demand on my devoted people. But they did not shrink, and a committee was formed in April to make the arrangements and issue the invitations.

When the Spring Meetings began on May 11th, I was in a pitiably weak and nervous state. I got my old friend, one of my first friends at Hampstead, Mr. Alfred Davies, to drive me down to the City Temple on the morning of the 12th, for my Address, and to drive me back. I had great difficulty in standing for the delivery, and when it was over I was completely exhausted. No one knew what a state I was in, and I was grateful for the relatively kind reception given to what was a very feeble effort. I spoke on Congregationalism and the Catholic Church, and if I had had my usual health, I think I might have induced Congregationalists to claim their right place in the Catholic Church, even if I could not have persuaded Catholics, Roman and Anglican, to recognize them. Feeling how my dart was but an *irritum telum* in delivery, I tried to go farther by print : I sent a copy of the address to the bishops whom I knew. It happened that in that year of my chairmanship I came into unusually close contact with the bishops. It was the time of Mr. Balfour's Education Bill, when Free Churchmen were in revolt and planning methods of passive resistance to the endowment of Catholicism in the schools.

I went down to Canterbury and spent a night with the Archbishop to consider whether a way of reconciliation could be found. I did not agree with the extremists on the Free Church side, who wished to see a civic education provided for all, without any religious instruction, and to have the Bible taught only as literature. The secular solution of the question was to my mind a *pis aller*, to be resisted as long as possible. The position of the Archbishop seemed to me the right one ; he asked for religious teaching in all elementary schools, but disclaimed any desire to force Church teaching upon them. In a correspondence with him, and in letters to *The Times*, I endeavoured all through this year to save the religious teaching in our schools. I was, and am, convinced that the people of this country are quite willing that their children should be brought up in a Christian atmosphere, and taught the fundamental truths and doctrines of Christianity. The peril came from a " Catholic " party, which did not consider that teaching was truly Christian unless the doctrines of Catholicism were included in it. I saw that those extremists played into the hands of the extremists at the other end, who would use the general weariness of the public mind over the religious controversy to make the National schools secular.

It was a real sorrow to me that my friend, the Archbishop, took exception to some statement in my address about the Church of England. Bishop Talbot (now of Winchester) made no comments. He had been for many years the kindest of friends to me, and now a few days after my May Meetings he asked me over to Newington, and put me up for the night with Canon Palmer, in order that I might meet the Archbishop of

York and Bishop Gore. Archbishop Maclagan talked to me most of the evening, and left on me a singular impression of simple piety and Christian love. Bishop Gore I had known since Oxford days, and this year I paid him a flying visit at Worcester, where I met the Vicar of Birmingham, who was soon after consecrated Bishop of Carlisle. Bishop Gore draws men to him by a humorous and caustic candour, which to me is very fascinating. I was talking about " A Raffle for Souls," which was held in Mexico ; he overheard the phrase, and asked if I was speaking of the method of selling advowsons in the Church of England. I always remember his putting his head in at the cab window to explain that it was " a domestic cab, which ran between the house and the station," with which I had no further concern than to ride in it. I was glad of these opportunities, presented by the Education controversy, of close talks with the leaders of the Anglican Church.

Visits that same year to my friend, Canon Streatfeild, at Fenny Compton, and to my old Oxford contemporary, Robert Ottley, who was vegetating at Winterbourne Bassett before taking up his Regius Professorship at Christ Church, filled me with sympathy towards the gifted sons of the Anglican Church, who find themselves in such strange corners and are passed over in ecclesiastical preferment. And then, as always, I was thankful for the Divine arrangement which called me to the Congregational ministry ; but I never felt anything but love for the Church of England as a whole. Lancelot Andrewes, George Herbert, William Law, if not Richard Hooker and Frederick Robertson, keep me always true to the National Church, of which I always feel myself a member, though, to my sorrow, a non-conforming one.

The Sunday following my address I preached at Shrewsbury, and went to see my old head master, Moss, in the new school above the Quarry. He showed me the beautiful chapel he had devised, and recalled to me the old chapel with its desk at which the head master read the prayers. He remembered Dr. Kennedy at that desk, when a boy, only just in time to get in, was propelled forward right to the knees of the head master, with the odd result that the words ran : " Dearly beloved brethren, the Scripture moveth us in sundry places—get out, you boy." I have heard that my old friend and master (who has died this February 1917) sometimes expressed regret that I entered the Nonconformist ministry and was lost, reversing his own course ; for I think he was brought up among the Methodists, and entering the Established Church, was found—head master of Shrewsbury School. But we are differently made ; and I am as contented with my position of freedom and opportunity in the Free Churches as he was with his in the Church Established.

On that occasion, when I was preaching in Abbey Foregate, something of a sensation was caused because an old college friend of mine, known in the town as a staunch Churchman and Conservative, actually came to hear me. We had a talk afterwards, and recalling talks we had enjoyed at New College thirty years before, I could not help being sad to find how little real and conscious faith may be found with a staunch and inflexible Churchmanship. I had been preaching on prayer : to him the whole experience appeared incredible.

I wonder if rigid Churchmen realize from what treasures of the spiritual life they exclude their followers by forbidding them " occasional Nonconformity." I would have all people attend at least once a year at the Church to which they do *not* belong. We are members one of another.

In June came the Convention. It was impossible for our one Church to entertain six hundred and fifty guests (that was the number of those who accepted the invitation), but all the Churches in Hampstead, and some outside all Churches, generously offered hospitality. Sneers at suburban life are not uncommon. But I like to think that my suburb has on more than one occasion shown all the vigour and concentration of a large provincial town in carrying out a public work. The Mayor, Mr. Pritchard, received the guests at the Town Hall on Monday evening, June 8th. All the necessary accommodation, and the £410 necessary for entertainment, were gladly supplied.

But it was easier to elicit the warm feelings of Hampstead than to get the physical strength needed for the week. I was still in that limp and nervy condition, in which active and determined leadership seems impossible. My dear friend stood by me in the most wonderful way, though she was herself, alas ! in a very broken condition of health : she assured me that I was suffering from nerves and not from real weakness, and she encouraged me to rely on Christ as certain to realize His promise of being present. On Tuesday morning my very weakness drove me to remit the whole management of the Convention. Accordingly, instead of taking the chair at the assembly, I left it vacant and explained to the brethren that it was left vacant for Him. Though I myself was far too weak to appreciate it at the time, this Convention, seen in the retrospect, was one of the crowning mercies of my life. It would be impossible to give a detailed account of it, but there was a note in it which many never found in any such assembly before. On the Monday evening, our Jewish Rabbi, Mr. Green, was present and made a profound impression by his glowing tribute to Jesus. The Old Testament led in the New.

My own guests were my dear friend Mr. Meyer, R. J. Campbell, and Mr. Loosemore, though I think the last named was prevented from coming. Each morning we met for prayer at 7.15. The rain poured, but the showers of blessing exceeded. On Tuesday morning at 10.30 we had a beautiful conference on the Practice of the Presence of God (Arnold Thomas, Meyer, Maxwell, etc.). In the evening at 7.30, P. T. Forsyth and R. J. Campbell spoke on Faith in Christ ;

and He was there. On Wednesday morning the Holy Spirit was the theme ; Dr. Goodrich, Pearson, Silvester Horne, brought help to us all. The evening was devoted to the Conditions of Receiving the Spirit. A. J. Palmer spoke with power, and then I tried to lead them all to that blessing of Pentecost. There must have been a great power of God at work ; I heard afterwards of men being in those few minutes filled with the Spirit " from top to toe," and some have witnessed how their lives and ministries were transformed from that time onward.

On Thursday morning the question was the means of reaching the outside. We chanced to have with us Dr. Taylor of Chicago, who gave us a thrilling address about his own efforts among the mixed masses of his city. In 1913 I visited Dr. Taylor at his Settlement in Chicago, surrounded by Jews, Greeks, and Roumanians, still holding a fortress of practical Christianity with un-tiring devotion, and I did not wonder that his words had moved us in that June morning of rain and blessing ten years before. One of my people gave a reception to our guests in the Royal Botanical Gardens, Regent's Park, that afternoon. The rain reached a climax. But that evening the spiritual showers reached a climax, when the subject of Conversion was handled by R. J. Campbell, J. H. Jowett, and Titmarsh and Bailey. The early prayer meeting of Friday was one steady flow of thanksgiving. At 10.30 the strain of praise was louder still. Howard Fry and Ravener made a deep impression. The Convention ended in an over-flowing gratitude for Christ's manifestation of Himself such as I have not seen before or since. At the Autumnal Meetings in Bournemouth, the ministers who had been present gave me an illuminated address of thanks ; but none knew better than I that no thanks were due to me. In my helpless and humiliating weakness of body Christ had taken His own work in hand ; putting me aside, He had fed the multitude with the broken bread and poured out wine of His own Person. The Communion on the Tuesday evening radiated its divine light on the whole week.

I was worn out, and my friend Joseph King came with us down to Sidmouth, to recover in that healing air and the magical beauty of cliff and moor and sea. We went to Collaton Ralegh to see the beautiful old house of the Raleghs, and found a rustic there who had never heard of Sir Walter Ralegh. Why do we let Englishmen alone grow up in ignorance of their great past? What would Germany or America give to have ancestors and a story like ours? Yet every German and American absorbs his meagre national history, while we alone leave our rich treasures unassimilated. By the 1st of July Nature and God had wrought invigoration. That morning He sent me a great sense of joy and hope in the thought of work, and seemed so sufficient for our human needs that I marvelled why we ever doubt Him.

In the gladness of returning strength I wrote the articles on Matutinus, Meridianus, and Vespertinus, which were printed as a booklet ; nothing I ever wrote has brought me more satisfaction in later years. It is a landmark of God's mercy, reminding me of His amazing way of meeting us with peace and joy in the Valley of Humiliation. That August I stayed at home, and had an August mission in the Church, which was attended with rich blessing. During the month my friend Arnold White, who was for a time a member of Lyndhurst Road, was in prison, and I visited him. In the Whitaker Wright case he had made a statement which incurred a fine of £100 or a month's imprisonment. Convinced that he was right, he refused to pay and went to prison. What an experience that was ! When I saw my friend, the very model of strength and uncompromising determination, in the prison dress with the arrow marks, and known no longer by his name but as a number, my heart sank within me. I returned to ask the prayers of the

Church. In a few days he was very glad to find the £100 paid and himself liberated.

How few of us realize the horrors of imprisonment ! For a high-minded man, rejoicing in life and work, conscious of integrity, it is an unendurable torture. That experience enabled me to realize what Christ endured on the Cross, the Just dying for the unjust. Depraved and unhumanized people may be content in a prison ; when the sense of shame is gone, the confinement and the regularity of life may seem a relief from the risks and disgraces of crime. But the saddest thought of all is that men should sink so low as to adapt themselves to the ignominy and servitude of a prison life.

In September we went to Sheringham, that in that fine strong air, and with Silvester Horne and his family, who had a house there, I might prepare my Address for the Autumnal Assembly.

Tempted as I was to handle the social questions which lay nearest to my heart, I felt bound to take the subject which came first in the Faith. I could not find that Foreign Missions had ever been urged from the Chair of the Union : afterwards, when my friend and elder, Ralph Wardlaw Thompson was chairman, the claim of Missions came by its own. I thought and read and wrestled, to show the Marching Orders of the Church as a compelling appeal to the Church to put the foreign work first. I tried to prove that the Church always flourishes or declines in proportion to the interest she takes in extending the Kingdom of God and preaching the Gospel of Christ in the Regions Beyond.

Early in October I paid a visit to Lancashire College, to the principalship of which I had been invited and urged during the time of my greatest weakness in 1902. My friend and elder, Dr. Adeney, had taken the place, and I rejoiced greatly in the promise of his work there. On my return from Manchester I had an amusing experience. Tom Ellis, the Welsh M.P. who rose to be the Liberal Whip, had been a pupil of mine at Oxford, and

I had written some recollections of him for the Memoir which was published when his premature death robbed the country of one of its most promising statesmen. On October 7th John Morley was unveiling a statue of Ellis at Bala, where shortly before I had visited the Ellis home, and seen the father, who was so Welsh that he could never read his son's speeches. I was to speak on the occasion of the unveiling. But my train was late at Chester ; I missed the connection, and I had to return to London. Much to my satisfaction I received a paper giving a full account of the ceremony, and my speech in full ! This was the cleverest thing I have ever known in journalism.

The Autumnal Meetings of the Union were at Bournemouth, and I was hospitably entertained by Lady Maxse. It was a pleasure that my duty brought me to a place which I remembered in childhood, when the railway came no farther than Poole, and a few villas among the pines of the New Forest and a few houses on the beach constituted the town which now runs in monotonous miles of beauty along the shore. As a child I had heard the waves break, with a certain musical murmur, on that sandy bay, and I realized that all my life I had expected the sound of the sea to be like that. As children in those primitive days we were not hindered from cutting houses and forts in the cliff, and I could remember the sense of commanding the world from a rampart thus excavated by childish toil. Thus childhood ran into manhood, and I was touched with a sense of the plan which is laid down for our lives, when I delivered my address in Richmond Hill Church on Our Marching Orders. That same day Mr. Mitchell, who had been principal of the Nottingham Institute, was elected as secretary of the Union. His life was prematurely cut short, but it was an auspicious election, and if he had lived his industry and thoroughness, together with his high standard of pastoral life, would have led the Churches in a favourable way. The meetings were all good. Dr. Forsyth and Campbell Morgan spoke well on that day. And a Mayor's reception in the Winter Garden I remember with special pleasure, because the band played a remarkable piece, which brought to my mind Napoleon's retreat from Moscow, and on looking at the programme I saw it was Tchaikovsky's " 1812." I recall also a wonderful paper on the Congregational Ministry from Dr. John Hunter, who too seldom appeared on the platform of the Union. I returned from Bournemouth with an overwhelming sense of gratitude that I had been carried through the year of my ordeal.

I felt that God had used me, even in the humiliation of my weakness, and that He had been good to me even in withholding from me that striking success which might have given me a dangerous eminence among my brethren. The more I have known of popular and successful ministers in the Free Churches, the more thankful I have been that God has spared me the snares, the feverish excitements, the overstrain, and the disappointments to which they are subjected.

I wonder whether there is any example of a great preacher who is not torn and racked with anxieties and misgivings. On more than one occasion I have met such a preacher in the height of his powers and influence, admired and envied by all his brethren, and I have found his own mind a prey to the most dismal shadows and discontent. Great and popular preachers are the modern martyrs of the Church. The strain on nerve and heart makes life a purgatory ; the good they do is secured at a cost to themselves which, if it were realized, would win the sympathy, the pity, of the whole Church.

During this year I worked with great satisfaction on another Commentary for *The Century Bible*. I took six of the Minor Prophets, and the other six were taken by Professor Driver, who had been my first master in Hebrew. Sadly conscious as I was of the difference between my own work and his, I found much delight in being, as it were, his colleague. I remembered how in Oxford days he had envied my faculty for getting at people, and how, when he was about to be ordained, he, the greatest Hebraist of his time, paced my room in nervous terror lest he should be ploughed in the Bishop's examination. He had trodden the scholar's path and had become the acknowledged doyen of Old Testament scholarship ; I had been plunged into all the distractions of ministerial life, and had worked at the desk only by snatches. But for a brief, and for me happy, moment, we were side by side as collaborators in the work of Old Testament study.

Another great joy of this year was that I was brought into close touch with Dr. Greville Macdonald, whose father, George Macdonald, I had repeatedly met in my early years at Hampstead. Greville Macdonald, though a physician in Harley Street, was deeply interested in philosophy and religion. He was writing books which had something of his father in them, but more of himself. Poet, story-teller, thinker, the earnest student of human life, he had much to tell the world if he could get it expressed. He came to lecture to my people. One Sunday morning he preached, and a man met us afterwards in the street, who came up to him and said : " Dr. Macdonald, I have been waiting for what you said to us this morning all my life." This warm-hearted, gifted man, generously pouring out his means, and himself, in help to others, came into my life and brought me treasures which I could not repay, for his deafness prevented him from hearing me when I preached or spoke. At the same time I met John Watson (Ian Maclaren) in Liverpool ; he was the man of genius ; his expression, his hand-shake, his talk, gave one a sense of distinction. I hope his books will last, because they give some slight impression of what he was.

But this year, begun in weakness, was to end in indescribable sorrow. My beloved friend, who had helped me unfailingly all through, had never recovered from the shock of leaving her home in Halifax and the racking anxieties connected with it. A painful melancholia settled upon her, and it was necessary to have a nurse always with her. When, after a drive, she told me what she was passing through, and said, "I have looked after you, and now I must ask you to look after me," and then offered up a tender prayer for me, I did not know what years of sorrow were before me, but all the joy of life seemed to wither at the root.

The anxiety and trouble were so great that when Dr. Macdonald invited me to go with him and a small party to Arosa for Christmas, I thought it was better to get the change of ten days, and she urged me to go. That was a wonderful experience. The high snow-cup in the mountains open to the glorious sunlight and moonlight, the sparkling frost, the strange beauty of the electric lights crossing the slopes, the tobogganing (for the first and last time), the skating (for the last time), the congenial companionship, enabled me to end the year, notwithstanding the sorrow and apprehension, with thankfulness and peace. "I believe God has blessed me," I wrote on the last day. "He has used me. He has given me three new friends : Mr. Rhodes, Mr. Sully, and Dr. Macdonald. And this holiday in Arosa, with all its charm and interest and stimulus, shows how He crowns the year with His goodness. May the New Year be better."

CHAPTER XIII

PRESIDENCY OF THE FREE CHURCH COUNCIL

1905

THE prayer that the New Year might be better was answered in a strange way. The experiences of the next few months were so heart-breaking that I shrink even from recording them. And yet, as I believe that they were sent by the chastening hand of my Father for a purpose, which was, I trust, fulfilled, I must not pass them over too hurriedly. When I returned from Arosa in the New Year our beloved invalid was much worse. Dr. Macdonald, with endless sympathy, took her in charge, and she was for some weeks in a nursing home in Welbeck Street. But when she returned home the symptoms became more alarming, and one terrible day in February a specialist, called in, said that the only hope was for us to leave the house and put her into the hands of trained nurses. Kind friends received Mr. Oakes and me ; within an hour of the doctor's verdict we were away. In carrying my large bag of clothes and books, hastily thrown in, to the house of my friends, the Flints, a few hundred yards away, I strained myself, with fateful consequences. An evening or two later I was summoned by a messenger to come quickly, for Mrs. Oakes was dying. The nurses on either side were fanning her and she did not know us. But our prayers were heard, and she recovered from the immediate danger.

In the middle of February my sight went wrong. I could not read. I consulted an oculist, who was a member of my Church. While I waited in the reception-room I took out my Bible to test my sight. Opening at random, I read 2 Sam. xxii. 29, " For Thou art my Lamp, O Lord, and the Lord will lighten my darkness." This swift message of God, coming from so unlikely a part of the Scripture, had an indescribable effect upon me. I was nerved to endure whatever should come. I did not take the promise to mean that my sight would be spared, but that in losing it I should keep the Lord as my Light.

But none of the doctors I consulted could do anything for me. There was a detachment of the retina, and all they could prescribe was long weeks—one said months, another said two years—of rest. I must, in the hope of saving others from such suffering, record the treatment I received from one doctor, who had a high reputation as an oculist. He had a breezy, rollicking manner. When my own doctor explained to him that I wrote books, he said cheerily, " Well, he won't write any more, but that will be no loss." Then he added : " You will be among the one-eyed, like Lord Nelson, Kitchener, etc." Before I left he actually swore in the presence of the lady who had come with me. His fee of three guineas was paid on the spot. But (by inadvertence, no doubt) some weeks later he applied for it again. My experience of doctors, and of the great consultants, has been so favourable, and this instance is so exceptional, that I do not like to dwell upon it. The explanation I afterwards received was that this great physician hated the clergy, but that he was overwhelmingly kind and generous to actors and actresses. Let him pass ! I forbear to name him.

I was now precluded from preaching, and was dependent on friends for reading and writing. At the end of February Dr. Harold Basden took the charge of our sweet invalid. We obtained a small house on the Warren at Crowborough, and there we had to leave her, with occasional visits, for two years and a half.

Early in March my dear friends, the Andrews, fetched me to their house, Everleigh, and there for weeks they did all that medical knowledge and unfailing tenderness could do to help me. Cut off from my work, and lying most of the time on my back, I got a young friend, Aldersey White, to come and write for me every day. The boy's goodness and patience I remember with deep gratitude. In this way I composed a booklet on *Hope*, and then a poem on *St. John*, which Mr. Dent published for me. The love and care of that dear family were an extraordinary comfort, and more hopeful news began to come from Crowborough. Our dear one was sleeping better, and began to take food again, and presently to walk in a way she had not done for many years.

On March 10th came a long telegram of sympathy from the Free Church Council Meeting at Newcastle, informing me that they had appointed me President for 1905. That seemed blankly impossible, but I was living by faith, and began to suspect that God had a design in the affliction which He was tempering with so much unexpected mercy and blessing.

While I was thus imprisoned, Mrs. Kumn came several times to see me, burning with zeal for evangelizing the Sudan. I encouraged her and her husband, Dr. Kumn, to form the society for the purpose, and promised that, if I could act as President of the Free Church Council, I would do all in my power to promote the project. In my blinded state the needs of darkest Africa seemed to appeal to me.

Sir Anderson Critchett, who now had my case in hand, insisted only on three months' complete rest. He had nothing else to do for me except mercury rubbings about the temples. My friends the Flints, whose interest and kindness overwhelmed me, were convinced that Pagenstecher of Wiesbaden might do for me more than our English oculists could. And on Sunday, March 20th, I awoke with the conviction that I must go to Wiesbaden on Tuesday. Then occurred another of those unforeseen events which have convinced me that a Divine hand guides our lives and arranges for us. My dearly beloved friend who would have taken me was herself utterly incapacitated. But Mrs. de Sélincourt, the widow of my old friend of Westminster Chapel, who had recently come to Lyndhurst Road, made the wonderful proposal to go with me and look after me. And my good and energetic friend, Arnold White, offered to convoy us both to Wiesbaden. Notwithstanding the warning of Sir Anderson Critchett, who declared that crossing the Channel was risky, my loving escort managed to convey me in perfect peace to Cologne (for the night) and then on to my destination. In the private cabin, as I crossed the Channel, the conviction came to me that I must, while I was away, prepare a Manual of Devotion for the Free Churches, as a gift to them, in case I could not occupy the chair of the Council. That was the origin of my *Open Secret*.

Pagenstecher held out hopes that if I would come into the klinik for a few weeks he might preserve the sight of the affected eye, and I felt it my duty to accept his proposal. When I found myself among the inmates of this hospital, cut off from my life and my work, and shut up with my sorrow and anxiety for my beloved friend, who could not write a letter or even send a message, my heart for the moment sank within me. But there were the other patients to sympathize with ; and Mrs. de Sélincourt engaged a room in a neighbouring pension and came in every day to help me. Not only was she ready to read and write for me, but she could pray, and as the days went on we tested the power of prayer to comfort and sustain us in the most trying situations of life.

I was to remain lying until midday, and have a daily injection in the eye ; then I was to be allowed to go out for a leisurely walk ; the rest of the day I was to lie still. Mrs. de Sélincourt in her girlhood had been a favourite of Thomas Binney, and once when he was laid aside with trouble in his eyes for some months, she had written, at his dictation, one of his books, *How*

to Make the Best of Both Worlds or *Money*, I forget
which. Now in her old age the task of her youth was
to be repeated. Two days after I was settled in the
klinik I began to dictate to her the *Open Secret*. In
the evenings she read me the necessary material ; in the
morning hours I dictated, and some times went on dictating
while the injection was made, vanquishing the pain by
distraction of thought. With so zealous and eager an
amanuensis the work made rapid progress. She helped
me immensely by her experience of prayer, and sometimes
by quotations which were in her mind. When the book
was finished, and in September published, I felt that
it was as much hers as mine, and her diligence in com-
mending it gave it a wide circulation. The book has
been the pivot of my later years, and is now filled with
facts about its own work in the world, with the record
of answered prayers, and with the aspirations after things
yet to be obtained, which make it a *journal intime* of
the last thirteen years of my life. Into that I cannot
enter here.

I was not left without visitors. My friend Frederick
Hastings, cycling through Germany, paid me a visit,
which did me good, though he wrote an article in a paper
which gave friends at home an exaggerated idea of my
suffering. My sister Constance and her friend came,
when their Easter holiday allowed them to leave their
school ; that was a great delight and encouragement.
Mr. and Mrs. Flint came to one of the large hotels, and
when I was permitted to be out for an evening, or
even for a midday meal, the change was most refreshing.
They talked to me much about the need of a book
showing the missionary message of the Bible. When
the *Open Secret* was finished, I began to dictate a short
volume which was published under the title of *The Bible
a Missionary Book*, in which I tried to show how the
Bible, treated by the methods of recent Biblical scholarship, became more than ever a call to missionary enterprise, and that the whole message of the Scriptures *is*

epitomized in the Marching Orders, "Go into all the world and preach the Gospel to every creature."

As the weeks passed, though the news from home was frequently very sad, and the grim fiend of depression had to be fought tooth and nail day and night, I became increasingly hopeful that my ministry would not be stopped by the calamity which had come upon me. At last Pagenstecher said that the detachment had been arrested, and that with care I might go on with my work. He approved of our going to Schwalbach for a few days to recuperate from the long confinement, and then I might return home. The day of release was one of great joy. And yet on looking back I find the whole period of my imprisonment fragrant with holy memories. In the great Markt Kirche every Wednesday there was a concert, which often brought me wonderful help. One day they sang a German verse which runs into English almost literally—

> Through the gloomy night of sorrow
> Breaks the joyful morning star,
> Soon shall dawn thine own to-morrow,
> God's dear help is never far.

That I had experienced. We had been allowed to present Christ to some in the klinik, and one experience abides with me : a lady of fashion was there for treatment, very charming, but apparently given wholly to pleasure. On the night before we left Mrs. de Sélincourt offered to read to the company my poem, *St. John*, which had just come to hand. It was very warmly received, and in the morning our fashionable friend came to bid us farewell. She was really affected, and after showing us a little of her inner life, hidden away, and so wholly unexpected, she said that never did any of the patients have a painful operation but she offered prayer for them.

Fellow feeling makes us wondrous kind, and the common suffering of the klinik opened our hearts to one another ; eyes were blind, but spiritual vision was quickened.

I was going back under severe restrictions. Not more than three hours' reading a day, not more than one sermon a Sunday, and many of the delights of physical exercise gone for ever. Sight was greatly impaired. It was difficult to read, and more difficult to recognize faces ; my preaching must be done henceforth without seeing, in the true sense of the word, my audience. The advantage of the rapport, which comes from the speaker reading what the hearer is feeling or thinking, must be surrendered. But, in spite of all, I was profoundly thankful to get back to work and to see if in any way I could make up for the faculties which were now lost or impaired. I had been away from my pulpit four months, nor was I allowed to begin preaching again at once. But the first Sunday in Lyndhurst Road again, June 5, 1904, brought me untold comfort. Dr. Josiah Strong of New York preached twice, and impressed us all with his Social Gospel, and his understanding of the Industrial Revolution and its effects. But in the vestry he gave me this singular encouragement : " Dr. Horton," he said, " let me just say this—I never had but one eye, and I can hardly see with the other." And yet he had become a great leader and had accomplished a unique work in the modern world. Yes, I took heart. At the Communion Service that morning, attended by some hundreds, I faced my people, and my heart overflowed with joy.

Only there was the vacant place in the house.

Other cheering evidences came that one-eyed people can be of use in the world. I had in the Church two ladies named Stoddart. One, Anna Stoddart, the biographer of John Stuart Blackie, was a very close friend. The other, Jane Stoddart, was well known, under the pseudonym of "Lorna," in a popular journal. Strange to say, the two Misses Stoddart, not knowing each other, found themselves living in the same mansions in York

Street. They made a mutual acquaintance in trying to sort out the letters which were constantly getting delivered at the wrong address. To their surprise they found that they were members of the same Church, and then, on farther inquiry, that they both came from Kelso, on the Scottish border. They became fast friends. It chanced one day that they were both calling on me at the same time, and the two literary ladies were trying to encourage me with hope that I might yet continue my work. " Pastor, dear," said Miss Anna, for that was the way in which she always addressed me, " I have only seen with one eye all my life." This, though encouraging, was not very surprising, for there was an odd look in the sightless eye. " I, too," said Miss Jane, " have only the use of one eye." This was surprising, because her two brown eyes had all the appearance of seeing.

A few Sundays after my return, my friend Dr. Bradford, of Montclair, New Jersey, came into my vestry and explained that he had done all his work and written his books with one eye. His injured eye, like my own, was a cause of confusion, making a double plane of vision, one clear and the other blurred ; he, therefore, in reading covered the bad eye with his hand. Here, then, was a reason not to lose heart and also to say nothing about my infirmity. I made a rule never to refer to my bad vision except to explain to my people that if I passed them in the street without notice I was not cutting them.

It was not till the first Sunday in July that I was able to preach twice and to take up something like my former life. The Church had not been idle in my absence, and its activity made me glad that I had not listened to an urgent plea from Allen Street, Kensington, in February, that I should go to the pulpit vacant by Mr. Silvester Horne's removal to Whitfield's. The Church had met and resolved to enlarge our buildings in order to make our institutional work more effective. The early prayer meetings in July were the last held in the Guild

Room, which had been consecrated by many memorable meetings and enterprises. The great block of buildings which now makes Lyndhurst Road, when the trees are bare, appear as large as a cathedral, rose to completeness, according to the excellent plans of one of our elders, Henry Spalding. This was not the only step of importance taken while I was at Wiesbaden. George Barrett, who was doing a fine work at Stroud, was invited to come and take up the Mission at Lyndhurst Hall ; to my surprise he consented to come, and the explanation of his readiness to leave a successful pastorate, in order to occupy a subordinate post, was a singular illustration of the interlacing of the threads of life. When he was a boy at Park Church, Halifax, he had desired to enter the ministry, and put it aside as impossible. One Sunday I preached in Park Church, and the result of the service was that he went home resolved at all costs to be a minister. Again, when he was leaving Lancashire College to begin his work, it chanced that I went to address the outgoing students. He was so impressed with the fact of my connection with his call to the ministry that, when Lyndhurst Road invited him to come to my aid, he never hesitated. I have had many assistants and colleagues, and am fortunate enough now to have Edward Shillito the poet, but no words can depict George Barrett as a colleague : his loyalty, his ardour, his boundless devotion, his loving appreciation of Church and minister, made his time with me a constant help and satisfaction. During those hardest and most torturing years of my life he was a cordial to my spirit, a brother beloved indeed.

When in July 1904 I took up my work again I saw that I must not shrink from the Presidency of the Free Church Council, which had been laid upon me for 1905. I had been at the first Grindelwald Conference, which aimed at the reunion of all the Churches, but actually effected that partial confederation of the Free Churches, which Mr. Shakespeare is now trying to develop into a real Federation. I knew Hughes, Sir Henry Lunn, Berry, Mackennal, Munro Gibson, and all the leaders of this movement ; and though I found myself in frequent disagreement with the spirit and methods of the Council, as they were developed and worked by poor Thomas Law, I never doubted but that it was our plain duty to find the points of connection between the Free Churches, which were only separated accidentally, and to aim at a reunion. It was a sore trial to me to be used, " put up," to use his own expression, by a secretary, to whom organization seemed to be everything, and the spirit quite secondary. But I worked with him as far as I could, and to me he was as appreciative and helpful as it was in him to be.

Just at the end of 1904 I began my *Devotional Commentary on St. Matthew* at the request of the secretary of the Religious Tract Society. Strange to say, when it was finished the Committee declined it, on the ground of supposed heterodoxy : what an anomaly it is that men do in the name of religion what in other connections they would call unfair ! Of course I said nothing, but allowed the Free Church Council to publish it, and found that it met a want ; and, if I had been encouraged, I should have gladly worked on other books of the Bible in the same way. About Christmas came the joy and encouragement that our beloved invalid began to write letters again, and though a year and a half had to pass before she could come home, there was a bright hope now, and she began at once to offer the spiritual counsel and help which had been suspended for a year.

The plan of campaign for my presidential year was, that after the great Annual Meetings of the Council in Manchester, the first week of March, I should endeavour to visit the whole country by holding a three days' convention in several selected centres. We divided England into another heptarchy ; the seven provinces were to be gathered in turn at some town that would invite the delegates from all the Councils and Federations of Councils. It was an alarming programme for one who was in the first bewilderment of confused sight, and who carried about a sorrow and anxiety which made the days heavy. But Mrs. de Sélincourt kindly offered to go with me in all the necessary journeys, and to help me with reading and correspondence ; and for the rest I had an inward assurance that another Presence would go with me, and that for the formidable demands of the year His grace would be sufficient. In February I filled the Mansfield pastoral office again for four Sundays. And at the same time John Mott from America was holding a remarkable mission among the undergraduates. I took the chair for him one evening in the Town Hall, and came into contact in this way with one of the most powerful personalities I have ever met. I was in Oxford in 1883 when Moody conducted a wonderful mission among the undergraduates, and saw the power given to him to turn scoffers into devout hearers and to change careless young manhood into apostleship for Christ. But John Mott's gift for work among students was far more specific ; and the Student Christian Movement, of which he seemed to be the centre, was destined to have an even more world-wide influence than Moody's great evangelistic services. One day I ran down to Birmingham, and at the house of my friend, Sir Hallewell Rogers, met Sir Oliver Lodge, who was now the President of the new University of Birmingham. Here, too, was a man of remarkable power : in appearance like Lord Salisbury, a man of science and yet full of literary interests, he made an unusual impression upon me. The new knowledge about the constitution of Matter was occupying my thought, and I asked him if the fairylike description of the atom, the invisible atom, as a cathedral in which the ion of electricity darted about, relatively the size of a mouse, was to be taken as an accurate scientific statement. He assured me that it was. And a remark of his, which has been made more emphatic by his recent book on the survival of his son Raymond after death, remained with me : " The ceasing of personality is one of the things which don't happen." It is a great sorrow to me that Sir Oliver has extended his ægis over the doings of Spiritualism ; for I am persuaded that the method of seeking communion with our lost ones through a medium and in dark séances is prohibited by the law of God and by the wisdom of men ; but Faith owes much to Sir Oliver Lodge—he has for many years made it impossible to say that Science and Religion are opposed. Sir David Brewster, Faraday, Clerk Maxwell, Lord Kelvin, Sir Oliver Lodge—they form a noble succession in British Science, and by showing that Science is not the enemy of Religion, they have encouraged us to preserve our religion from being the nervous enemy of Science. In my work among the undergraduates that year I found how puzzled they were about the Atonement ; indeed, the students for the ministry seemed inclined to leave the doctrine out of their teaching. I gave them three addresses, which were published under the title *Does the Cross Save?* afterwards enlarged into *How the Cross Saves.* My own personal experience, and my constant need of an objective Atonement as the ground of any subjective at-one-ment in myself, my absolute dependence on Divine grace for my salvation, and my certainty that nothing which I had done, or could do, offered me a sure foundation for acceptance with God—always prevented me from surrendering the doctrine of the Atonement. Besides, I had seen again and again how conversion resulted from apprehending that truth more frequently than from any other presentation of the Gospel. It was therefore a real anguish to me to find my little book reviewed in the *Congregationalist,* the organ of my own Denomination, by a young minister who had, I knew, abandoned this central truth, and afterwards went the length of writing a book to show that Jesus never lived. It is that anarchy of the Free Churches, and the lack of support which one experiences

in every attempt to defend their central and fundamental
doctrines, that we hope to alter by the new movement
of Free Church Federation.

After the month at Oxford I was, as always, exhausted,
and went for a few days of recuperation to Llandrindod
Wells. This was my first acquaintance with that lofty,
invigorating umbilicus of Wales, which three months
later was to be the scene of one of the most inspiring
episodes of my life.

In the first week of March we went to Manchester
for the Annual Meetings of the Council. I stayed
with Mrs. Rylands at Longford Hall. Horne and
J. D. Jones were among the other guests. I was
very uneasy in prospect of the meetings. I knew
I should not be able to read my address, nor to see
the faces of my audience. I tried to think of Paul,
used in Galatia, *owing* to the defect of his eyesight.
My address aimed at two things : to enlist all the Free
Churches in the Missionary cause, and to bring the
Churches into a new touch with organized Labour. Oh !
if only I had my sight, I thought, and the vigour and
heart-ease of earlier days, I might accomplish something !

But on that Tuesday morning I ,woke at five o'clock,
with the peace of God in my heart, and He told me
to let Him preside at the Free Church Council. I
went down reassured, and when I stood up before the
crowded Free Trade Hall, I was calm and happy. I
asked the people to put our Lord in control of it all,
and the vast audience bowed in reverent prayer. The
programme seemed to unfold beautifully. Principal Rainy
preached the sermon in the evening, and next morning
I went on my task light-hearted. Rattenbury spoke on
Institutional Churches, and I had the joy of welcoming
him as a worthy successor of Hugh Price Hughes. And
that same day W. T. Stead made a great speech which
impressed the whole assembly. Stead was a true apostle
of purity and of social justice. Working in the medium
of journalism, he did not entirely escape the snare of

sensationalism ; but he was a true man, and if he had only kept clear of " spooks," and such elements of imposture and self-deception as necromancy and automatic writing create, his influence would have been entirely good. When he went down in the *Titanic* it seemed to me that his death was the tragedy of that disaster ; but it may have been God's way of delivering him from the spiritualistic entanglements in which he had become involved.

That Wednesday evening " Gipsy " Smith swept the outcasts of the city into the hall and preached Christ to them. About one hundred and fifty of them seemed to be saved.

In the exhausted atmosphere the Thursday meetings were difficult, but Arnold Thomas conducted the Devotional Service. On the Friday I lunched with the Bishop of Manchester and recalled Oxford days. When I returned from Manchester, and looked back on this typical assembly of the Free Church Council, I could not help regretting the mistaken notion shared by many that the Council is a caucus of ecclesiastical politicians. The error is due entirely to the Education Controversy, which raged from 1902 onwards. Dr. Clifford and his friends strove with all their might against the Denominational settlement of the schools. Dr. Clifford's amazing eloquence and power of leading, together with the childlike innocence and sweetness of his character, put him in the forefront of the Council work. But the dominant note of the Council from the beginning was spiritual : the great object was to save souls and to work for a happier and a holier England.

In April I was made president of Browning Hall, and tried to help my friend, Herbert Stead, in his long struggle for the enlightenment and uplifting of the people in South London. The same month Rabbi Green took a Thursday evening service in Lyndhurst Road. I had addressed his people on the Old Testament at the West Hampstead Synagogue. And this return visit was deeply interesting. Regarding the Jews as the great Nonconformist race, and Jesus as the greatest product of Judaism, he seems in an address to a Christian Church very near to us. When I asked him to close with prayer, he did so, and prayed beautifully, but he told me how nonplussed he had been at my request, because he had never before offered an extemporary prayer.

At Easter my visitation of the heptarchy began. The West of England representatives met at Plymouth. There were three hundred delegates. Jowett and Rattenbury came and addressed crowded meetings ; and Thomas Phillips of Bloomsbury there for the first time revealed himself to me as one of the prophetic voices of our day. Coming back from Plymouth, as Law had mentioned the *Free Church Hymnal* that he was compiling, my hymn, *Father of Mercies*, wrote itself in my mind, and on my return my organist, Douglas Macey, set it to a tune. Of innumerable efforts at hymn-writing I have made, this is the only one which has found a place in a hymn book. Unfortunately the crowded meetings had brought on laryngitis, and I had to go to Bourne-mouth to recover.

But by May I was ready for Llandrindod—that was the centre for Wales. The Welsh people were still trembling with the emotion of the Revival, which was connected with the name of Evan Roberts. Also the high clear air seemed to favour spiritual exaltation. The singing was spontaneous ; the people did not wait for hymns to be given out, but went on from one to another, and repeated, and recommenced, until the whole audience seemed to be a single organ, breathing out its worship, its exultation, its confession and its faith, as from one mind with harmonized voices. I remember feeling in the midst of one of these acts of choral worship : this will probably be the lasting atmosphere of heaven ; this deep full joy is prophetic.

The members of the Convention took rambles over the mountains, and held missionary meetings, and poured their contributions in, while looking out over the glorious

scene they sang : " O'er the gloomy hills of darkness,
Look, my soul, be still and gaze." The Welsh certainly
have a genius for religion, to which England owes much.
It is impossible to estimate the results of a Convention
like this ; but if I were to judge by the effect on my
own heart and life, I should put that assembly at
Llandrindod as a high-water mark of spiritual experience.

On coming back I had an unusual pleasure. King
Edward gave a garden party at Windsor. It was the
only time that I was able to accept the invitation which
was sent to me for that kind of occasion, and I greatly
enjoyed it. I saw the distinguished people of the
country, and others like myself undistinguished, in the
grounds of the historic castle. The intellect and beauty
of England were there on the green sward, as I have
not seen them before, nor shall again. The King and
Queen moved down the midst to receive the greetings
of their loyal subjects. I had, as I have said before,
a sense of personal loyalty to King Edward ; and though
I find myself incapable of admiring rank and station
and wealth, my love of England gives me a thrill of
enthusiasm whenever I am able to realize her on her
ideal side. That afternoon, June 14, 1907, was therefore a notable point in my life.

The East Anglian Convention was at Lowestoft, beginning June 17th. Here I had a wonderful encouragement. My beloved friend had been able to write letters
for some time, though it was not yet wise to go and see
her except at long intervals. But at Lowestoft I had
a letter containing a beautiful suggestion. She urged
me to get the young people around me as a " Bodyguard," and to try to impress on them the ideas of
the Convention, so that when I left they would carry on
the work. Accordingly, after the service on Sunday
morning, I appealed for a Bodyguard. The first who
responded and acted as secretary has remained a close
friend ever since ; she is married, and has boys of her
own, but she refers to me as if she were still working

with me in the Convention. Another of that little group
went out as a missionary. All through these Conventions
Dr. Kumn and his devoted wife were present and kept
the claims of the Dark Continent, where the Crescent
was outstripping the Cross, before our eyes. Timothy
Richard also came to Lowestoft and urged the claims
of China. The plan of appointing a secretary to form
Missionary Study Circles was mooted, and my friends,
the Flints, made the most generous offer for carrying it
out. But my year of office was too short and crowded
to get the work established.

For Northumbria the Convention in July was at Sunderland. Before starting on Monday morning, July 3rd,
my friend and elder, Eliot Reed, called to tell me that
he had met a man the day before who said that I was
the best-loved man in London ! The dear hyperbole
was a strange comfort and help in facing the strain of
another Convention. I stayed with Mrs. Backhouse,
whose husband wrote the Church history which shows
the Early Church in a clear dry light, free from ecclesiastical prejudice. We met in the Bede Hall, and the
influence of the venerable historian of England seemed
all about me. Campbell attended this Convention, and
so great a crowd came to hear him that I had to preach
to an overflow in a neighbouring church of eight or nine
hundred people. We had a wonderful meeting on the
sands, and Dr. Clifford came and gave us one of his
breezy and stirring addresses. How wonderfully, little
things are remembered ! I said good-bye to one of the
ministers in Sunderland, and, it seems, prayed with him ;
eleven years later he came to settle in London and recalled that prayer, as if it had been an event in his
life. I suspect the really important things and moments
in life, seen from the heavenly side of the tapestry,
are those which have seemed to us trifling or wearisome.
If only we could see !

On returning from Lowestoft I attended a meeting
in the Mansion House for Dr. Barnardo, July 10th. I

had known him since 1874. That day he seemed anxious and worried. I was glad to speak and point out what a work he had done for London and for the country ; no one else thought it worth while to breathe a word of gratitude to him. When he died in September I was thankful indeed that I had delivered my soul. Why do we save our wreaths of praise for the biers of our best? If we told them while they live we might not only gladden their hearts but multiply their effectiveness.

In July we opened the new buildings which completed the pile of Lyndhurst Road. It was a fancy of mine to name the rooms after men who would suggest to us the ideals to be realized in them ; there is a Kingsley room, a Coleridge room, a Toynbee room. It was my wish also to have an oratory always open for private prayer. That will perhaps be realized when I am gone.

In August, at the request of my friend Mr. J. A. R. Marriott, I attended the Summer School of the University Extension work in Oxford, and delivered to the assembled students a lecture on Calvin, which cost me an infinity of toil during the year. Then Mr. Oakes and I went up to Scotland and stayed with my friend Miss Stoddart at Kelso. We saw the ruins of Jedburgh and Dryborough and Melrose, that strip of country which, as Ruskin showed, was the supremely cultivated part, agriculturally and spiritually, in the later Middle Ages. We visited Flodden Field, and the lonely Hermitage Castle, famous for Queen Mary's ride to find her lover, Bothwell, and the whole length of the Roman Wall, and there at Hexham had the oddest encounter with a burglar. We visited Yarrow and St. Mary's Loch, Abbotsford and Eildon Hill and the Lammermuirs ; in a word, had the full flavour of the Borders, and of the Lowlands, and of Sir Walter. Then I went to my friends, the Glanvilles, at Braemar, and from the summit of Lochnagar saw the whole of Deeside as the clouds lifted for a moment ; we seemed to look down from a parapet of heaven on the sunlit, heather-clad earth. Then we went down

the canal to Fort William, and thence to Mallaig, where
the wild September gales refused us the " bonny boat " to
go over to Skye. We could only see the ridges like a
bird's wing in the glory of stormy sunsets. Then coming
down to Callender on a day between the storms I climbed
Ben Ledi, and had the widest view of the whole of
Scotland I or any one else will ever obtain. During
this holiday I passed through the press a volume of
sermons entitled *The Hidden God*, containing some of
the recently discovered sayings of Jesus. And at the
end of September I was allowed to see our beloved
lady, and to find that she was making steps towards a
(yet distant) recovery.

In October my heptarchical conventions began again.
We tried to draw the Midlands together at Cheltenham,
where a fine " Bodyguard " gave me a hope of the
work continuing. Later in the month we had the Convention for London and the South of England at Hampstead. I enrolled a Bodyguard at Lyndhurst Road,
which, under the name of the Active Service League,
continues to this day. Again I had to ask Hampstead
to help me in entertaining the guests, and the Mayor gave
a most kindly reception. There was a beautiful flow of
spiritual power in those meetings, and in all my presidential work I felt that my own Church benefited most,
and most lastingly. That was their reward for letting
me undertake the wider ministry.

In November I went to the Channel Islands to meet
the Free Church Councils of Jersey and Guernsey. I
arrived on the rollers of the great storm in which the
steamer had been wrecked at St. Malo. It is difficult
to keep the close contact with the Churches in the Islands,
and the stormy visit was worth the effort that it cost.

The last of my seven Conventions was for Yorkshire.
It began on November 18th at Harrogate. The Bodyguard there mustered a hundred strong, and one of them
afterwards became a missionary in Central Africa. When
I left Harrogate on November 24th I had a feeling

of deep gratitude for the grace of God which had carried me through the extensive programme. I published the addresses I gave at the Conventions in a little book called *The Law of Spiritual Power*. It stands on my shelf, the monument of a year which in prospect seemed impossible, and in retrospect seems suffused with Divine life and joy. An entry in my journal for October 12th runs, " Felt that God had given me at least *one* happy day." But looking back I know that the whole year was crowned with mercy.

The work of my presidency was brought to an end at the Annual Meetings in Birmingham, where my final word was a sermon on God is Love. But before I laid down the seals of office there were two things which I recall with interest. We had a New Year's Conference of all the Free Church missionaries that were at home on furlough. Before the great Edinburgh Conference of 1910 the opportunities of the missionaries of different societies meeting and conferring were rare. We hoped that this was a piece of missionary work which the Free Church Council might legitimately attempt. The other occasion was a dinner at the Hotel Cecil on March 2nd. The new ministry of Sir Henry Campbell-Bannerman was entering on its momentous career, and in the new House of Commons there were a large number of Free Churchmen. We invited them all to dinner ; on my right hand was Professor Bryce, on my left Mr. Lloyd George. We had no wish to form a Free Church clique in the House of Commons, but we felt that by realizing the number of Free Churchmen returned by the constituencies, and by hearing such leaders as the two who addressed us that evening, we might make the Nonconformist conscience a power instead of a derision in the counsels of the nation. The positions which both Lord Bryce and Mr. Lloyd George have since taken in our public life show how much the country owes to her convinced Free Churchmen.

One amusing memory lingers from the close of this

eventful year. I had met Mr. Kingscote, the King's butler at St. James's Palace, in the work for the better observance of Sunday. On December 14th he asked me to lunch, to meet Bishop Potter, whom I had met in 1893 in New York. As we were conducted through the rooms and cellars of the palace, a housekeeper accompanied us, demure and reverential, evidently feeling a mysterious awe of a bishop. The Bishop in his friendly and unconventional way was telling me how much more familiarly an American bishop is treated by the public than our own prelates. " As I was leaving New York," he said, " a friend patted my back and exclaimed, ' Well, Bishy, how are you? ' " I caught sight of the housekeeper's face as she heard this sacrilegious speech. I shall never forget it. That any one could address a live bishop in that familiar way, and that a live bishop could tell the story himself—she felt that the heavens would fall.

But I am not sure that the American treatment of bishops is not kinder to them than ours. When men rise to the highest authority in the Church of Christ, just in proportion as they are true men they become more humble than ever, and with one exception, and that was abroad and not in England, I have always been struck with the genuine humility of the Anglican bishops. It must, I think, be infinitely distasteful to them to be addressed as " My Lord," and to feel that atmosphere of court etiquette and adulation always about them. The King may be forced to live in a world apart from his subjects, and to maintain the divinity which hedges a throne by artificial barriers, but I should think a chief pastor in Christ's Church must long for simple and natural relations with his fellow-men, and to excite in them not awe but love. That bishops, with all their dignities and pre-eminence, are as godly as they are, is a striking evidence of God's grace.

CHAPTER XIV

THE RETURN OF JOY

1906

WHEN I was released from my duties as President
of the Free Church Council, eager as I was to betake
myself again undisturbed to my pastoral duties, there
was another concern upon me also. The failure of
my sight reminded me that if I wished to see other
parts of the world I must not lose time. There were
two places which I felt bound to visit, the Holy Land
and India.

In January 1906 I went down to Thanet to help
my friend Joseph King in contesting the constituency
against Mr. Marks. The electors preferred Mr.
Marks, but that was for me a fortunate choice.
It liberated Joseph King to come with me to the Holy
Land. The year opened for me with joy and hope.
At the first church-meeting there were forty new
members before the Church. February 10th is an
entry : "A week of constant joy." The truth was,
our beloved lady was slowly mending, and we began
to count the months before she would return. I had
discovered that my loss of vision was not at present
a decisive bar to work, and during the year of sorrow
and strain God had visited me with the treasures of
love in Christ Jesus. The pilgrimage to the Holy
Land seemed happily timed, and my friend who
would go with me was the best of travelling companions. We set off on March 12th, and did not get
back till May 2nd. We had a day at Avignon, where
the vast palace of the Popes, with the faded frescoes

of Simone Memmi, brought vividly before me those seventy years of the " Babylonish Captivity," Petrarch lauding Laura, and Catherine of Siena at last bringing the Popes back to Rome. Avignon, Arles, and Nîmes are to me the most interesting part of France. There the Roman influence has been preserved in picturesque vividness by the recession of the tides of life from the district. At Nîmes, too, Protestantism does not seem hopelessly impossible for France as it does elsewhere.

The voyage from Marseilles to Alexandria on a Messageries liner was the most delicious time at sea I, up to that point, ever had. There was ample room ; each of us had a cabin to himself. French courtesy pervaded the ship. I had with me some French gospels, and they opened up many pleasant talks with passengers and crew. I remember a Belgian gentleman of real culture who had never seen St. John's Gospel, and was most interested to accept it. The cloudless skies and the deep blue of the Mediterranean made Corsica and Stromboli very beautiful. And Etna ! we saw the white cone fifty miles away to the east, then beat up against a wind in the Straits of Messina ; but the sea became more blue and tranquil than ever when we had passed them, and at sunset Etna was still in sight fifty miles away to the west, purple against the saffron sky of evening. We left Sicily and Italy in crimson and gold. On Sunday, with the help of a most charming Dutch countess and her husband, whom we met afterwards both in Cairo and Jerusalem, we got a service in the saloon. There were but few English people on board. But French ships have no Sunday service, and the readiness of the captain to afford us religious liberty made one feel that Republican France has become, if not Christian, at least tolerant, a claim which never could be made for monarchical or imperial France.

On the fifth day I looked out at the porthole. Fez and turban, brown and black faces, flowing robes of red and yellow and green, told me that I was in the

East. We were at Alexandria. Cairo and Shepheard's Hotel are a surprise and fascination, at least on the first visit. The Pyramids, approached by a tramcar running parallel with strings of camels, and riders jogging on them just as they did in the time of Abraham ; the tombs of the Caliphs ; the sleeping faces of Seti I and Rameses II in the Museum ; the gigantic prostrate form of Rameses II on the way to Sakhara ; those tombs in the desert, fresh as if they were finished yesterday, after six thousand years ; the step-pyramid already a thousand years old when the pyramid of Cheops was reared ; the Bazaars ; old Cairo and the Coptic Cathedral with its priceless sculptures and treasures preserved from the early Christian centuries ; the inscription over the entrance, A, Ω, Ἰησοῦς Χριστός υἱὸς Θεοῦ, holding its own under the inundation of Islam ; all made this glimpse into Egypt and Africa a rich experience, and a fit approach to the Holy Land. On Monday, March 26th, I rose with the dawn from the hot berth ; the sun was rising over Palestine, the land where our Saviour was born. That was one of the thrilling moments of my life. How crooked, dirty, and corrupt Jaffa seemed ; not even the house of Simon the tanner could keep our spirits above the mud and the human refuse. Yet on returning to Jaffa, we thought it looked quite civilized in comparison with the towns and villages of the interior, as Islam and the Turk have made them. But our steamer left at noon for Haifa, for it was our plan to see Nazareth first, and to follow, in His steps, up to Jerusalem. The tents, horses, and dragoman were waiting for us, and we were instructed how to put our things round the tent-pole, because thievish hands might slip under and seize anything within reach. Early next morning we climbed Mount Carmel, carpeted with flowers—we were with Elijah, and heard the " choose ye this day whom ye will serve." Then from Elias to Jesus : as we rode towards Nazareth we passed a carpenter's shop, and presently a mother riding on an ass with her child before her, as if Joseph, Mary, and Jesus were going down into Egypt. O the wonder of the young green and the flowers on those Galilean hills ! At Nazareth we saw the women drawing the water from Mary's Well, and walking gracefully with the pitchers on their heads down the street. We met a bright-eyed boy of twelve, who talked freely with us, for he had been trained in a mission school. He was very beautiful and engaging. Did Jesus look like this?

The dogs barked all night, and it was hard to sleep in the tents ; but at 6.30 next morning we climbed the hill—that was where they meant to throw Him down !—and presently Mount Hermon came in view. There on our left was Cana. This was the way He often travelled. It was like a day in June ; the flowers —iris, orchid, cyclamen, anemone—were everywhere. There was a long flight of storks. There was a Bedouin curveting on his Arab steed across country. Over the Mount of the Beatitudes the larks were carolling. Presently, far below us, opened the Sea of Gennesareth, still and blue, encircled by its caressing mountains. No wonder, that early Galilean ministry was buoyant and hopeful in a scene so fair. We camped outside Tiberias, and rowed to Capernaum, where the ruins of a synagogue convince you that it was Roman, the one built by the centurion. In the evening we bathed in the lake, and the crescent moon hung over our tent. But in the night the thunder roared, and after sleepless hours we climbed up and crossed the mountains in rain to a khan, where we lunched in the open court surveyed by a taciturn and curious sheikh, who was well rewarded with an empty bottle. Then we reached the summit of Mount Tabor, and talked with the Franciscans who have a convent there. Descending in torrents of rain we met a stream of patient Russian pilgrims ; the men looked like Tolstoi— the popes were riding ; the peasant women in their thick clothes and carrying all their utensils appeared infinitely pathetic. But they were all thrilled with the thought that they were on the soil which Jesus trod ; and it is pleasanter to meet them than travellers— American, German, and English—who forget that the reason for visiting the Holy Land is that their Saviour lived and died there.

> Tabor we climbed in mist, and had no sight
>   Of Esdraelon or of Carmel—rain
> Came pelting down and blotted all ; in vain
> The weary Russian pilgrims sought the height ;
> Then at the foot our tents gleamed warm and white.
>   But darkness fell, and the night howled with storm,
>   Drowning the heavens, the earth, the mountain's form,
> Preaching the brevity of the world's delight.
> Pondering we slept, and took a brief account
>   Of wonders that had place when Christ had worn
> Our flesh, and been transfigured in the fount
>   Of Light Eternal. Then the day was born
> Cloudless, and this Transfiguration-mount
>   Brought us transfiguration with the morn.

We started early, and in the slow ride over the plain, uninhabited and ill-cultivated, for the tillers of the soil have to crowd into the squalid villages surrounded with thick thorn hedges for safety, I realized perhaps for the first time what blessings railways have brought to men. We rounded Little Hermon, leaving Nain on our left, through Shunem, in its ineffable neglect and filth, up to Jezreel, where we lunched, surrounded by a curious crowd. Looking northwards we saw Nazareth across the plain, white on the hillside, and Carmel closing the west.

We camped that night at Jenin, and next day rode through the spring freshness of winding valleys strewn with flowers, under the olive-trees ; and the note of the cuckoo sounded across the vale, as if we were in our English Lake District. Soon the storm gathered, with such ferocity that the horses could not face it. We were in a wide, shelterless plain ; we turned their heads and waited, while the thunder rolled round the hills of Samaria, and the hail lashed horse and man. We had lunch at a sweet spring which it was safe to drink. How much sweeter was that water than the wine ! Sebaste (Samaria), with the pillars of Herod's colonnade, we visited after lunch, and came down to Nâblus in the afternoon. That evening we climbed Mount Ebal, and watched the golden sunset on the hills, and the moon, a blue sparkling crescent, shine out through the purpling night. The Sunday was a welcome rest, for riding day after day, up and down, over unmade tracks, was very tiring. We read our John iv at Jacob's Well, and had a beautiful Protestant service, not in English, held by a Syrian named Karey ; we celebrated the Lord's Supper with the little community. Christ had His own in that haunt of Moslem fanaticism. And yet how few—though the fields were already ripe to harvest that noon when He sat by Jacob's Well ! Next day we started on the road, which abruptly ceases. (The Bey who had received money for the work carried the road out of sight of Nâblus, and pocketed the remainder of the grant himself !) The lunch at Lebonah was delightful—all the women of Samaria were coming to the spring for their water. That sight of the graceful creatures in their brilliant colours, drawing with joy the water out of the wells, would, I think, never lose its charm.

But when we reached Sinjil the rain fell in torrents, so that the tents, which the camp-followers had pitched, were swamped, and had to be repitched on ground instead of water. We looked into a house where the women were grinding at the mill, and the women let my friend try his hand on the millstone.

Next day our ride through the mountains of Ephraim was very grand, but we were lashed by storms of sleet, and were thankful for a brazier in the khan at Beeri where we lunched. We reached Jerusalem chilled to

the bone. But in the grand New Hotel (as it is jocosely
called) we were warmly welcomed by Mr. Selah
Merrill, the American Consul, and we found our Dutch
friends, the Comte de Leyden and his charming wife,
whom we had met last at Cairo.

How can people be disappointed with Jerusalem?
Perhaps we were fortunate. Torrents of rain cleansed
it, and the narrow streets were sweet. The colour and
the charm are everywhere. Never did I find a crowd
so fascinating as the motley, international throng that
presses through those narrow arteries. The camels, the
asses, the veiled women, the Jews with their long
ringlets, grown to avoid cutting the head square (vide
the Law), the olive-coloured Syrian, the jet-black
Nubian ; the runners swinging the corpse on their
shoulders hastening to the Kidron Valley ; the sorrowful
lepers trooping to their pens, thankful for a word or
a smile ; the vast bastions of Herod's Temple, and the
lofty crypt ; the Mount of Olives, carpeted with
flowers, and Bethany just as it was ; the circuit of
the walls and the solemn depths of the Valley of
Hinnom, and Siloam with its Hebrew inscription ; and
the views over the land, down to the Dead Sea and the
Mountains of Moab, from any elevation ; and always
the Russian pilgrims crowding the Church of the Holy
Sepulchre, climbing its roof, and kissing their way
round its dome—no, the whole kaleidoscope of beauty
and interest would fascinate and satisfy the weariest of
globe-trotters. Why, then, are people disappointed?
I think only because they spend their time in looking
at fictitious sites ; or they are upset by the Mohammedan
occupation of the Temple area, the Mosques of Omar
and Achsah, with squalid superstitions and fanaticisms,
where once was Solomon's Temple or Justinian's Church.
Shut out all the talk of dragomans and the discussions
of scholars, forget the Turk and Mohammed, and
with your Bible in hand go round Jerusalem and tell
her towers, and I defy any Christian with eyes and a

heart to be disappointed. It is an overflowing cup of
wonder and delight.

We drove down to Bethlehem, and our black driver
ran over a poor woman. The dragoman and he were
terrified because we got out of the carriage and made
them carry the injured peasant into Bethlehem. He
was brought before the mouhid, who offered us
cigarettes and coffee, while we explained what had
happened in German. The man might have been
thrown into prison, and then, as the dragoman explained,
might never, in the absence of bribery, have come out.
But he was released at our request. When we entered
the carriage we found the windows smashed ; this was
the revenge of the injured woman's son.

Then we went down to Jericho, accompanied by a
Bedouin, who curveted on his Arab horse before, behind,
and around us till we reached the Inn of the Good
Samaritan. He belonged to the troop of Bedouin that
used to rob travellers on the road, and keep up the
traditions of the spot. But very wisely the robbers
are now engaged as escorts, and for suitable baksheesh
afford not only security but a charming exhibition of
horsemanship. We put up at a Hôtel Belle Vue, in
what was once the city of palms. And " beautiful
view " is an appropriate name. Ruined and deserted
as it is, that 'valley of the Jordan is yet a paradise :
the waters were out, and we rowed over " the swellings
of Jordan " to reach the river-bed ; the stream was
tawny like the Tiber. I tore my hand on a rusty nail
in the boat. But remembering what Holman Hunt
said about the healing qualities of the Dead Sea, we
bathed in the sparkling waves, and my wound gave me
no more trouble. The plain is barren and encrusted
with salt ; weird branches of trees are thrown up by
the 'waves and look like the bones of the earth's skeleton.
But the mountains of Moab stand round the sea, as if
cut in agate and topaz and amethyst. Northward you
see the white crest of Hermon far away, and westward

the Mount of Olives at a distance of fifteen miles rises from the level of the Dead Sea to a height of 4,000 feet.

How insufferable it is that the land which flowed with milk and honey should be under the corrupt and inefficient misgovernment of the Turk ! The Khedivial Line wished to make a harbour at Jaffa, at a cost of two millions, but the Sultan would not have it. It is not, therefore, possible to land or embark unless the sea is calm. Mr. Pierson had come from America to attend the Mohammedan Conference at Cairo, and had spent the spare days in a visit to Jerusalem. He went down to Jaffa to take ship for Cairo, and could not embark. He came back to us, his plan in crossing the Atlantic frustrated by the crass stupidity of Turkish rule. It was the irritation with all that cruel incompetence, and that alone, which made me glad to leave the Holy Land. I carried away with me undying memories ; and I think it would be worth while to send all theological students to visit the scenes of our Lord's life before they enter on their ministry. It is, as Stanley said, a fifth Gospel. If people go ignorant of, or indifferent to, the other four Gospels, like a very interesting American lady whom I met in Jerusalem and travelled with to Jericho, they cannot feel the wonder and joy of Palestine. But a Christian, who wants to understand how Jesus lived among men, finds all the toil and risk of travelling in an uncivilized country well repaid. Every town and village, every turn of the way, is a fresh illustration of the narrative of the Gospels.

Returning to Alexandria we had some difficulty in getting a passage to Athens. When we got on board the boat was thronged from end to end, and it was difficult to move. The fact was, an Italian opera company were leaving Alexandria, and half the young men of the town were there to see them off. Even when the enthusiasts had left the ship we were very crowded. The saloon was so full at night that we had hardly room to lie down, and the Italian singers kept up their conversation till the morning. We passed Crete at sunset, and saw its lofty cliffs and mountains against a pale gold sky. In the morning Cape Sunium was in sight. The sea was a deep blue, the land was purple, and the sky was clear. The approach to Attica filled me with indescribable enthusiasm. There was the Piræus, and Thucydides seemed by my side, describing the long walls which once connected the harbour with Athens ; and there was Lycobettos outlined against the eastern sky. The flags in the harbour were half-mast high. We thought at first that some notable was dead. Then we remembered it was Good Friday. Those signs of reverent mourning were for Him who died on Calvary. As soon as we were settled in the Grand Hotel Pateros, we set off for the Parthenon. Athens took us by storm. We were to stay only two or three days and go on to Constantinople for a week, but we at once determined that the week must be in Athens. I knew the Acropolis was beautiful, but I found it gigantic too ; the marble of Pentelicon, honey-coloured with the weather, the absolutely symmetrical columns, the Erechtheum with its Caryatides, the glorious Propylæa, and restored temple of Nikè Apteros, and above all the ground covered with marbles inscribed with Greek letters easily legible ; the whole majestic and glorious record of the greatness of Greece moved me to tears of joy. In the evening from above the Stadium we saw the Olympieium, and the Acropolis in the splendour of the sunset—the first of seven indescribable sunsets—and so I entered on the week richest in interest and charm that I have had in my life.

That view from the ambulatory of the Parthenon impelled me to try for the first time to sketch, because no photographs are taken from, but only of, the Acropolis. And failing with my pencil, I tried to fix the wonder of it in my mind by the following sonnet—

> See Salamis, o'er which Athenè fought
>   With spear and helm against the Persian ships ;
>   That is Cithæron in the half-eclipse
> Of sunset ; and with but a little thought
> Behold the Long Walls to Piræus cross
>   The tilth, securing access to the sea ;
>   And there, between the fluted columns, free
> To all the winds is Nikè Apteros ;
> And through the fluted columns on all sides
>   The clearest curves, and purple of the hills,
> Parmès clear-cut, clear-cut Pentelicon,
> Hymettus purple, as the sunset spills
> Its glory over plain and flowing tides—
>   Such is the vision from the Parthenon.

O that λαμπρότατος αἰθήρ of Attica ! No wonder the Athenians produced the greatest poetry, and sculpture, and architecture in the world. What sunsets they were night after night ! One from Lycobettos abides with me—

> O miracle ! 'Tis but three days ago
>   I watched the sunset from this lofty hill,
>   This Lycobettos, splendours calm and still,
> The steely waters and the rosy glow :
> And here again I watch the sunset, but
>   Different, as if the whole fair scene were changed,
>   A dusky west, the hills in darkness ranged,
> The sun red peering through a door half-shut—
> O opulence of beauty, always one
>   Yet always different ! In a series grand
>   Of changing glories God works out His scheme,
> This orchestra of colour from one sun,
>   This shifting drama from one sea, one land,
>   Eternity a full fair endless dream !

Then Easter in Athens ! From the Areopagus, under the Acropolis, Paul preached Jesus and the Resurrection. And on Easter-eve the great square was thronged till midnight. On a raised platform, lined with coloured lamps, were all the magnates of the city, king and court, judges and generals. The priests brought out the great silver-backed Bible, and all kissed it. They chanted their Gregorian hymns, and the whole vast crowd joined in. Then a light was passed from the altar, and every one ignited his candle, until the square, the windows, balconies, and roofs, all gleamed with the thousands of candle-lights. At midnight a salvo of artillery announced Easter-day, and all quietly dispersed with mutual greetings, Χριστὸς ἀνέστη, " Christ is risen." On Sunday, after reading Paul's speech on the Areopagus, and realizing what he meant by the statues of gods made with hands, for the glory of the Propylæa and the gigantic figure of Athené were before his eyes, we went to the service in the Metropolitan Church, where John xx was read in eight languages ; the English reader was in a pulpit close to us, and looked uneasy when he saw two Englishmen standing near. And, indeed, his English was less intelligible than the Greek.

On Easter Monday we climbed Hymettus in three hours. How astonishing is the view of Greece from a height of 3,300 feet ! Snow peaks in Eubœa, and in the Morea, and Parnassus in eternal snow ! We went to Eleusis and examined the Temple of Demeter. Every moment was filled with beauty and joy. But, most thrilling of all, in the Ceramicus, where the Dipulon carries us back to Themistocles, we came unexpectedly on those mysteriously beautiful tombs, the Χαῖρε, the veiled figure seated, with the exquisite arm bent, and the ministrant offering the box to her mistress. And these were standing there when Pericles delivered on that spot the immortal speech over the dead in the first year of the Peloponnesian War.

But the week in Athens was so full that a book would be required to describe it. We sailed from Piræus foot-sore and weary, but satisfied. Yes, Athens is the one place on earth which, to one who knows the classics at any rate, is absolutely satisfying.

Constantinople is a nightmare in my memory : roads dangerous by day and impossible by night ; dogs and offal everywhere ; a population half destined to massacre, the other half their murderers ; every one venal and insolent ; the danger of mentioning the Sultan's name, for spies were everywhere. And yet the view from the Fire Tower is magnificent : Pera and Galata at your feet, across the Golden Horn Stamboul, stretching into the Bosphorus, the domes and minarets of the mosques outlined against the west, " like a Turk-verse along a scimitar," and across the strait Skutari, with its white lighthouse at the point, and memories of " the lady with the lamp." The islands in the Sea of Marmora shut in the west. And the Bosphorus is exquisite, with memories of Jason on the Argo coming through the Symplegades with the Golden Fleece.

Still in the dim apse of St. Sophia you can from the gallery discern the form of Jesus, which the Turks have not obliterated, though they have covered the majestic walls with their ugly texts from the Koran, and have twisted the interior, putting the carpets slant-wise, that in praying they may face towards Mecca. What a sigh of gratitude would rise from humanity if Justinian's Church were again in Christian hands !

What a relief to escape from Turkey and to travel through the rich plain of Bulgaria between the Balkans and the Rhodopé ! The second morning we were at Belgrade and on the Danube. I remember Buda Pesth, the stateliest city in Europe, and the shameless profligacy of the café to which the guide took us to hear a Hungarian band. I remember Vienna chiefly in rain, and only gleams of beauty in the picture gallery —a beautiful Caracci, I think, of the woman of Samaria and Christ—a visit to Dr. Fuchs, for advice about my eyes, and a rather alarming verdict. I remember Nuremberg, Dürer's house, and the people in the street just like the people in his pictures four centuries ago ;

and St. Lawrence, with the vast pulpit piled on the crouching form of Hans Sachs, the sculptor of it—a proud humility—and a sermon, the best I ever heard in German on the Good Shepherd who gives His life for the sheep ; I remember the castle of Frederick Barbarossa, with its colossal proportions and rustic simplicity ; the appalling collection of instruments of torture, the well 320 feet deep—six seconds for a drop to reach the water—Nuremberg, an epitome of the German people and the German character.

When I returned I was thrown into the struggle against sweating, which was absorbing attention ; and I made my first close acquaintance with Christian Science, because an enthusiastic friend wished me to get the help of a healer for our beloved invalid. But in July came a great joy. She was able to return home. Coming back from preaching at Prestatyn I found her there. Our joy was transfiguring. For long months she still suffered much ; but for the rest of the time she was spared to us, she got progressively better, and was able at last to enter into everything again. We all, and she most, were convinced that her restoration was given in answer to long and believing prayer. Her gratitude and love to her Saviour were unceasing. This signal mercy brought a great and solemn joy into life ; everything regained the interest which for a time had been lost.

In August I went to Clayden, where my friend Sir Edmund Verney wanted me to give an account of the Holy Land to his tenants and neighbours ; it was the first of several interesting visits to that historic house, and I occupied the rooms which were full of pictures and reminders of Florence Nightingale, who was a frequent guest there. In October I had the satisfaction of preaching to the Baptist Union at Huddersfield, a late amendment for the rebuff delivered to me when I was a young man nearly twenty years before.

At the end of the year I was writing letters to the

Tribune, the short-lived but able Liberal paper, and *The Times*, trying to prevent the secular solution of the educational difficulty, which grew in favour, owing to the " passive resisters." I myself was a passive resister at first, accepting joyfully the spoiling of my goods for conscience' sake. But when the Liberal Government came in, committed to make the changes which justice demanded, I felt that passive resistance was no longer a legitimate weapon ; and I was increasingly convinced that a religious atmosphere in the schools is more worthy of consideration than the doctrinaire dislike to religious teaching of a certain sort.

In December I had an encouraging account of a conversion. Florence Martindale was on the way to throw herself into the Hampstead pond ; she was attracted by the stream of people entering Lyndhurst Road, went in, and was saved. Such incidents make a preacher able to go on, in spite of all discouragements. " The happiest Christmas Day I ever remember. God be praised ! " is the entry for December 25th. Of that light Christmas Day 1910 was to be the dread shadow.

In travelling from Edinburgh to Blackpool for the memorable Union Meetings under the Chairmanship of Sir Joseph Compton-Rickett, on October 13th, I opened my bag and dropped out my diary. No advertisements availed to restore it, and thus there are nine months of 1907 for which I have no record but the uncertain faded hieroglyphs of memory. But the year was filled with mercies. Our dear lady made steady progress ; to occupy her mind I got her to collect some fugitive poems of her own and of mine, which Mr. Dent very kindly printed for us—*Poems by two Friends*—in the summer. It was not a commercial nor even a literary venture, but it brought us much joy, for loving appreciations came from many quarters. I think myself that some of these poems, interpreted by what I knew of her life and of their origin, are the most beautiful things I possess. My own productions in this kind have only been the products of leisure moments, and alone were unworthy of publication. But together the records of our long, unsullied, friendship make a little volume which, as my friend Dr. Courtney said in his review, is one of the most precious things in life. That friendship was to me strength, inspiration, and joy; and the poems keep it always, in these sorrowful years of separation, fresh and green.

This year I wrote for Messrs. Jack of Edinburgh my little study of the Early Church. This year also my missionary sister returned for a time and lived with my other sister, Mrs. Ross, who had come to Highgate, that her husband might be near to Somerset House.

All through the year, after my return from the East, the work in the Church went on with a song of praise and blessing. At the end of the year came another instance of the way in which a great joy and a great sorrow are allowed to coincide. On November 26th, in order to clear the debt which still rested on our completed premises, I adopted the novel plan of sitting all day in the vestry and asking the people to come with offerings which would represent their thanksgiving for their church. On my way down through the chill November fog a policeman met me, and gave me £3 to start the fund, and God's blessing. All day my dear people came in one after another, and gave me such a demonstration of their affection and appreciation as I had never had before. The gifts amounted to £2,315. But on the day when this noble giving was reported at the church-meeting, November 28th, the Church experienced an irreparable loss in the death of Thomas Minshall. I can render no adequate tribute to this devoted man. He was one of those who moved with his family to Hampstead in order to help me in my ministry. For long years he was my never-failing helper. His loving care of the people, and his readiness to take trouble, in order to find them situations, or introduce them to each other, or gather them together for spiritual fellowship, created an atmosphere in the Church of which every one was conscious. For years he saved me by taking my correspondence in hand, and never offended a correspondent by his handling of it. He edited the *News Sheet*, and made it a bond of union for the Church and a constant guide and encouragement to me. He passed away amid the blessings of all who knew him ; and I trust that as long as Lyndhurst Road stands his memory may be cherished.

CHAPTER XV

THIRTY YEARS OF MINISTRY
1880–1910

THE two years which closed my thirty years in Hampstead were like a St. Martin's summer, before the cold of winter sets in. During that period I came nearer to having a real home than I ever did in my life. Our beloved lady made an atmosphere, and, as she gradually recovered, she gave to the house an influence which every one who entered it could feel. She put up in the hall a motto, worked in silk, " This tent is God's ; it is no more ours than yours ; enter and be at peace." I have been told by a newspaper man years after how, coming to interview me, this welcome impressed him. For me there was always at hand a warm sympathy and an eager co-operation in my work. For many, many years she had made extracts for me, found incidents and illustrations, which she arranged under headings, and called my attention to books which I had not time to read. But now she was always helping, reading to me, and reading for me. The rare evening free from engagements became a rich delight. She recovered her power of playing and culled pieces from Beethoven, Mozart, and works of Mendelssohn which are seldom heard. And this soft and sweet accompaniment of music in the home was rest and inspiration to me. As far as her strength went she took a lively interest in all the services and organizations of the Church, and welcomed to the house all, but especially the poor. When she went out in her bath-chair she distributed Bibles and Gospels on the Heath ; her heart yearned especially over the forlorn women that haunted it, and she pleaded with them to go to the Shelter which we had opened in the neighbourhood. I felt for the first time that the house was becoming what it ought to be, and illustrating the principles of giving and sharing our possessions, which I had always taught. I went out to engagements all over the country strengthened and returned home to be welcomed and encouraged. I counted it a singular mercy that my thirty years should be crowned with this rich and undeserved blessing.

In January 1908 I went to the Students' Conference at Liverpool, and met John Mott again. In the concluding address of the conference, which I delivered, a remarkable influence came on the meeting and brought all to their knees in intercession for the world. It seemed to some the foretaste of the great Missionary Conference of 1910 in Edinburgh. I set about a book this year, which was published under the title of *My Belief*, in order to meet the difficulties which I found in the minds of those with whom I talked, and the book met with just the success I desired. It was translated into Japanese and Chinese, and (part of it) German. Repeated evidences have come to me that it has helped others to find a secure basis for their faith. That seemed to me a crown of blessing. In February the death of my friend, Lady Rogers, in Birmingham, gave me an exquisite vision of a brave and beautiful life ending in triumph. Sir Oliver Lodge, who was at the funeral, wrote to tell me that it had deeply impressed him. To enter the other world singing the dear familiar hymns, and serenely blessing every member of the household, and then saying a joyful farewell—that is what I would choose.

The ex-chairmen of the Congregational Union endeavoured this month to draw up a manifesto of the things which we must surely believe, in order to help those who were in perplexity through the promulgation of a New Theology. I felt myself peculiarly able to promote this effort, because my whole ministry had been a struggle for a Theology which could grasp the future without surrendering the essentials which had made the past. Then at the end of March, Mr. A. G. Gardiner, who was a member of my congregation, wrote an appreciation of my work in the *Daily News*, afterwards published in *Prophets, Priests and Kings*, which enabled me to understand my work itself and my place in the life of our times, better than anything that had ever come to me. "Oh wad some power the giftie gie us, to see oursel's as others see us!" I had received the usual criticisms and laudations, but never before had I read an appreciation which I recognized as in any sense accurate. I wonder whether all the men whom A. G. Gardiner has delineated have received a similar benefit. If so, he must feel richly rewarded for his toil. In April the noble and unselfish Campbell-Bannerman died. I attended his funeral in Westminster Abbey. He, more than any statesman I have met, illustrated to my mind the supreme value of moral qualities, and the secondary place of intellectual gifts. His settlement of South Africa was the greatest triumph of statesmanship that occurred in my lifetime. All the influential voices were against it. His seemed the one sane voice in a blatant land. When in the Great War of 1914 South Africa proved to be a strength instead of a weakness to the Empire, I felt a glow of satisfaction that history had justified that emotion of gratitude which I felt when standing by the grave of the brave, pure premier in Westminster Abbey.

June was a very beautiful month to me. A new vicar came to Hampstead, Mr. Brook Deedes. Influenced by the prayers and visits of Mr. Landel Jones, a retired minister, who was a great strength at Lyndhurst Road, he called together the clergy and ministers of Hampstead, and formed a Fraternal, which has continued to exist, though he and his successor have gone. A monthly meeting for prayer and conference keeps the two sides of the Church, the Established and Free, in sympathetic touch. We have arranged together for such public lecturers as William Temple and T. Reavely Glover to come and address the borough on Christian Apologetics, and for other speakers to instruct us on questions of Social Reform. It was a great satisfaction that after thirty years I saw this kind of unity among the Churches, for to me Free Churchmanship never meant division from the Church of England, it was only the attempt to supply elements in our common faith which the Established Church omitted or depreciated. Thus the relation of the two sides at Hampstead at last realized my ideal.

Then at the end of June came a singular experience. I went to Cambridge to preach at the Speech Day of the Leys School, and two curious coincidences occurred. I spoke in the afternoon on the three characteristics of the English : (1) the love of Truth, (2) the obedience to Duty, (3) the passion for Liberty. Lord Cromer came to distribute the prizes, but did not hear my sermon. He delivered an address to them on these lines : (1) speak the truth, (2) love your country, (3) don't dawdle. There was a boy in the school who had been during the term convicted of untruthfulness. The poor culprit thought that the head master must have instructed both Lord Cromer and me to preach at him. That afternoon the last window of a series in the chapel, illustrating the Life of Christ, was to be unveiled. I chanced to go into the gallery, and found myself standing by the artist, Mr. Salisbury, who exclaimed : " How remarkable that you should be here to-day ! " " Why? " I asked. " Because," he replied, " I owe the whole thought and plan of doing this series of windows to you. I heard you once at Lyndhurst Road describing Giotto's frescoes in the Arena, Padua, and I was so delighted with the thought that I applied for this commission to design these windows. And," he added with deep earnestness, " the close study of our Lord's life, in order to sketch the

series, has been one of the great blessings of my life."
That was one of those harmonies in the mosaic of life
which convince one of the Master-hand that executes
the whole design.

July had a double though related interest. The Pan-
Congregational Council was held in Edinburgh, and I
went to take my part in it. And the Pan-Anglican
Congress was held in London. That afforded me one
of the most interesting hours of my life. I was asked
to meet the bishops at Lambeth to state the standpoint
of Congregationalists. An American bishop was in the
chair, and on my right was the saintly Bishop of Lincoln,
whom I had known as Canon King in my later Oxford
days. It seemed to me that I did more to reveal the
bishops to one another than to explain our own position
to them. I mentioned how the doctrine of Apostolical
Succession created a barrier between the Episcopal Church
and ourselves, and an American bishop exclaimed in
astonishment, that surely that could not be. I turned to
my old friend Bishop Talbot and asked him if it could :
he replied that he was afraid it was. Then referring to
the fine sermon in St. Paul's, which opened the Congress
by recognizing the oneness of the Churches, I remarked
to the presiding bishop, the Bishop of Albany, I think
it was, that those sentiments exactly met the position of
us who were Congregationalists, but I feared that they
would not meet with the same approval from, for instance,
the Bishop of Lincoln, who was sitting by me. He with
reluctance admitted that I was right.

And yet I was glad that the bishops were seriously
considering the question of Reunion. In that conclave
of a dozen or so I recognized the promise of a better
day. It is not Episcopacy that erects the barrier, but
an exaggerated claim for the Episcopate as belonging
not only to the *bene esse*, but to the *esse* of the Church.
And the chief hindrance to Reunion in England arises
from the difficulty which Anglicans find in recognizing
any *raison d'être* for the Free Churches, or any claim

they can make to be of the Church of Christ. So soon as the English Church sees the right of Free Churchmen to be, she will be in the way of making their existence unnecessary.

At the end of July we were able to pay another, a final, visit to Norway. A friend came with us who carefully watched and tended our dear lady. She was, but for one or two sad moments, her own happy self, overwhelmingly grateful to be again in the land of her love. The Kviknes welcomed us, and then we went to Turtagro, three thousand feet up in the Jotunheim. We had always longed to see the high peaks and snows of the highest mountains in Norway. This joy was given to us. And as the book of our Norwegian travels was closed, we acknowledged that it had been complete and wholly good. I picture heaven and reunion as something like the climb up into those clear regions, and seeing the high rejoicing ridges of the mountains emerging sharp and purple out of the eternal snows. I fancy that the new world will have kindly hearts like the Norwegian, and simple ways free from " the contagion of the world's slow stain." I recall one of those mountain peasants who came to us one day on the verandah, not to sell or to beg, as one might expect in other countries, but only to show us some verses which he had been writing. He brought his wife the next day, and we sang together in that high air some of the hymns out of their Psalmen-bog. It was altogether characteristic. The simple people always opened their hearts to that blessed lady ; and her command of Norwegian made them forget that she was a stranger. The glorious road through Myrdal, connecting with the railway from Bergen to Christiania, was a new and final experience of those amazing valleys of interlocked precipices, and roaring cataracts, which had given to us our best notions of grandeur and loveliness in harmonious combination.

In September I began to write a series of essays on different aspects of life, which Mr. Fisher Unwin finally

published under the title *Great Issues*. This was a
source of great interest and joy to me ; it gave me
a chance of discussing Literature, Art, Science, Philosophy, Politics, Socialism, etc., subjects which fill so
great a part of life, and yet have only an incidental
place in preaching. It has meant for me a severe self-
discipline for many years, to refrain from these pleasant
fields which were opened up to me by my education.
Literæ Humaniores always fascinated me, and Science
cast its spell on me when it was already too late for me
to gain a scientific training. This book therefore was
to me a great relief, and I had one great joy in connection
with it. One of my boys, Maurice Basden, who went
with me in my last journey to America, and then joyously
gave his life in the Air Service in France on May 23,
1916, made *Great Issues* a kind of *vade-mecum*. I
knew no one else to whom it meant so much, but it
was reward enough to write a book, if one young mind
in the making could find it a help.

In the early autumn of this year, 1908, the Atheists
were very active in holding their meetings on the Heath.
They complained that I did not come out and meet
them on Sundays. I invited them to meet me in our
church-room. They responded ; the hall was thronged
twice with four or five hundred men, and I invited
their speakers to say what they would, promising to do
my best to answer them. Strange to say, their chief leader
was an unfrocked Russian priest. He was extreme in
his hatred of the religion which he had discarded, and
it was painful to see English working-men led by one
who was so ignorant and so prejudiced. But at that
time the masses were ready to listen to any one who
would denounce the Churches and the ministry. One
of these speakers a good many years earlier greatly
amused the crowd on the Heath by a sally at my expense,
which was turned against him by the facts of the case,
" There's my friend, Bob Horton," he said in his familiar
way, " I met him the other day, and I said, ' Bob,'

I says, ' how long are you going on preaching what
you don't believe? ' " (Needless to say the whole scene
was a fiction ; I never saw him or spoke to him in
my life. " ' That's all very well,' " said Bob, " ' but
there's the missis and kids to consider.' " This caused
great amusement in an audience which knew that I was
a bachelor.

In that October I undertook with my younger friend,
Harold Brierley, a tour to several towns in the south-
east of England, to advocate the claims of the London
Missionary Society ; and next month we attempted at
Lyndhurst Road a novel form of missionary propaganda.
The year had been notable for the Missionary Exhibition
in the Agricultural Hall, Islington, opened by a great
speech from Mr. Winston Churchill, and marred by a
pageant, which was a lamentable use of theatrical methods
and effects in the cause of religion. The training of
the stewards for that exhibition was one of the most
delightful tasks I ever undertook. And now for a week
we tried by conferences, Bible-readings, etc., to engage
the interest of all the people in the great world-wide
enterprise. That week is entered in my records as one
of the happiest of my life. I wonder people do not
devote themselves more to the missionary task for the
undiluted joy that it brings into life. But like the honey
in the flower which is protected by all the devices of
the structure, the purest and sweetest joys of life are
hidden away, and are only found by accident in the
discharge of duties which at first repel.

The year closed with the usual blending of interests and sorrows. The Tercentenary of Milton was
being celebrated, and the Bishop of Hereford asked
me to go and stay with him, in order to take part
in a united commemoration service in the Cathedral.
The Bishop's intentions were good, but his Dean
and Chapter were too much for him. I left my
own Church and supplied the pulpit, and travelled to
Hereford and back at my own expense, for the privi-

lege of reading the lesson, Ecclus. xliv., in the afternoon service. I was not even asked to sit in the chancel, but was placed in a chair in the nave. It had all the appearance of a studied slight—and this, to commemorate Milton, the great Independent ! I have made many sacrifices to promote unity and to preserve peace between Christians, and I am not sorry that I made this. But I cannot help a feeling of pity for good men who are bound so straitly in the fetters of a system that they are compelled to perpetrate solecisms of this kind.

At the end of the year George Barrett left me to enter on a ministry of his own at Lincoln. The gap left was very painful. And then the world shuddered at the appalling earthquake which laid Messina in ruins. I remember a Christian Scientist who had come to talk with me about the gospel of *Science and Health*. When he had explained to me the method of healing all diseases by demonstrating the oneness of God, the perfect love and wisdom, which make evil of all kinds impossible, and therefore prove evil to be only a delusion of our own minds, I said to him : " Then, Mr. L., on that principle you would be able to prevent the earthquake of Messina? " " Certainly," was his amazing reply. I cannot help wishing that some thinker of the first rank would take the trouble to show to Christian Scientists the fallacy that underlies the teaching of Mrs. Eddy. Such a book as my old schoolfellow, Stephen Paget, wrote, from the standpoint of the outraged medical man, is not satisfactory. There is a good in Christian Science, practical and palpable : why should it all be lost or ultimately corrupted by the intellectual limitations of Mrs. Eddy? In October 1909, at the Union meetings in Sheffield, Mr. Stephen Paget gave a brilliant paper in criticism and derision of the movement. I stood by him and spoke, trying my best to disentangle the good from the evil, and to secure for the Church those truths and powers, long neglected, which Christian Science has brought to light.

It was an interesting experience for me : we who had been in head-room together at Shrewsbury, and had walked, and talked on most subjects that interested boys, stood, he a Harley Street doctor and a Churchman, I, a Congregational minister, side by side after so many years. How we are all parted in life ; how little we know of each other ! O for the all-reconciling country !

My thirtieth year at Hampstead—1909—began and ended in joy. The first week was closed with an entry : " It has been rich in mercies, and I am enabled to yield myself to God for my ministry here, with the fervent prayer and hope that I may be allowed to finish my life in this task and to find the greatest blessing at the end." The entry at the close runs : " The year ends with intense gratitude in my heart for its mercies, especially for the measure of blessing and success in my work. The prayer goes into the New Year, make me fruitful." Ah, how that New Year needed the prayer ! It is tragical in looking back to see how unconsciously we approach the rapids which plunge us over the terrible waterfalls of life into the roaring gulfs. In January I spent a week at Mansfield College. Dr. Fairbairn, that intense fire of passionate erudition, had gone. Mr. Selbie, in whose appointment I had taken a rather prominent part, was standing in the shoes of his great principal. This was the visit to Mansfield which seemed to me, of all I have made, the most fruitful. I have learnt to be very glad that Selbie was elected. He has filled a most difficult place with conspicuous modesty and efficiency.

My eldest sister this January returned to the mission field. This was a joy to me. She has always said that she was my missionary ; I have been for many years her committee, board of directors, and paymaster. This time she went to Jaffna, in Ceylon ; thence she went to Galle, where for six years she has worked single-handed among the Tamil-speaking Mohammedans. It is one of the singular facts of life that she seems nearer to me when she is doing mission work in Ceylon than when she was living just across the Heath at Highgate. The distances and ties of the spiritual world are more real than those of the physical. In February Dr. Eleanor Shepheard went out from Lyndhurst Road to Almora. There were circumstances which made me think that of all the missionaries we have sent out she made the greatest intrinsic sacrifice. I keep very close to her in her noble and unstinted work in Almora. March brought me a sad and yet beautiful task ; I had to bury Judge Bompas. He had been one of my earliest friends in Hampstead : his optimistic spirit, and genuine humility and kindness, had made him invaluable to me; in those early days, and his family had been to me a great interest. I loved him much, and his peculiarities, especially his gift of convincing himself that what he was doing was right, caused me constant and affectionate amusement. A convinced Nonconformist when he went to Leeds, he attended the parish church with his family, who did not share his principles. That was intelligible, but my friend's defence of his action to me was : " I incline to think that I am acting on true Nonconformist principles in joining with the body of Christians that is nearest to me "—the Headingley Congregational Church was five minutes' walk farther on. But I loved him, and was grateful to say the last words of love at his grave.

In April I went to Glastonbury to preach for the Somerset Union. Is there a more fascinating place in England? Joseph of Arimathæa, and the exquisite remains of that monastery which Henry VIII dissolved ; the Museum, with the relics of the lake village perfectly preserved—the evidence that those prehistoric men stopped their teeth with gold, and those prehistoric women used rouge ; then the ride to Wiveliscombe over Sedgemoor, where the last fight on English soil was fought, and Athelney, where Alfred burnt the cakes ; a drive up to Exmoor, and the sight of the deer that range over the moor and sometimes raid the villages, completed this glimpse of the endless charms of this dear, dear land. Every acre of it seems to have a meaning ; its storied past hides modestly in shy monuments, or just beneath the surface ; to be English, with none but English blood in your veins ; to be born, to live, to die in England is the greatest birthright that God gives to a man.

But I was very fearful that the happiness of my home in these years should prevent me from doing my duty abroad. And this feeling led me to accept the invitation of Principal Mackenzie to visit Hartford, Connecticut, this spring. The seminary was celebrating its seventieth anniversary, and he thought I might say something to help the students. On May 4th I started with my old friend, Frederick Hastings, in the *Saxonia*, for Boston. It was a leisurely and delightful voyage. Never did I address such a congregation on shipboard as assembled that Sunday morning, May 9th, in the saloon. They came from all parts of the ship ; three hundred out of the twenty-one hundreds on board were present. The storm was raging all the time, and I spoke to them on " He loved me and gave Himself for me." In the evening we got up a voluntary service with the help of the stewards. The captain's name was Pentecost. He moved about among the passengers, chatted with the ladies and nursed the babies, and made the large ship a home. The surgeon was a good man, too, and fetched me to see sick people in the other parts of the ship. One night he operated for hernia on a steerage passenger, aided only by a stewardess. I tried in vain to make the stolid Lancashire operative realize what he owed to that doctor's skill and courage. Another day the doctor brought me to a Norwegian who had meningitis ; I tried to rouse the sufferer with a few words of Norsk, but the calm face remained motionless until his body was slipped into the Atlantic. Just as we reached Boston I was fetched to a man in the second saloon, whose wife had been taken ill, and was unconscious. He, too, was a Lancashire man ; I never saw a more desolating grief. I had to leave them, for we were disembarking, and I never heard the issue. The nine days were a constant joy ; there was more varied work to do for Christ in that little world than in my charge at home.

.We visited Toronto and Niagara. At Hartford the society of the professors was charming. American hospitality is the most lavish and resourceful in the world : I am ashamed of the imperfect way in which we return it. Bushnell's Hartford is a beautiful and attractive town, crowned with its gilded cupola. Among the speakers at the celebration was President Woodrow Wilson. Hearing and talking with him I formed an opinion of his qualities which made me understand his action during the Great War better than they could who knew him only as a politician. It is a splendid tribute to the American Constitution that such a man is brought to the top and to the front.

When the happy days at Hartford were over, and I had visited Montclair again, to see my old friend Amory Bradford, and to take part in the ordination of his son, we very reluctantly said good-bye to the United States. Each visit I make raises my admiration of the great Republic higher, and fills me with larger hopes of its destiny. We returned by Montreal and Quebec. The return voyage was in the *Empress of Ireland*, which four years later foundered in the St. Lawrence after a collision. That June there was much ice in the Atlantic, and as we were embarking I received a letter from my friend, John Oakes, describing the perils of the sea. On the Sunday evening, the 6th, at sunset we entered a dense fog-bank off Newfoundland. I had taken a service in the saloon and we retired to our cabin at 10.30. My friend said to me, after we had prayed : " We never know what may happen at sea, but what a comfort it is to commit ourselves to our heavenly Father, and lie down in confidence." Hardly were the lights out when we heard a foghorn from

another ship, and almost immediately came a terrific
crash, which brought the *Empress of Ireland* to a stand-
still. We rose and partly dressed, because, as Hastings
said, it is horrible to take to the boats in pyjamas.
He put his head out of the porthole and exclaimed : " We
have run into an iceberg : I see the ice floating past."
He went on deck ; the passengers were in great agitation,
but no one could tell what had occurred or was likely
to occur. Only there was a wild rush of water, which in
the silence of the night sounded as if the ship were filling.

I lay down in my berth and committed myself to
God, feeling that but for beloved friends at home I
should be well content to go in that way into the land
of my desire. In perfect peace I fell asleep. Waking
at seven I still heard the foghorns, and we were not
moving. Going to the bath I spoke to the steward
and urged the necessity of faith in Christ as the preparation for unexpected death. I was grieved to find how
the man's mind was set against any personal decision
for Christ. When the daylight came and the fog lifted
we were surrounded by icebergs. Happily what had
brought us to a sudden stand was a floe, which the good
ship clove asunder without injury to herself. If we had
gone on we might have crashed into those bergs ! The
next Sunday I spoke on the Heath and recounted this
experience ; it was the means of the conversion of a
young man who was passing and just heard the story.

The remainder of the voyage home was delicious.
Earl Grey, the Governor of Canada, was on board, and
asked us several times to dine with him ; there was
with him Mr. Fielding, the Canadian Minister of Finance.

It is remarkable in looking back to see what an
opportunity a voyage is. You get busy people at leisure ;
acquaintances are cordial, because, leaving the ship they
will probably never meet again. Differences of rank
are laid aside ; we are all citizens of the world, making
the voyage of life together. I know my own tendency
to live my life apart, and my disinclination to come

into too close quarters with fellow-creatures. A voyage therefore does me spiritual good.

That summer we went to the Black Forest ; another lady friend accompanied us, and our dear lady was much better than she had been the previous year. In May I had sailed down the Hudson from Albany to New York ; in August I sailed up the Rhine from Cologne to Wiesbaden. I thus had the opportunity of comparing two famous rivers of the old and the new world. I had to admit to myself that, notwithstanding all the beauties of the Siebengebirge, Drachenfels, Bonn, St. Goar and the Lürlei, beauties that seemed greater than when I first saw them thirty years before, the Hudson is a finer and grander river than the Rhine. My friend Hastings took sketches of the river in our rapid descent—the Catskill Mountains, West Point, the Palisades—and the album is a delight. And though the Hudson is modern compared with the Rhine, nothing can surpass the romance of its discovery, when Hudson sailed up the broad waters believing that he was in a channel of the sea, and had come almost to where Albany now stands before he knew that it was a river. I always wonder at the things Americans praise in America. About the true beauties and glories of their country they are as reticent as we English are about ours.

That time in the Black Forest comes back to me infinitely sacred in memory. At Titisee, on August 29th, we missed the service ; we therefore climbed into the wood behind the hotel to what we called The Pavilion of His Presence. We worshipped together, and heavenly presences were around us. As we came down from the wooded hill, that loved companion and I observed how, " when we talk about our Lord's things together, we two, Jesus himself draws near and talks with us."

I recall also the way down the Höllsteig, and the emergence into what seemed the heaven of Freiburg, and then Strasburg—incomparably glorious. We passed through the Ravennaschlucht, a narrow ravine with a brawling stream, up to a sunny upland. Returning to

the Sternen we confronted the sunset. The valley, closed
to the west by interlocked hills, whose serrated pines
were sharply outlined against the sky, was bridged by
one long level cloud, the upper edge a braid of gold,
shooting up censer-like protrusions, from which radiated
shafts of shadow. Between the hills, under the cloud,
opened a vista of faint red gold, which seemed like
a faery seascape, dotted with drifting cloudlets as ships,
with a coastline of mountains surmounted by snowy Alps.
As the sun descended the censers burnt themselves out,
but the visionary sea and mountains glowed with a
warmer light. We returned in silence by the spiral road,
in one loop of which a solitary cross stood on a wooded
hill. The west burned solemn and inspiring, the lit
sky framed between the ridges of the purple hills. At
night the moon rose over the eastern hills, and in company
with a red planet shone down the vale.

But the whole of the Black Forest holiday was an
undimmed joy, the last but one of those times which
that beautiful and brilliant spirit had made the great
restoring and recuperating influence in a busy and strain-
ing life. She had such a gift of enjoying, equal to
her capacity of suffering, and she had the still rarer
gift of imparting her joy to every one else, equal to
her power of keeping the suffering, the depression, the
haunting fears to herself.

In September I payed a visit to Clayden, and on
November 15th Sir Edmund Verney came to me, in
order to give us his lecture on old Bibles. It was the
last time I saw him. He was one of the most sincere,
the most modest, and the most truly religious men I
have known. In earlier days, before he unexpectedly
succeeded to Clayden and the baronetcy, he had been
a sailor, and he carried the sailor characteristics—the
openness, the seriousness, the fun—to the end. I loved
his yarns and stories ; I loved his religious confidences ;
I loved his complete naturalness. These old English
families might be, if we knew how to keep them, the
strength of the future. The deep fibrous attachment

to the soil, the habitual breathing of an atmosphere rich
with the honours and the struggles of the past, the
courtesy to all, and the special care for dependents,
tenants, neighbours ; these characteristics are far too
valuable lightly to surrender. The newly rich, or the
newly titled, cannot be expected to have these qualities
in the first generation, but they may prepare their
descendants to acquire them.

On November 21st I had a great pleasure. I was
present at the celebration of the centenary of Queen
Street Chapel, Wolverhampton. A book was prepared
telling the story of the hundred years, and there was
recorded more fully than ever before the work of my
father. His energy and enterprise, his genial and loving
ways, and his faithful preaching had built up the spiritual
Church, and had raised the new material building. It
was a joy to me, as my own thirty years of ministry were
rounding off, to go back in thought to my father's work.
If I have been able to walk in his footsteps, and if
I have been permitted to do anything in the Church or
in the country, I owe it not only to his example, but
to the foresight and determination which made him give
me the best education that was possible. It would have
been to him a coveted privilege to be at a public school
and at Oxford. What he could not enjoy himself he
gave to his son.

That same month *Great Issues* came out. And the
thirty years ended. All the way I had been brought
by Divine goodness and mercy ; untold blessings and
encouragements had been given me. Never, I imagine,
did a man have so faithful and wonderful a friend as
the one who had been my mentor since boyhood, and
now at last was actually living in my house, inspiring
my work, and affording me constant joys in hours of
rest or relaxation. How often I said—

> My bark is wafted to the land
>   By breath divine,
> And on the helm there rests a hand,
>   Other than mine.

CHAPTER XVI

THE VIA DOLOROSA

1910-1914

THE year 1910 opened with much joy and encouragement. Mr. Shillito had come to me in September, and the church had undertaken a final enlargement of the Mission buildings in Kentish Town. On one day in January I was in the vestry to receive gifts, and by a most remarkable series of unexpected events the whole sum, over £7,000, was cleared off. As at the same time the contributions of the Church to the London Missionary Society reached more than £3,000, I could not but be grateful and hopeful. God was with us, and there was no reason for apprehension. I set to work also this year to present to the people the New Testament in chronological order, as it is given in Dr. Moffatt's *Historical New Testament*. There was encouragement in that effort from the beginning, and Dr. John Brown, who had become a constant worshipper at Lyndhurst Road, persuaded the Congregational Union to publish these studies under the title, *The Growth of the New Testament*. But shadows fell. Owing to an unusual number of journeys in February I was seized with influenza in March. A humorous incident lit up the gloom at the beginning. For the first Sunday of the month my lecture had been announced as "Optical Illusions." I was going to speak about Norman Angell's *Europe's Optical Illusion*, for that book I had eagerly received as a gospel of peace coming from an unlikely quarter. But I was taken

specimen of the ways of justice even in England. The prosecutor was allowed to bring an action, though he was unable to pay the costs which the court commanded. The defendant was mulcted of £600 for a slight error, which, as appeared in court, was not only natural but almost inevitable. A generous public came forward and helped me with the costs ; and the penetration of the jury, one of whom was himself a Roman Catholic, and wrote to me afterwards in genuine sympathy, gave me a happy feeling of the security which lies in those twelve men to correct the prejudices of judges. But I had to admit the wisdom of the advice given by a famous lawyer : " Bear anything rather than go to law."

This unsavoury incident was followed at once by an event of the greatest interest, the World's Missionary Conference in Edinburgh. I had taken part in preparing for it by a visit to Edinburgh the year before, and I had ventured to predict that Edinburgh would be remembered and referred to, like Nice, Ephesus, Constantinople, etc. as the place of a General Council. I think the event justified the prophecy. For in that great conference, to which came fifteen hundred delegates from all missionary societies and all countries, the task of evangelizing the world entered on a new and final stage. John Mott presided, and the lines were laid down on which the whole work of the mission field has been reviewed, co-ordinated, systematized in the last seven years. The great movements in India and China are directly connected with that conference ; but its full results are not yet visible. It was one of those quiet, unostentatious incidents which, in the counsel of God, give a trend to the whole future of the world. Nothing was more remarkable than the presence of bishops, like Talbot and Gore, taking part in the discussions with the leaders of the Free Churches. There was no jarring note. The hour of intercession each morning, which introduced a new method of guided prayer, brought all into the conscious presence of God, and seemed to set the whole missionary work under the direct control of Christ.

I count it the greatest privilege of my life that I was called on to speak three times at that Conference. On Sunday, June 19th, at the men's meeting, under the presidency of the Archbishop of York, I spoke on the resources of the Christian Life, and was thus brought into contact with Mr. Trumbull of Philadelphia, who induced me in consequence to write on Christ's Victorious Power for the readers of the American *Sunday School Times*. And that reminds me that this year I was president of our own English Sunday School Union, and visited several parts of the country to advocate the new method of grading the schools. That address in the Synod Hall, Edinburgh, was, I believe, the most fruitful that I ever gave.

Then on Tuesday, June 21st, I was allowed to address ministers in the Tolbooth. And finally, with Bishop Brent on Wednesday evening in the Free Church Assembly Hall, I closed the conference with The Sufficiency of God.

I came home to the death-bed of one of my oldest and most trusted elders, Mr. Henry Spalding. But that week in Edinburgh remains in memory as a Mount of Vision, from which were discernible not only the Celestial Mountains, but the kingdoms of the world becoming the Kingdom of our Lord and of His Christ.

I put up a board this month outside the Church asking, " Whosoever you are, enter and receive a welcome," and at once a stranger was brought in and helped by one of my young deacons, Allan Wyon, the sculptor. Thus the World's Missionary Conference told on my own personal work at Lyndhurst Road.

In July the National Council of Public Morals, on which I have worked as far as my time allowed for many years, held a very important conference at Westminster. My own part in it was the discussion on the Press. It was a great discovery to find how eager publishers and editors (on the whole) were to purify the Press, and to make it a power for good and not for evil. And the work of the Council, under the devoted guidance of James Marchant, shows constantly how much can be done by drawing together thinkers and workers of different schools, parties, and Churches, and directing the attention of Governments and subordinate authorities to flagrant evils. All our troubles come from the enterprise and daring of money interests, which pander to the vices and weaknesses of men. The love of money, over-riding all moral considerations, is a driving force of immense power ; but if only the love of purity, of sobriety, of goodwill, that is widely dispersed in the community, can be brought to bear on the right spot, a power is generated before which the powers of evil tremble. There is no evil so old, so strongly entrenched in the practice of men, so apparently lucrative and necessary as the slave trade. Yet, that is overthrown. Duelling survived into my own time, and was defended by the unwritten code of honour. But in England that has gone. I have come to believe that vice, drunkenness, and even war can be overcome, and that it is God's purpose to root them out from human life. This glorious possibility has dawned upon me partly through my connection with this National Council of Public Morals.

On July 21st we started on what was to be our last tour on the Continent. Again we took with us a lady friend, who was a help and comfort to our beloved lady ; but during these weeks she was so much herself, and so radiantly happy, that the hope was in our hearts that there might be yet many more of these glorious times. I was still very nervous and shaky from the experiences of the spring and summer ; the severe strain of the trial had also made me uneasy about expenses ; and now I often grieve that in that last year there was so much to tax her patience. What

would I now give to have her back, and to give her
a holiday in which the thought should be not for me
and my work, but only for her? But despite my own
shortcomings, all went very well. We had a gay visit
to Berne, which was *en fête* for a shooting contest ; and
then we climbed up to Beatenberg. On the third
morning the sunrise was amazing ; the Mönch, Eiger,
Jungfrau, stood out startlingly clear, like vast jewels
of agate lined with white. It was one of those trans-
porting visions which give you the liberty of the
mountains and of the heavens. We found here our
friends Professor Armitage and his wife : he came to
us with a large *Aquilegia Alpina* in his hand, which
he had found just below the glaciers of the Mönch.
The dear lady was enraptured. Unable to climb
herself, she enjoyed the flowers and the things within
reach as nobody I ever met besides could. It was
at Beatenberg that we realized in our quiet talks that
we were growing old and white. That led her to
write a poem for my birthday on September 18th,
which bade me take heart, because white hairs need
not mean decaying powers, and she thought that my
best work was yet to be done. How I have clung to
that prophecy and prayed for its fulfilment in these
sad years ! We went on from Beatenberg to Château
D'Oex, where she entered into the life of some hard-
working ladies, teachers and nurses, that were enjoying
a holiday in the pension. There we had a glorious
week ; a fine sermon from the pastor on the Good
Samaritan—the Vaudois still worship and throng their
churches ; a grand climb to the top of Mont Cray,
from which, to my astonishment, all the chief mountains
of Switzerland can be identified ; wonderful drives
under the Glumflüh, and up to Lecherette ; another
noble French sermon, on Pourquoi ; and then we had
to leave the enchanting valley, and come down for a
night at Montreux, en route for Geneva.

After a day or two on the tracks of Calvin, and

rejoicing as never before in the meeting of the rivers, we went to the quiet lake of Annecy, and then drove up to Mégève, under the shoulder of Mont Blanc. The little French village gave us much delight. It was wholly Catholic ; every man, woman, and child went to church in an ordered procession ; the church could not quite hold the twelve hundred people, but those who could not get in knelt outside. The bells rang out their carillons on the hot August air ; the great " Calvary " led you up the hill with large life-size scenes of the last days of our Lord, represented at successive stages. A huge impressive cross dominated the vale. The Mass was singularly simple ; the bread was handed round to the crowded congregation in paniers. Where the Church was so plainly in possession it was odd to hear the curé in his sermon, from the text " The Gates of Hell shall not prevail against it," tell the people how the Church was persecuted by the French Government, and was only not apparently defeated, in England ! (The sermon gave a special force to the brochure which I published this year in collaboration with Joseph Hocking, *Shall Rome reconquer England?* To the curé of Mégève it seemed certain that she would, as the only hope of fulfilling Christ's promise to Peter.) Delightful as this dominance of religion seemed, as compared with the apparent godlessness of villages in England of the same size as Mégève, we were not quite satisfied to go by surface values. The main occupation of the Church in the announcements of the week seemed to be offering Masses for the dead. From talks with the people we found that the absorbing thought was the suffering of their dead relatives in purgatory, and their anxiety by lavish payment for masses to curtail their time of torture.

Our dear lady was able to drive along the valley, and we got a cumbersome bath-chair to give her more of the Alpine air ; one day when we had walked up to Christomet, and had obtained a glorious view of the piled masses of the Mont Blanc range, she attempted, from my description, to sketch the view which she had not been able to see. I have that brave endeavour before me as I write ; no masterpiece of art is dearer to me. Sweet, strong, brave soul, always finding consolation in her infirmities and limitations out of the inexhaustible resources of her fancy, her ideals, her projects, her dreams ! I thank God that in that last holiday she had, and gave, all the joys of former days.

Then we went on to Chamounix, where we stayed in a small hotel kept by an old guide who fascinated her by his descriptions of daring feats in ascending the Aiguilles ; and as we took our *déjeuner* in the garden, those vast needles of rock, ribbed with snow, looked down upon us with their smile of awful calm. We had a glorious day on the Glacier des Boissons ; she was happy to have her feet on the river of ice.

On September 3rd, Cromwell's great day, I started up the Brévent in a peerless morning. After two hours' climb I ate my lunch on a snowfield. The whole range of Mont Blanc blended with my foreground, so that I seemed to be on Europe's highest mountain, and yet looking at its whole mighty outline. Beyond the Mer de Glace stood out the vast Jorasses. The Aiguilles, chocolate coloured, with their streaks of snow were pencilled against the living blue, and visited by fleecy clouds, which assumed the forms now of snow mountains, now of winged ministering spirits.

I descended straight down the valley, free of the pine-woods, and found beds of blueberries and delicious wild strawberries more than I could eat.

Never do I remember Nature, pure and simple, coming to me in such gracious succour. But better still, that beloved lady, notwithstanding a serious accident, which alarmed us much, girded me with my armour for the coming return to work ; and I obtained a definite grasp of Jesus Christ as sufficient, which makes me think of Chamounix—the place which

organic community, with a municipal life of its own. It was the only occasion I can recall on which, even for a moment, the sense of corporate life gave a faint thrill to the suburb. Then Mr. Bitton and I reported to the Union the wonderful doings in the Edinburgh conference ; and in the evening, Edward Powell, the son of Mr. George Powell of Cedar Lawn, one of my earliest friends in Hampstead, presided over a valedictory meeting for missionaries. Thursday was equally full and interesting.

On the Friday, just as the great week was over, Charles Ross came to tell me that my sister Beatrice that afternoon, at 4.25, giving tea to a visitor, suddenly bowed her head, and was gone. She was forty-eight, two years older than my mother had been. For years her only son, Horton, had been gradually dying of locomotor ataxia ; she had nursed him, and as he grew helpless, had tried to lift him ; and the heart gave way. It was so swift and unexpected a blow that all the joy of the Union meetings was forgotten. It was a training in sorrow for a heavier blow still which was coming.

Those were days of great national excitement. The death of King Edward, Mr. Asquith's appeal to the country to curb the power of the Second Chamber, and all the agitation of a critical election, filled the public mind. But I was being led down into the valley of the shadow of death.

Our beloved lady, who had entered joyfully into the Union meetings, had also started a Monday afternoon meeting for intercession on behalf of missionaries in the house. Her whole heart had been in the mission cause from her earliest days, and her poem *To my Sisters* had stirred many to the same interest. Many came to those Monday meetings who can never forget her bright welcome, her strangely beautiful prayers, and the sense of a presence filling the room. Wonderful things happened, conversions and miraculous answers to prayer. That meeting still continues, and her influence, many feel, still gives it an atmosphere unlike that of any other prayer-meeting. For her those closing weeks of the year were happy. She was present at the communion on the first Sunday in December, and then she was busy in painting Christmas cards and arranging presents for everybody. On December 18th she had a cold ; but on Monday, as usual, she went out with me. In Golder's Hill Garden she got out of her bathchair and walked a little on my arm, saying that it did her good, in her own bright and encouraging way. A little bronchitis developed, but we were not alarmed. She had instituted a Young Men's At Home on Friday evenings, and thus I had come into close and happy contact with many, whom she drew by her happy ways. But that Friday she was not well enough to see them. She always saved my sight by reading to me for an hour each morning : but that Friday she got some one else to read. On Christmas-eve the distress increased rapidly. The doctor had to come, and in the evening he said she must have a nurse. She yielded, against her own wish, to please him, and I heard her say under her breath : " If a nurse comes it will not be long." At the Saturday prayer-meeting there was earnest prayer for her ; many who attended it had learnt to know her beautiful spirit ; and on my return she seemed better. But, the nurse told us afterwards, she did not sleep that Christmas-eve, and talked to her most of the night about her father, and the happiness of her life. In the morning she gave me as her Christmas present the beautiful sketch of St. Maclou, framed in dark wood, and said that the rest of her present was in crocuses, which she had sown in the garden to appear in the spring. O the anguish when her flowers sprang up, but she was not there ! That day I had three services ; and though she seemed very ill and grew worse, I never dreamed of the worst. But coming from the evening service, where I had struggled to preach on " The Word became flesh and dwelt among us . . . full of grace and truth," I found two doctors, who had done their best, but said that the end had come. The blow was terrible in its suddenness. She was in her chair, and always anxious for me on Sundays, she showed that she wished me to go and rest. They said that her eyes followed me to the door with an expression of indescribable concern. When I was fetched again she was lying unconscious. When I touched her hand and it did not respond, the desolation that fell upon me was like passing through death. She had, while I was out of the room, murmured " Jesus, Jesus " in an attempt to pray. I read and prayed as well as I could, thinking she might hear, though she could not speak, and knowing that God would hear, and take her into His care. It was eleven-thirty on the Christmas-day, which she loved so much. Just before the day of her Saviour's birth was over she entered into life.

Next morning the room was filled with the flowers that she loved ; the whole house seemed luminous ; and the sweet face lay so calm and glad that it might have been a reassuring smile from the other world upon it. On Thursday the 29th the sunshine gilded the sorrow, as we laid the sacred body in the grave,

> Winter slumbering in the open air
> Wore on his smiling face the dream of spring.

Those lines of Coleridge she always loved, and spring, her own spring, was always in her heart, however wintry times might be.

In the church, which she had regarded with such devotion, and enriched with so much prayer, I spoke and tried to tell what she had been, and a little of what she had done for me.

*   *   *   *   *

I went right on with my work, feeling that I should dishonour her if I let my sorrow, which I knew must be lifelong, hinder me in the service of her Saviour and the preaching of His Gospel. On the first Sunday in 1911 I preached on *Endurance* in the morning, and in the evening on, *And Then*.

But it was a crushing sorrow that had come upon me, and life could never be what it was. For nearly forty years—we hoped to celebrate the close of the forty years by a visit to Yorkshire in August 1911— she had been to me a guide and counsellor, always a perfect human friend, and often like a ministering angel. In the early days she had established my faith, through my life-work she had heartened and counselled me, always discerning the eternal significance of the labour, which is so often hidden in the dust, and lowered by the pettiness of daily cares. For more than thirty years her letters, and for the last few years her presence in the home, had been the strength and recreation of my life. And it was over, and life must be faced without that dear and trusted friend.

And now I had to experience that inevitable, and perhaps salutary, cruelty of the world, which hitherto I had not known. All people, and especially the young, shrink from one who bears in his heart a great sorrow. I tried my best to be bright, and to keep to myself the anguish and the sense that life for me was over, but, of course, the thoughts in my mind tinged all I said and did. I had the added sorrow of people falling away from me, and of the Church declining, because I could not show the brightness and eagerness of happier days.

But there were some—God bless them!—who understood, and came forward with unobtrusive sympathy and divine compassion. They brought me love to heal the wounds, and rich appreciation of the one who had gone. To these I owe a debt of gratitude which I cannot hope to repay. I pray for them, that in the times of their desolation they may have such help as they brought to me in mine. Nothing in retrospect seems more marvellous than God's mercy to those whose hearts

seem broken : just as Nature covers ruins with ivy
and traveller's joy, and stonecrop, and wallflowers, so
God covers the bereaved heart with flowers of His own.
The loss remains, the anguish of it enters into life and
abides ; but new interests and affections are brought
in. Duty calls and makes a forward view necessary.
For two long years the grief continued unassuaged ;
then gradually the thought of the life to come over-
mastered the memories bitter sweet. My beloved lady
was no longer the sufferer of long ago, but became a
living presence, coming to me always in the aura of
Christ, with whom she is. The thought of communications through a medium in arranged séances is unutterably repulsive to me. I could not ask her to stoop
to those dubious and suspicious ways. But in the
glorious faith of Christ she seems always to be one of
His ministering spirits sent out on her unreluctant errand
to help and encourage me, as she used to do. The
loss, which at first seemed to shatter my life and make
the grasshopper a burden, has resulted in giving me a
sense of communion with the unseen world, a confidence
in the eternal life, a joyful expectation of entering within
the veil, which has not only blessed me but also enabled
me to succour others in the dread time of bereavement.

The years 1911 and 1912 I pass over rapidly,
because, though there was much to do and to strive
for, the shadow was upon my life. She had greatly
valued Carnegie Simpson's *Fact of Christ* and David
Smith's *In the Days of His Flesh* ; and I set to work
on a life of Christ for the young, which brought me
untold comfort. It was published with lovely illustrations, under the title of *The Hero of Heroes*. In
the spring my friend, Joseph King, took me off to
Holland. In the towns made famous by Motley—
Alkmaar, Leyden, Haarlem, Delft—I found the heroic
interest singularly consoling. In June some of those
dear friends who had come to my aid took me to East
Runton ; and mingling with young life, throwing my

whole interest into the careers of those who had a long future, I tried to recover touch with this present life which had lost, not only its charm, but its reality. In the summer my sister Constance came with me to Brittany ; the attempt to enter into the life of the Breton peasants, and the strange fascination of Carnac, the menhirs and dolmens, the mysterious suggestion of half-human giants who in the dawn of life on our planet reared those vast monoliths, split by thunder-bolts, and planted those endless avenues of stones, brought a kind of relief. We came over to Dartmoor and compared the two Brittanys on either side the channel with their kindred peoples and identical saints, and then at the Lizard I made my first acquaintance with the seas and sun, and the flora, of Cornwall. That was the severest test of all—a holiday without that dear companion who had made so many foreign places home, and so many places at home romantic, by her presence. A second visit to Cornwall in 1912, and a third in 1913, with the dear friends who had come to help me in my distress, gave to the great heaving seas of the Land's End, St. Michael's Mount, Marazion, Penzance, some sweet suggestion of comfort—of reaching at last the land's end of life, from which we strike out into the glorious sunset —the home where we would be.

In the course of three or four years I was again able to feel the charm of Nature, as I had learnt to feel it with her. I could recall how she often quoted " Nature never did deceive the heart that loved her," and I found that in this sorest loss and most crushing sorrow of my life God could still speak through Nature, as through grace, His divine word of an incredible consolation.

But there was much in the call of my work which summoned me to efforts, constantly renewed, to rise above the depression and gloom. The Manual which came out in the spring of 1911 showed that there were 1,238 members on the Church Roll, and that the people had given during the year £21,000. Such devotion made me ashamed of private sorrow. In November we opened the completed buildings at Lyndhurst Hall, and there was a reunion of old and present workers, which was so rich in memories and promises that I recognized the signal of God that my work was not done.

And then came an interruption. Pagenstecher was in London that month. I asked him to examine my eyes, and he said that the difficulty I felt in my one sound eye was due to a threat of choroiditis. He urged me to pay a visit to Wiesbaden, that he might try to arrest the disease, which otherwise would make reading impossible. My heart was at the time too broken to feel this new blow ; but there was mercy in it. Mrs. de Sélincourt was willing to go with me again. And the loving hand of God had provided unexpected alleviations in the klinik. We found almost the first evening Mrs. Lefroy, the widow of Dean Lefroy, and her daughter, who was there with trouble in her eye. They were both, as they said afterwards, more cast down than ever they had been before ; the imprisonment in the klinik is, at first, unbearable. We were able to cheer them ; and here sprung up a new and delightful friendship. Others in that home of despondency were waiting for sympathy ; and the days became full and useful. It was also a singular grace that on the dreaded anniversary, Christmas-day, I was far from home. The German Christmas, with the trees and presents, and other festivities, was very interesting, and gave the impression that the Germans were a Christian people. The treatment was for me very tedious and annoying, hot-air packs and rubbings with mercury, which took much time and produced no perceptible effect. I tried again to dictate a book on the Inner Life. But seven years had lessened my dear old friend's power of writing from dictation ; and the attempt to dictate during the treatment was not successful. When at the close I examined the MS. I felt that it was not fit for publication ; and I do not know that I shall attempt to rewrite it, for undoubtedly the extreme dejection of that time gave the work a colour which is not quite normal.

My friends the Flints also came again to Wiesbaden ; and times with them in the Quisisana Hotel, and sleighing when the snow came, brought a sensible relief. As that year closed I was amazed at the merciful ways of God. Chastisement is the proof of His Fatherhood ; but the consolation He gives in the severest trials is a revelation of tenderness which is infinitely reassuring. I suppose we learned to understand it through Christ. I am not aware that apart from Christ this point of view was ever gained by other religions. But from my experience as a Christian I have come to a clear perception of this fact, which is illustrated by my whole life : *God is dealing with us in a way of discipline and training, which requires that life here should never seem complete; and yet He tempers every sorrow, breaks every calamity, sends relief and encouragements, with such a set purpose that the chastisement can always be recognized as the work of Love.*

I find that no joy is allowed to last long without some balancing of pain or sorrow or loss ; but that no trouble ever comes which is not accompanied with certain compensations. As the outcome of the long and crowded years I have learnt, as age comes on, to believe implicitly in God's goodness, whether joy or sorrow be the experience of the moment. The blow which had shattered my life had revealed shoots of joy among the ruins, which at once began to grow ; and the exceeding goodness of God produced an ever deepening conviction that our beloved, who leave us, are not taken from us, but are allowed to mingle with our lives at all points, and to wait for us in the spiritual world to offer us a welcome which will overwhelm us with joy.

Browning's glorious thought of reunion with his wife, and then " With God be the rest ! " seems to me one of the surest fruits of Christianity. For this Christ came, to take away the fear of death and the agony of loss.

CHAPTER XVII

INDIA, AND LAST VISIT TO AMERICA
1912–1914

ONCE more in the Markt Kirche at the Orgel Concert I heard that old strain which had breathed hope into me seven years before, ringing through the lofty nave—

> Durch die Finsterniss der Klagen
> Bricht der Freude Morgen Stern,
> Bald wird auch dein Morgen tagen,
> Gottes' Helf ist nimmer fern.

And in the third week of January 1912 Pagenstecher said that the danger was averted. A patient whom I met in the klinik, disabled by choroiditis, showed plainly to me the disaster which was threatening me. But now the doctor assured me that I might go back to my work with a firm hope that my sight, such as it was, would last out my time. This was a new call to renewed diligence in my ministry.

On January 21st I preached to my people on "My grace is sufficient for thee," and in that confidence I plunged into work again. I have often noticed how soon a joy or relief is followed by a crowd of troubles. On the 23rd my friend Dugald Macfadyen from Highgate came to me heart-broken at the sudden death of his wife, and I had to go over and take the funeral service ; I saw my dear nephew, Horton, my one hope for a succession in the ministry—the fourth Horton—though not of my surname, obviously declining towards the grave ; and at the end of the week my friend John Oakes was summoned to Halifax by the death of his only brother. Early in February my friend Dr. Fairbairn died ; he had played a considerable part in my life, and his death left our Congregational ministry strangely depleted, as if the most prominent headlight of the ship had gone out.

But there was a project in my mind which my repaired vision encouraged me now to fulfil. I had always felt a kind of duty to visit India, not only to get some first-hand acquaintance with missionary work, but because I knew that we English are responsible for that vast country, and show, in the main, a culpable ignorance and neglect of its needs. The way opened for me to do my little part in lessening the indifference and apathy. My dear and faithful people eagerly welcomed the idea of the visit, and promised to follow me all the way with interest and prayer ; and the London Missionary Society gladly planned a tour in which I might visit all their chief stations. From the first I felt that I was obeying the call of God, and had no hesitation in leaving to His care my work at home and the loved friends from whom it was a sorrow to part. My oculist, Dr. Knox Shaw, did not think that the journey would hurt my sight if I obtained the Euphos spectacles, which exclude the dangerous violet rays ; and Sir Havelock Charles went with me through the proposed tour before-hand, giving me the most minute directions and pre-cautions, to which I undoubtedly owed my immunity from illness during my travels. Then a delightful arrangement was made for a fellow-traveller ; Nathaniel Micklem, the son of my old College friend, was now at Mansfield, preparing to enter the ministry. He was released for part of two terms, and I think his visit to India was not the least important episode of his ministerial training. From February to October I was making the necessary arrangements, and planning for an absence of five months. As far as I could I read about India and studied its problems. On Whit-Sunday, May 26th, I did what I had never done before, nor ever since in my own pulpit have I repeated it : I preached entirely *ex tempore*. The entry for the day is " On the Spirit, and by the Spirit, with clear blessing." And yet I never venture to enter the pulpit unprepared, knowing the danger of presumption. Indeed a chance remark of a candid friend, who hinted that my sermons were sometimes ill-prepared, and quite unworthy, has made me for the last five years take much more pains with them than in the earlier years of my ministry. But I believe the ideal would be, by constant work, and study and prayer, to be always prepared and always preparing, but always to preach *ex tempore*, allowing the Spirit to speak as He would through lips and heart and mind " always ready."

In July I carried out a strong desire of Mrs. de Sélincourt and went with her for a week to Fontainebleau. How thankful I was that I did not evade that opportunity, for I was not, on my return from India, to find this kind and faithful friend alive. Then the dear friends who had come to my aid in the time of desolation gave me a lovely and invigorating time at Mullion ; soon after the holiday final preparations were made ; with only the sad anxiety about my sister Constance, who had just undergone an operation for appendicitis, on Friday, October 11th, my young friend and I embarked on s.s. *Oesterley* for Colombo.

Those five months seem in retrospect an unbroken chain of mercies, interests, and delights ; and the visit to India, which ought to have been twenty years earlier, made so deep and lasting an impression on me that I must not pass it over. When I set out I was resolved *not* to publish a book, but certain articles that I contributed to the *Daily Chronicle*, the *Contemporary Review*, etc., were put together by Messrs. Cassell, and I wrote two or three additional chapters, with the result that a volume entitled *Three Months in India* did appear. But the inwardness of my visit could not come out in that book, and the lasting effects were not apparent at the time. Without therefore quoting from the book, assuming it as read, I shall set down some things which entered into the very fibre of my life : India has become part of me.

To begin with, we had an ideal voyage out, with ideal company. We were fog-bound in the Thames for twenty-four hours, but that was the last as well as the first of our troubles. I know from the return voyage how exceptional the outward voyage was, and I can believe that many people have gone backwards and forwards to India for years without ever receiving such a series of delightful impressions as was granted to me. The Bay of Biscay was absolutely calm, and then we circumnavigated Spain, in full view day after day, from Cape Finisterre to Gibraltar, and then, in sight of the glorious Sierra Nevada, up to Toulon. I seem to know Spain from that week. Then we entered the Bay of Naples, and I saw that you never understand the saying, " See Naples and die," until you approach and leave it by sea. We had time for a visit to the Greek sculpture, and to the delicately carved chapel of St. Januarius. Then passing Sybaris we put in at the ancient Taventum, and got another splendid impression of Southern Italy. Our course then gave us a good view of Corcyra, the scene of those memorable incidents related by Thucydides in the Peloponnesian War. We then had a fine view of Crete as we passed.

Meanwhile the ship's life was intensely interesting. We had a Bible-reading in the saloon each day. One glorious Sunday evening I had a great open-air service on the deck. Not only fellow-passengers, but all the officers and crew on the Orient liner, seemed bent on making the necessary voyage a prolonged summer holiday. In the Suez Canal brilliant moonlight, cloudless sunrises, and the glows of sunset, made the desert mysteriously beautiful. And quails brought to us at Port Said made us think of the Israelites in their desert march. The Red Sea was of course hot, but we were

in sight of the Arabian coast, and could mark where
Mecca and Medina were, so that we seemed at the birth
of Islam, and before reaching Perin Island we made
out the triple peak of Mount Sinai, and were present
at the birth of the older religion, Judaism. The African
coast, especially in the splendid and awful yellow sunsets,
was overwhelmingly grand ; we saw the natives on the
beach of Somaliland, and the lofty mountains stretched
endlessly down the coast towards Cape Gardafui. The
dolphins were leaping in apparent joy all day, and
presently in the Indian Ocean the shoals of flying fish,
gleaming silver-white among the crests of the waves,
like swallows flying south in the autumn, gave me a
new sensation of the sea as homelike and fairylike, rather
than vast and terrible. The unimaginable beauty of
the full moon on those Indian seas seemed to open
out to me all the wonders and fascinations of the East.

When Colombo was reached I was reluctant to leave
the good ship and the delightful company, but there
was my sister from Galle to meet me, and our fellow-
travellers, Mr. and Mrs. Aitkin, laid themselves out to
give us a beautiful impression of Ceylon. But Mr.
Ferguson had dissuaded us from staying in Colombo,
which at that time was in an insanitary state, and I had,
not unwillingly, surrendered Ceylon because the surrender
enabled me to visit Travancore. We therefore, Micklem,
my sister and I, crossed at once to Tuticorin.

Old Indians forget, and visitors as a rule are too
interested in greater things to note, the sudden magic
with which India captures the heart. The beauty of the
human forms, clothed only in their brown, black, or
tawny skins, with the brightly coloured saris, and the
jewels in the women's ears, that have drawn out the
lobe into long loops to sustain them, the feeling of a
humanity, unlike our own, but at once eliciting a sympathy
and a wish to claim kinship, and in Ceylon or South
India, the luxuriant tropical vegetation, and enchanting mountain scenery, are lost for the conventional

traveller who arrives duly by a P. and O. boat in Bombay. But it is by these subtle combinations of form and colour that India masters the heart, and afflicts one with a strange nostalgia when one leaves it.

No one can know the full charm of India who misses Travancore. This small native state at the south-western corner of the great peninsula remains more untouched by modern civilization, and yet is more penetrated by Christianity, than any other part that I visited. My sister was with me, and in the long journey to Quilon by rail, and then to Trevandrum by the fascinating backwaters, on which we were propelled in wallums by nude natives, we renewed the companionship of our childhood, and talked together of God's wonderful ways with us in joy and sorrow. For the first fortnight in India I had the advantage of her intimate knowledge of the country ; then we parted at Madura, wondering whether we should meet again on earth. Travancore is so beautiful that all India by comparison seemed dull and flat until we reached the Himalayas. The Western Ghats, which form the eastern boundary of the little state, are beautiful as you cross their wooded ravines, with dashes of bright colour from the *lantana*, on the way to Quilon ; beautiful also, as you thread the pass in the south, jolted in the pitiless bullock bandy for fifty miles ; but most beautiful of all, rising in ridge and peak, softened with the lights of the sinking sun, when the broiling day is over, all the way from Trevandrum to Nagercoil. The roads along which you run in rickshaws, or creep in bandies, are always charming, arched by the spreading banyans, or shaded with palms, while the green paddy-fields on either side afford a margin of brilliant colour. Delicious birds flash across the road—orioles, wood-peckers, king crows, and others quite unknown to a dweller in temperate latitudes ; still more delicious children, clad only in their innocence, survey you with soft shy eyes from every village. There is the great *lingam* for Siva worship by the wayside, and there is a decayed building, which proves to be an old Syrian church, presumably of the time of the Apostle Thomas, and the frescoes around the altar make you fancy yourself in an old Italian city. Another reason why Travancore puts one a little out of conceit with the rest of India is that a third of its population is Christian, and the London Missionary Society's churches and schools at Trevandrum and Nagercoil, and especially the splendidly equipped hospital at Neyoor, give one the feeling that the Gospel of Christ is really gaining the day in South India. Crossing the beautiful Ghats again by the road along which Ringeltaube entered to evangelize Travancore a century ago, we came upon the equally promising work of the Church Missionary Society at Palamcottah and Tinnivelly, where Rhenius is buried. Then on to Madura, where, if the vast temple is the most splendid monument of Hinduism in South India, the missionaries of the American Board have established a Christian work of unexampled thoroughness. Dr. Jones and Dr. Chandler made India seem like home. And a great Christian Endeavour Convention, representing twenty thousand endeavourers, gave one the eager hope that even there Christianity was in possession.

I had a day at Salem among the Shevroy mountains, and then stayed for a week in Madras. One of the great interests of my Indian visit was that Dr. Mott was there just at the same time, giving effect to the resolutions of the Edinburgh Missionary Conference by holding a series of conferences in all parts of India. I joined him at Madras. All the missionary societies were represented ; the methods of work were carefully reviewed, and the lines of future co-operation were laid down. By attending these conferences at Madras, Allahabad, and Calcutta, and by taking part in the final conference in Calcutta, which drew together all the threads, and shaped the missionary policy for the future, I was enabled in three months to get a fuller view of the work in India than otherwise I could have obtained in several years.

Lord Pentland had just come out as Governor of the Madras Presidency, and as his wife, the daughter of the Earl of Aberdeen, had in college days attended Lynd-hurst Road, I had the pleasure of dining with them, and there I met Sir Pardy Lukis, the Surgeon-General of India. He took me to see the Tata Institute at Bangalore, and from him I got my first real insight into the great way in which the British raj tries to care for the interests of the vast country. At home I had often listened to the accusations brought against the Government and Governors of India. The haughty manner to natives, the self-indulgence and irreligion of Anglo-Indian life, and the inconceivable modesty and reticence of those who have administered India since the Mutiny, had completely misled me, as it has done a large part of the public at home. But I came to see in India itself the presence, everywhere and in all depart-ments of life, of a steady and enlightened administration, dealing bravely and unselfishly with the vast problem of governing 300,000,000 people, of various races, tongues, and religions. The more I saw the more con-vinced I became that if English civilians are not Christians, they have made a very successful practical application of Christianity. I recognized two great missionary movements in India, one trying to proclaim to Hindus and Moslems the great truths of Christianity, for the regulation of individual life and the salvation of the soul ; the other trying to show how the Gospel of Christ, accepted as a national religion, works out in a government, just and merciful, securing life and property and public decency as the material conditions of spiritual development.

At Bangalore I enjoyed the hospitality of that en-lightened missionary, E. T. Rice. With Mott I laid the foundation-stones of a Union Theological Seminary for training native pastors, a very notable precedent of combined action on the part of the societies. And through inquiries and conversations I got some impression of the native state, Mysore, which is perhaps the most enlightened and progressive in India. At Bellary the natural beauty of the rocks and the fort, combined with the delightful reception of the missionaries, and the talk of interesting ruins of old cities and temples within reach, made me begin to feel that my tour would be too hurried. There a Hindu, Gopal Swami, explained to me the three things which prevent Hindus from becoming Christians : first, the strength of the caste system ; second, the Hindu philosophies which make truth doubtful and enable men to explain everything away ; and third, the dense ignorance of the people. This a Hindu judgment on the situation ! There too I saw the touching spectacle of the girls in Miss Haskard's school, representing the Pilgrim's Progress : the Slough of Despond, the Strait Gate, the shining ones, and the rest of it. Would that John Bunyan might have seen that !

Bombay, with Dr. Mackichan, genial, overflowing with information, the rarest combination of dignity and kindness ; with the Towers of Silence and the mysterious vultures ; with the watered garden in the early morning on Malabar Hill ; with Elephanta, the temple cut in the rock, and the monstrous image of Brahma ; Allahabad with Bishop Westcott, and the meeting of the Ganges and the Jumna, where the monstrous Mela, attended by a million Hindus, takes place, and Khusru Bagh, with the Moslem tombs large as temples ; Benares, with the Cuttings and the delightful missionary group, making a centre of Christian light and joy and fun in the central home of Hinduism ; Sarnath, with its stupas marking where the Buddha first preached, and the column of Asoka recalling the great Buddhist monarch ; Benares, with its Ghats and the endless coloured beauty of its worshippers, and its Doms, scorned even by the outcasts, and gathered in by the Christian missionary ; then Bankipur and Patna, Asoka's splendid capital, all ruins or vanished wholly, the Holy Land of Buddhism ;

Calcutta, under the friendly roof of the Le Quesnes, with Kalighat and its unspeakable doings hard by, the " Black Hole," the great college at Serampore, where Carey baptized his first convert, and where two converts from Mott's Mission were baptized while I was there ; Berhampore, with the Stursbergs, close to Plassey, where the Mutiny broke out ; the Nawab's palace at Moorshedabad ; the elephants, the cemetery crowded with great monkeys, where Suraj-ud-Dowlah, the perpetrator of the Black Hole murder, lies in his simple tomb—the fireflies and the exquisite green bee-eaters wheeling in the air, the jackals howling round the veranda at night ; Mr. Joyce giving a lantern lecture in the open air to the crowd from the bazaar, and Mrs. Stursberg telling the thrilled audience in fluent Bengali the story of the Prodigal Son ; Lucknow, with the appealing beauty and clothed ruins of the Residency, and the tower where " ever upon the topmost roof the banner of England *flies* " ; then Almora, on the lower spurs of the Himalayas, with my own missionary, Dr. Eleanor Shepheard, and the vast snow range 23,000 feet high in view, whence all the gods descended to the plain of India ; then Agra, with the Church Missionary Society missionaries, and Bishop Durrant, and the fort and the unimaginable beauty of the Taj ; Delhi, where the attempt on Lord Hardinge's life had just been made, Stephen Thomas, a Baptist missionary, but a great citizen of Delhi, the statue of Nicholson, that Kashmir Gate, remaining as it was, when they heroically blew it up, that ridge on which the besiegers were besieged ; then Baroda and the cordial Gaekwar, and my kindly friend Dewan Samarth Bahadur, who asked me to visit his state and address the *élite* of Baroda, when I first preached in Bombay ; what a succession of fascinating images, what scenes of religious interest, what talks and pleasant evenings with devoted men and women living in India in order to win it to Christ, are brought to my mind by the names !

When on the eve of my departure from Bombay Sir Neryon Chandavarka, Judge of the High Court, entertained us at the Taj Mahal Hotel, and introduced me to the leading citizens of Bombay—Hindus, Parsees, Moslems, Somajists—I found my heart so drawn to the country, and my interest in its future so permanently engaged, that I knew, as I say, that India had become part of me. Little as I can serve her, she has done great things for me. She has deepened my love of human nature, she has taught me the place of courtesy in human life, she has convinced me that when Christ said, " other sheep I have which are not of this fold," He was thinking of India and China and Japan, with their (even then) ancient systems of ethics and religion, with the hearts searching for One whom they knew not. When I went to India my one thought was India's need of Christ ; when I left, there was another thought, Christ's need of India.

On our return journey we lingered for a week in Egypt, and under the direction of Mr. Gairdner, the Church Missionary Society missionary, we had a glimpse into Moslem life, and also into the Christian work among Moslems. The feast of Mohammed's birthday was being celebrated : we got through the crowd to the Mosque-el-Monayad, the oldest in Cairo ; for two hours the procession of devotees passed, twenty thousand at least, the groups each led by its sheikh, with banners and weird music, endlessly repeating " Allah." Why cannot Christ win such enthusiasm and devotion from men as Mohammed does? Is it because His demand is Purity? Moslems do not aim at purity.

On my first visit to Egypt the natives had seemed attractive, with their long robes—blue, white, etc.—coming down to the feet, covered sometimes with a loose toga, and the picturesque tarboosh on their heads ; but with Indians fresh in my mind they seemed rude, self-assertive, and devoid of the spiritual element. The women, too, in black, with the gilt nose-reel supporting the veil, are ungraceful to look at. An ungraceful Indian woman is hardly conceivable.

The Sakhara tombs, of Ti and Ptah-hotep, seemed more wonderful and incredible for a second visit after an interval of ten years. The pictures and sculptures of these tombs in their liveliness, humour, delicacy, surviving for five thousand years, fresh as if they were finished yesterday, are the most amazing witness in the world to man's passion for a life after death. The Ka could not live unless the body were preserved ; therefore, embalming was made the chief art of Egypt ; and the tombs were built, in which were delineated all the employments of a man's life, endless provision of food and other necessaries, and gigantic portraits of himself, to secure the happiness of the released Ka in the other world. The colossal tombs did not preserve even the bodies ; the tombs were pillaged and the bodies stolen ; not along that line could immortality lie. But Egypt is the eternal witness, in the undecaying records of its rainless climate, that man demands, if he has not, Forever.

At Marseilles my friends, Mr. and Mrs. Flint, met us, and we loitered for a few days at Avignon and Nîmes ; a day at Petrarch's Vaucluse was the charming conclusion of a wonderful journey.

One incidental result of this Indian visit was, that in the opening of 1916, when the London Missionary Society, obliged to retrench, proposed to withdraw from Mirzapore and Calcutta, I was able to make an appeal, through *The Times*, for the relief of Mirzapore, which I had visited, with the result that the £1,300 necessary to save that station was immediately subscribed, and by God's goodness Calcutta was also saved. I was thankful that the dear missionary folk who had received me so warmly, and entertained me so royally, regarded this little service as some return of all their kindness. God bless them !

I got back just in time for the Livingstone celebration.

The service in the Abbey about his grave, and the great meeting in the Albert Hall on March 19th, were a glorious reminder to me that India was not the only field of successful missionary enterprise.

The sadness of the return, deepened by the death of Mrs. de Sélincourt in my absence, was relieved by having with me over Easter two of my young people, whom I had known and loved from infancy, the younger of them from birth. They seemed sent by God, and by that ever watchful guardian, as it seemed, who was with me, though unseen, to cheer my solitude and hearten me for work. It is difficult to say what the old owe to the young ; and when a childless man finds in his declining years warm youthful hearts trusting and loving him, he takes a new lease of life, and knows that though much is gone, enough remains in the mercy of God to make life sweet and worthy. The demand which young, opening minds make on an older friend is singularly stimulating ; it wakes old memories, draws on the resources of the past, and makes the life which has been toilsomely lived serviceable again to warn and to guide a new generation. The young will not listen to the old because they are old, but when they love them they will listen for love's sake.

On April 29th an important decision was taken in Oxford Convocation, and I went up to record my vote. A proposal was made to open the Divinity Degrees and examinerships to competent men, irrespective of their religious denomination. It was an interesting instance of growing intelligence, that the two ablest supporters of the proposal were Professor Scott Holland and Dr. Locke, the Warden of Keble, who thirty years before had strenuously opposed my own appointment to the unimportant examinership in Divinity, because I was not a member of the Church of England. And the value of their argument lay in their generous recognition of the place which Mansfield College had taken, and the work which its professors had done, in the theological schools.

It was pathetic to see the crowd of country clergymen and others mustering in the Sheldonian Theatre, just as they did thirty years before. And by two to one (860 to 430) they decided that Oxford theology should be only Church of England theology. They were exactly in the position of Parson Thwackum, in Fielding's novel, " And when I say Religion, I mean the Christian religion ; and when I say Christian I mean Protestant ; and when I say Protestant I mean Church of England." I have always avowed my admiration and love of the Church Established in this country. But on these occasions, when the cry of the " Church in danger " is raised, she appears in a peculiarly unattractive light ; like Germany, convinced of her own intrinsic superiority to all other countries, the English Church then seems only convinced of its own intrinsic superiority to other Churches. Christianity apart from her is of no account ; the fact that there are Nonconformists in England makes no impression on her ; she dismisses them by ignoring them as Martin Chuzzlewit ignored Mr. Pecksniff. It is on these occasions that one sees the point of Charles Buller, when he exclaimed against the proposal of disestablishment : " Disestablish the Church of England ! Why, it is the only thing that stands between this country and—true religion." To " the Church " in this mood all Free Churchmen are Pecksniffs.

In May I visited Cliff College and saw with delight the work which the Methodists are doing in my aunt's old house. In a large marquee I told the company of her zeal and prayers, and I counted it a privilege to pass on to another generation the memory of one of the most devoted Christians I have ever known. In returning I slipped from a dogcart and jarred my leg, with the result that for some weeks I was more or less incapacitated. But in September came another occasion of extraordinary interest to me : our London Missionary Society was in great straits with a vast accumulated debt, and the need of retrenchment was apparent, for the

Churches were impatient of the constant deficits. Hearing of the splendid results of a conference at Swanwick, in which by simple prayer the Church Missionary Society had liquidated an even greater debt than ours, I made a private suggestion that a few who believed in prayer should meet for three days at Swanwick and ask God to deliver us from our difficulties. The meeting was arranged. No one who was there could doubt but that God met with us ; for my own part I was startled by the immediacy and directness of His guidance : there were one hundred and fifty present ; they were brought to one mind, and a message was sent to the Union Meetings at Southend, which led to the extrication of the Society out of its dilemma. I suppose we shall never know what malign influence it is which—though it is demonstrated that God can and will answer united and believing prayer in Christ's name—keeps us from adopting the only infallible way of doing God's work.

At the end of October I gave another day to waiting in the vestry to make a final clearance of the debt on the new church we had built at Cricklewood. Mr. McEvoy did the same on the spot. We had the satisfaction of declaring the beautiful buildings free of debt.

And then came a disturbance which made a greater demand on me than I had ever experienced in my life. In November John Mott offered to preach for me, and he gave us a great discourse on the work of the Student Movement in the East. The people were fairly carried away by the noble vision of Christian service opened before them. But he was not so innocent as he seemed. Two days later he came to breakfast and said that his object had been to get me to America for the great Quadrennial Convention of the Students, and he had wished to conciliate the Church and to gain their consent. His diplomacy was completely successful. I was weary of travelling, and since returning from India in March had been trying to get into my work again. Here was another interruption. Besides, I felt ill-fitted for a long journey in the winter, first across the Atlantic, and then 1,500 miles across the Continent to Kansas City, where the Convention was to be held at the turn of the year. Moreover, what he wanted me to do was only to open the Convention on the first day, take a devotional hour, and preach at the Sunday morning meeting. The labour and cost involved to render so slight a service seemed to me incommensurate ; but Dr. Mott had so ingeniously captured my elders, that they met and urged me to go. My reluctance amounted to a positive aversion, and for the first time in my life I had a presentiment, that I should not return. However, it was settled by the Wisdom that orders our lives for us, as I learnt afterwards to see. My friends, who had done so much to help me during the last sad years, proposed that their younger son, Maurice, should go with me as my travelling companion, and another generous friend came forward to pay his expenses. Maurice was just about to leave Mill Hill, and when I went over to carry the suggestion to him, he received it with boyish glee. It was arranged that we should join Mott and his party at Southampton and embark on the German liner, the *George Washington* ; unfortunately I had to leave on Sunday morning. It was December 14th, and Maurice's family, with some others, came down to Waterloo to see us off.

That was a memorable voyage over the wintry sea, which seemed to be calmed and tempered for us, and the beautiful, well-ordered liner remains in memory as a proof of the way in which Germany was already gaining a command of the sea, if only she had been content to rely on peaceful progress. Dr. Mott was bringing with him for the Kansas meetings, Warneck from Germany, and Zwemer from Egypt. He was hard at work all day preparing the syllabus and the directions for the great Convention, but we had an hour's united prayer in his state-room each day. It was this that rendered the voyage memorable. Warneck had been a missionary in the East, he represented Asia. Zwemer represented Africa. Mott represented America. I Europe. We agreed to pray by continents. At Kansas there were to be a large number of Chinese and Japanese students, and from the first we tried to bring East and West together. I have never felt such enlargement in prayer. The December sea was exquisite, sometimes like daffodil fields, sometimes like a silver mirror. The seven days seemed too short ; the world's needs too great.

When we arrived, Maurice and I went to Niagara for Christmas, as we were not due in Kansas City till the 29th. He did not enjoy the place, he missed his home ; and even the beauty of the snow and ice on the falls and the tumultuous rush of the rapids were no compensation for human society. But he was beautiful in his care of me ; I felt that I had a son. We went to Chicago for the Sunday, and Professor Shailer Matthews made us almost in love with that vast hive of industry, and the University in which he gloried. We lunched with Miss Addams at Hull House, and visited Graham Taylor at his settlement. I remembered Stead's book, *If Christ came to Chicago!* and, from what I saw, I felt that He had come. I spoke at the Sunday Evening Club, and heard Bishop Williams speak, to a large audience. Maurice went to hear Dr. Gunsaulus. The problems of a vast cosmopolitan city like this would stagger us in the old world ; but Americans face them with courage and confidence. Christianity will ultimately prevail even there. Late on Monday evening, December 29th, we reached Kansas City, and joined Dr. Mott and the rest at the Coates House.

But now came the trial of my faith. Here were five thousand students assembled from all the colleges of the United States and Canada ; about two thousand of the public would also be present, and I was to speak at the opening session, December 31st, on the Lordship of Christ. On Tuesday, the 30th, I was taken ill, and had to remain in bed. I felt that I had undertaken this long and bitter journey at Christ's call, but the presentiment that I should not return had laid hold of me. All that night I was awake in pain, and fancied myself dictating a farewell letter to my people at home. A great peace came over me. Might I not say that I had died in "following the gleam"? What more could I desire? Then my boy Maurice was an unspeakable comfort to me. He applied the hot fomentations, and carried out the instructions of the doctor, with the fidelity of a nurse. He read to me, and knelt down and prayed for me. On Wednesday I rose, very weak, and walked to the Convention Hall. Before that vast audience I could hardly stand, and thought I had no voice. But I remembered that my people had agreed to meet at that hour, making allowance for the five hours' difference in time, and to pray for me. A strange accession of strength came to me, and when I sat down Mott whispered to me : "Your long journey is justified." I went back to bed. But by Saturday I was fit to take the intercession, and in that brief quarter of an hour I knew why I was sent to Kansas.

On Sunday, January 4th, I preached on "The Message," and Robert Speer on "The Messenger." Afterwards Sherwood Eddy addressed those in that audience who had definitely volunteered for the mission-field, fifteen hundred in number. The great map over the platform showed the lines going out into all the earth from Kansas City, and I got the definite impression that the missionary enterprise will be carried to victory during the twentieth century by the lead of the young manhood and womanhood of America.

It was an amazing experience to meet there in the centre of the Western Continent several of those whom I had met, less than a year before, in India. East and West now touch, and in Christ they meet.

In the train, returning from Kansas to Chicago, there were many students, most of them from Indiana. Led by Campbell White, we held a meeting in the car. We

spoke about the Vine, Christ, and the branches, which
bear fruit from Him. Something led me to show how
the results of the Convention would be preserved by
the indwelling of Christ, and to propose that all present
should form a society, " The Branches of the Vine."
Maurice, who had been greatly impressed by the whole
Convention, took the thought home ; he went on our
return to Germany, to prepare for his business in the
future ; he took the thought there and imparted it to
those whom he lived with in Hamburg. When the war
broke out he took the thought into the army and lived
it out among the men, and his fellow-officers. He
entered the Air Service and took the thought into his
perilous training. When in April 1916 he went to the
Front, that thought was still with him. On May 19th
he wrote to me a joyous letter showing how he was
supported by my prayer, and was absolutely happy in
his life offered for his country. The next day he went up
and was brought down by an enemy aeroplane. He
fell in their lines, they buried him with military honours,
and sent over to our lines two packets of photographs
showing the whole ceremony of the funeral and the grave.
It seemed as if even the enemy had been touched by
the fair and gallant boy—who in his daily prayers remembered the Germans, as well as his own country, who
had never cherished hatred in his heart, but had loved
and been loved by all. He was a branch in the Vine,
and death had no power over him. When this great
sorrow came I understood why I had been sent to Kansas
City. To have loved and helped one of the least of
Christ's brethren is its own reward.

We returned from New York by the large French
liner, *La France* ; we sailed on Wednesday, and on
Tuesday morning we were just off the Scilly Islands.
The comfortable state-room, with beds instead of berths,
the tasteful beauty of the saloons in the style of Louis
Quatorze, the exquisite band which played daily, the
effort of captain and crew to treat all the vast company

as guests, the daily paper printed on board, the warm, calm weather, with brilliant sunrise, sunset, and moonrise, Maurice's brave faithful spirit, and our talks and prayers together, made this voyage home a prolonged joy.

I came home to a real sorrow. My gifted and devoted neighbour, Dr. Newton Marshall, died the day before I arrived, January 13, 1914. He was an accomplished scholar and writer, as well as a faithful minister. In the visit of the ministers to Germany, seeking to establish better relations between the two countries, he and my other Baptist neighbour, Mr. Rushbrooke, were the only two English ministers of any denomination who were able to preach in German. Perhaps God mercifully took him in order to spare him the agony which would have come to him in the autumn of this year. Then I heard of my friend, Joseph King, who had gone to visit India, laid up seriously ill at Agra.

On the other hand, I was greatly cheered by a large number of my Active Service League meeting me, and ready for service. Their prayers for me while I was in America had drawn us together, and here I saw the promise of a better future for the work. I had no presentiment then of the dread event which was to call all the lads away, some never to return.

On Sunday, February 8th, I was preaching in Leicester, and my hosts were reading with delight Jonathan Brierley's article in the *Christian World*, " Life's Loose Ends "—that weekly article, they said, was their joy and strength—and just at that time he was called suddenly away at Westcliff. Jonathan Brierley had played a beautiful part in my life. He taught me courage and cheerfulness in the midst of the most difficult circumstances. He had been for many years the most loyal member of Lyndhurst Road. In the place where he sat every Sunday morning Joshua Harrison had sat after his retirement from Camden Town, and before him, for many years, William Urwick. I can testify to the great blessing that a retired minister can be to a pastor craving

sympathy and encouragement.   Retired ministers are the
most interested and indulgent of hearers.

At the end of the month Professor Driver died, at
the age of sixty-seven. I had known him for forty years,
a reserved, unfathomable man, but a scholar of the very
highest type, so thorough, so cautious, with so retentive
a memory and sound a judgment, that when he spoke
decisively, which was not often, one could accept his
decision with the utmost confidence.   I never forgot
how he helped me with my *Inspiration and the Bible,* or
the strength it gave me when he said that my treatment
of the Pentateuch was quite satisfactory.   As an influence
in my life I put him among the first. In May came a blow
which I felt more personally.   Silvester Horne had been
delivering the Yale Lectures at Newhaven (that Lyman
Beecher lecture on preaching which I had delivered
twenty-one years before), and on Lake Ontario, going
to Toronto, he was pacing the deck, talking to his
beloved wife of the happy time they were enjoying,
when he suddenly sat down and was gone.   That was
an ideal death for him ; but the gap it left for us was
shown in the masterly speech of Dr. Clifford, the greatest
funeral tribute that I ever heard.

Then on the 10th of May, my elder, G. H. Turner,
whose sight had given way just when mine did, and who
had borne the privation with heroic cheerfulness, had
been at the Saturday prayer-meeting and taken his part
in it—strange to say, the hymn sung had been, " There
is a land of pure delight "—and early on Sunday morning
his son came to tell me that he had gone. To these and
other losses I came back ; but now it seems as if
these righteous men had been taken away from the evil
to come.

CHAPTER XVIII

THE WAR

1914–

THE year opened with a great effort which we were making to cleanse the Heath. The gross indecencies and immoralities in our public places were part of the evidence that God's chastening hand would fall upon our country. I saw the Chief Commissioner of Police, and found that the authorities would support us in any plans we might make. The mayor called a meeting to consider it, and our local council of public morality did its best. I was rather struck by the fact that the Chief Commissioner of Police at Scotland Yard, and our local mayor, were both Roman Catholics, and the realization of their attitude on this moral question was some comfort to me in the obvious growth of Catholicism which is the marked feature of present-day religious life. But our plans for combating the evil were brought to an abrupt end by the great cataclysm of August.

I began a series of sermons on the Springs of Joy, which were taken down in shorthand, and put in type for publication. The publishers held them back, though it seemed to me they struck the very note which was needed in that sad autumn. They did not appear till 1916.

But the chief project of the year was a reunion to celebrate the thirtieth anniversary of the opening of Lyndhurst Road Church in July. The people entered into the preparations with ardour. We obtained, so far as we could, the addresses of all old members, and issued an invitation to them to spend the first Sunday of July with us. A great many responded. On Saturday afternoon my dear and loyal friend, McEvoy, preached a sermon of rare beauty. Then we had a reception at which we had heart-warming speeches from my friends Micklem, Frank Chaplin, J. G. Stevenson (called away since, alas, too soon!), Workman, Travers Buxton, Highton. The old members reminded us of the days when the Church had been crowded and an eager interest was felt in every service. Perhaps they exaggerated the glories of the past. But they also saw the possibilities of the future, and filled me with the hope that, notwithstanding age and infirmities, the best was yet to be. On Sunday I preached to them on "The Cloud of Witnesses," recalling the faces and the labours of some of our former helpers. And in the evening—the thirty-fourth anniversary of the Monthly Lecture—I spoke on Reconstruction, sketching the lines of theological readjustment, which I worked out and finally published in my latest book, October 1915.

Monday was one of the crowning days of my life. I had an extraordinary feeling that my beloved lady was looking down from her heavenly home and smiling on all our proceedings ; if ever we can be conscious of the dear unseen presences, I was conscious of her that day. She had loved and prayed for this Church, and supported me in the ministry all those years, and in her closing days she had believed in its prolonged prosperity. Among all the invisible spirits who gathered round us she seemed first, the choragus of an exultant choir. We had an early prayer-meeting, on which showers of blessing seemed to fall. Then we assembled for breakfast at the Town Hall. Affectionate speeches were made, and we presented a chair and a purse to our caretaker, who had been the most loyal servant of the Church ever since the building was opened, thirty years ago. Then our kind neighbour, Mr. Hancock Nunn, offered us his garden for a party : our church-room opens by an emergency door into the garden, which is a little paradise, and there was a cheerful time of welcoming old friends and forming new ties. Then the evening meeting was unique in my experience. Joseph King, who had returned from India, thank God ! and was comparatively strong, spoke of the old days, when his father had been the most generous giver towards the building of the church. R. J. Campbell spoke of the way in which I had stood by him at a time when he was surrounded by foes and his back was against the wall. He said other things which it would perhaps be ungenerous to recall now. Finally Dr. Courtney, always ready to give me his sympathetic aid, made the speech of the evening. It was so vivid a presentation of what the services had meant to him, and so warm and affectionate an appreciation of me that, just for a moment, I entertained the hope that he might be saying what would be the final and impartial verdict on my ministry. But that I could not permanently think. He was indulgent on such an occasion, as all speakers are ; and as he had taken a considerable part in shaping and moulding my mind, he naturally regarded with too much favour his own handiwork. Still, those warm and generous words from old friends are among the richest rewards of life.

There was one curious coincidence which came out in this review of the membership of the Church ; it made a deep impression on me. I had often bemoaned the fact that my work did not result in large harvests and impressive ingatherings. But, strange to say, we found that the number of members who had joined the Church from the beginning represented exactly one for every Sunday service that had been held. The slow and steady work of my long years was permitted to produce just what was effected at Pentecost in one day. *Laus Deo!* Thirty years now to do what then required a few hours.

read our declaration of war I said at once : " Germany will never forgive this : she will always say that we struck in just when she had her hands occupied with France and Russia, because we thought our turn would come when she had secured herself against them." But on August 4th I read the White Paper through, and my eyes were opened. I was absolutely convinced that Sir Edward Grey had striven for peace with all his might, and I realized that Germany had willed the war, and the toast of *Der Tag* had represented a settled purpose to fight us when the day should come, and the day had come on us at last by the violation of Belgian neutrality. Could any responsible minister, I asked myself, shrink from the duty of defending Belgium? Germany knew that would be a *casus belli*, and she had dared it.

I was very thankful to be away in that remote place though the battleships were in Lough Swilley, and an Austrian prize was brought into the Lough before we left—for I had to wrestle through to a clear position before I could be of any use to my people. When I got back for Sunday, September 13th, I was able to take a firm stand. I published three sermons in which I tried to hearten my people in facing a task which we, as a nation, could not evade. Already when I got back a large part of the young manhood of the Church had enlisted. With one poor exception, none, in the Church or mission, shrank from this supreme ordeal. Those who were most active in the work of the Church were most unflinching in response to the country's call ; and long before compulsory service came in all the men of military age in the Church were either in training or away, except, of course, those who were exempted on the ground of health or on that of doing necessary work.

One boy, Douglas Sully, went out almost at once, and in October laid down his life in trying to save a comrade. Thus the war had at once come right home to the heart of the Church. His father had been with us before his marriage, and Douglas, whom I had known all his life, used to run up and put his little hand in mine whenever he saw me, and talk in the most engaging way. He was a true Christian, eager to take his part in the work of the Church.

Immediately a great task opened before me. The Roll of Honour steadily grew until it approached four hundred ; and I determined to keep in touch with them all by regular correspondence. All the young men of my Active Service League were gone, but the girls were splendid ; and by their aid I began to send out a letter every two months, enclosing a sermon which I had printed for them. Before a year was out the effort began to reap its reward in the surprising response of the men. They felt the sympathy and prayers of the Church. We then arranged that each name should be given to a member of the Church, who would undertake to pray daily for that one. The letters from the men, and their visits when they were on furlough, soon assured me that this was the best thing a Church could do in time of war. It was useless to protest against a war which was inevitable ; still more useless was it to attempt a revolution in the Christian religion in order to justify war, or to cultivate a Christian Chauvinism, with the new dogmas, that the enemy were the devil's horde, and we were the New Crusaders, and therefore that our men, dying on the field of battle, would go straight to heaven, whatever lives they had lived, whatever faith they had held. This neo-Mohammedanism might safely be left to the new allies of the Turks. But a Church could keep the home fires burning, and by prayer and faith hold all her sons on service in the warm embrace of her love. The worship in the thinned pews could be vicarious, as the vacant places were, in faith, filled with the absent boys. Many of the boys became members, and loved to feel the corporate unity. Then, as one after another of our very best was missing, or reported killed, a great task developed of comforting the bereaved families, and presenting the truths of Christ, and the Gospel which brought life and immortality to light, as the one real consolation and support in these sad times.

> The world's a home of sickness, where each heart
> Knows its own trouble and unrest;
> The truest wisdom there and noblest art
> Is his who skills of comfort best.

As the conflict in Europe developed and the manifold problems, of enlisting the whole country, caring for refugees and wounded, economizing and saving, coping with the vice which came in like a flood, considering the kind of peace which should be sought and how it could be obtained, unfolded one after another, I found every hour filled and every energy demanded in order to guide and help my people. First, there was the surprising experience of Mons, when our small army escaped the annihilation which seemed inevitable from the overwhelming superiority of the enemy. There could be no doubt here about a Divine intervention, and the stories of the vision of angels only represented the deep sense of awe and wonder among our men who escaped. Mr. Machen, whom I had known in the *Academy* trial as the writer of the article which led me to think the paper was Catholic, now came forward and wished to explain the Angels at Mons as the result of a tale he had written, " The Bowmen of St. George." He did me the honour of interviewing me, and reminding me, as he left, how we had last met in court, when he was in the witness-box. This creator of angelic hosts was indeed enough to shake one's faith in what actually happened at Mons. But the recent book, *The Chariots of God*, by " A Churchwoman," reviewing all the evidence, makes it quite plain that God delivered us in that fateful moment by just such a host of spiritual powers as He sends forth to minister to His people in all ages. If we are victorious in the war it will be because God saved us at Mons and on the Marne ; if we are not, it will be because we, as a country, blinded our eyes to His mercy, and would have none of Him in our public and national life.

Month after month it became more necessary, and more enthralling, to speak the words of hope and warning to my people. In 1915 I arranged evenings of rest and refreshment for those who were overstrained, or lonely, or despondent. When the Zeppelin raids began and the streets were darkened, it became increasingly difficult to hold evening meetings, and the evening service, if the weather was bad, dwindled to a few hundreds. But never did the pulpit and pastoral work seem so real, so worth while, as it did now. It was more like the work of the prophets of Israel, who had to interpret and apply the facts of the moment, and the shiftings of national events, to warn or to comfort the people. It was all a new discovery of the meaning and the value of the ministry, the sacred task of " justifying the ways of God to men," or when the enemy came in like a flood, of lifting up the standard against him. Now I was thankful day by day that I had been for so long in the Church, that I could help and cherish the people with a full knowledge of their needs ; still more thankful was I that I had known Christ so long, and so tested His resources, that in this time of unrest, doubt, anxiety, and unbelief, I knew whom I had believed, and was sure that He would stand triumphant at the end.

When my book *Reconstruction* came out at the beginning of 1916, I hoped that it would help, not my own people only, but a wider circle. In that book I wrote my own experience of finding Christ, and of finding in Him the solution of the difficulties raised by Biblical criticism. I was not wholly disappointed ; for evidences began to come in, that agnostics and unbelievers were finding their way to faith by the argument there advanced. I tried therefore in January 1917, by an article in the *Contemporary*, to get the book into the hands of those whom it might help. But, of course, the attention of the reading public was occupied, either in books about the war, or, increasingly, as the war went on, in books which offered a complete diversion from the subject. A book on theological reconstruction could hardly find readers.

I turned therefore with renewed earnestness and zeal to my pastoral work, the pulpit, and the visitation, in which I saw my best hope of rendering real service. To keep the Church living and the fire on its altar burning was, for me, the task of the time. I remembered with joy that old Roman, Fabius, who went through the desperate war with the Carthaginians, when Hannibal was ravaging Italy almost to the gates of Rome. They honoured him because in the darkest days he never despaired of the Republic. If I am permitted to live through the war and to look back upon it as an event in the past, I believe that I shall regard it as the most fruitful period of my ministry. When the Church seemed to melt away ; when pacifists deserted me because they charged me with " supporting the war," and Chauvinists turned away because I wanted peace ; when people were so overstrained that they could not listen to sermons, and grumbled, in the same breath, that they would not go to church because they got no teaching, and because they could not listen to the teaching they got ; when everything had become un-natural, feverish, aguish, through the anxieties which pressed upon the public mind ; and when even the kindest friends and loyalest members of the Church were always complaining that the Church had missed her opportunity ; when if you prayed for the country and the war and the soldiers, people said that they wanted to escape the war for a moment in church, and if you did not pray for these objects they said that you were outside the thoughts of the people, shut up within a narrow circle of private interests, when to quote the Lord's command to love our enemies was regarded as "unpatriotic," and to express confidence in those who were managing our national affairs was thought to be pro-German ; in that time of almost unimaginable difficulty, it was an unspeakable mercy to be allowed to go on, week by week, whether people would listen or not, whether they criticized or were indifferent, declaring that God was over all, and the issue would be right ; that He would judge the nations impartially, and give His award in equity ; and that through all our blindness and blundering, our suffering and sin, there was the everlasting Gospel of Jesus and His love ; nay, there verily in our midst was Jesus Himself, with heart open for all our needs, a sacrifice for all our sins, a hand held out to save us from sinking in the waves. To be a minister of Christ in those days, and the pastor of a people whom one knew already in a second generation, was a grace of God for which I must always be thankful.

It is quite possible that the new world which will emerge from the war, with new outlooks and new conceptions, will require ministers of another kind. I can well believe that one who belonged essentially to the last quarter of the nineteenth will be totally unsuited for the second quarter of the twentieth century. When it appears that my task as a minister is done, and my place at Lyndhurst Road can be better occupied by a younger man, I shall retire with nothing but gratitude for the life I have been permitted to live, and the task I have been called to do.

Reviewing my life, as I have done in these pages, I have been led to ask, and to state to myself more clearly than I ever did before, what were the objects I had in view when I set out on my life-work. I find them to have been essentially (now one more prominent, and now another) four : first, to be a witness of Christ Jesus ; second, to form and shepherd a Church which should be an integral part of the Holy Catholic Church ; third, to promote social reform ; fourth, to carry the Gospel to the remote ends of the earth. Imperfect and ineffectual as my labours have been, those objects have always been before me, and in the order named.

To preach Christ was the object of entering the ministry ; for me, at least, that seemed the way in which I could make my life the most constant, if not the most attractive, witness of Him. Though I tremble to think how wavering and inadequate my witness of Him has been, I cannot in looking back see in what occupation or profession I could have made my witness better, unless I had been a foreign missionary ; but, strange to say, that possibility was never presented to me until it was too late. Could I have served Christ better in the Church of England? Here, again, I see that to enter the Church of England, when I left Oxford, would have been to compromise with principle ; I should have taken the easy, the popular, the fashionable path ; I should have looked on the way of honour and promotion and national influence, and have been persuading myself that I "should do more good in that way." I do not blame those who have acted otherwise, but for me to have done that would have been to introduce into my life at the beginning a principle of self-seeking, which would have rotted inward and destroyed all. Jowett, the Master of Balliol, used to say that for one blind to worldly ambition, he thought the Nonconformist ministry offered one of the most favourable careers in life. I have found his judgment singularly shrewd and sound. In that direction certainly no promotion lies, as Burke would say. Society knows you not, and you know Society only by the most occasional incursions into its sacred enclosure. But Ruskin's advice to an artist, to be "fit for the best society and to keep out of it," has its application to a minister. The exclusion of any possibility of worldly advancement, the obscurity in which one is not recognized by authorities, social or political, the complete escape from all the blandishments of great personages, are conditions not unfavourable for serenity of mind, and for the testimony of Jesus, whose own earthly life resembled that of a Nonconformist minister rather than that of a prelate in a State Church.

My failure to render a faithful witness to my Lord has been due, not to my position in life, but to my personal inadequacy. I fancy, of course, that I might have done better if I had been endowed with the brilliant qualities which I see in my younger contemporaries, or if my eyesight had been spared, or if I had been allowed a peaceful and consoling home-life. But these are delusions. My failure to serve my Saviour lies at the door of my conscience, and I can only abide in perpetual repentance and sorrow before Him that I have been so unprofitable a servant.

The object, to make and lead a Church which would be an integral part of the Church Catholic, was attained in a fuller sense than I dared to anticipate. For twenty years, from 1884, when the buildings were opened, to 1904 when my sight failed, the Church at Lyndhurst Road was blessed beyond measure; there was a steady inflow of members; a spirit of unity and mutual help pervaded the community; the generosity of the people was incredible; and there was an eager activity, attempting great things at home and abroad, which gave the Church an enviable reputation far and near. And even during these trying years, though the Church seems depleted, and unable to do what once it did, the spirit is the same; new-comers have taken up the heritage of the past; and the solid core of faith and hope and love gives promise, that I may some day hand the work over to a successor, chosen by God, who will make the future of the Church better and greater than its past has been.

That eager hope of Social Reform, which I brought

with me from Oxford and the Toynbee circle, has never died away, but, except in the institution of the Kentish Town Mission, and such work as I could give to the Union for Christian Social Service, the National Council of Public Morals, and the varied movements for the betterment of the people, which have come my way in the course of the years, I am sadly conscious of my failure to accomplish anything. I could not command the time to study and master the facts. I remember Professor Thorold Rogers, whose lectures on Political Economy I attended at Oxford, handing back an amateur essay I had written for him, with the remark : " You must read, my young friend." The amateur in social questions is not only of no use, he is a danger. I have therefore refrained from stepping in where I felt unqualified to tread, and have kept my opinions to myself. All I could do was to urge the great Christian principles which are the only sure motive for lasting reforms ; and once I was greatly encouraged by a remark which has remained with me. I had in my congregation for some years Mr. Alfred Harvey, the manager of Glyn's Bank. His was one of the most active and vivid intellects I have ever known ; seldom did I get a talk with him without returning a wiser, if not better, man. One day I was deploring to him my inability to take part in those social reforms which I knew to be necessary, and he said with great and kindly warmth : " But you must remember you are giving us Sunday by Sunday the motive powers which urge us all to do our part in the world." And I have to find my comfort in that. Certainly many of the members of Lyndhurst Road, men and women, have wrought nobly and effectively in the causes which I should wish to serve. But looking back over my public life I feel much disappointment at the very imperfect and hesitating steps which have been taken to heal the sores of our body politic. Education has not yet gained any adequate recognition in the State ; but for the effort of Churches to obtain or to retain the religious teaching, the subject would hardly attract public attention at all. The upper classes, preferring sport and pleasure to education themselves, are not conscious of any malevolence in denying to the masses a good which they do not value. Our public schools create in our boys a sort of contempt for mental excellence, and lead boys seriously to think that the world can be possessed and governed by athletes. The teachers in elementary schools are overtasked and underpaid, and they are only too conscious of the fact that they cannot teach to their bulging classes what they have to teach, nor if they taught it would it be of much use. The country refuses to think out the question of what an educated community means, or how it could be secured. A faint hope lingers in my mind that the war may accomplish what all the arguments and appeals of the instructed have failed to do. It may open to our belated eyes the revelation that education means efficiency, and efficiency is the one condition on which a nation can, or ought to, survive, in the world which will emerge from the seismic convulsion of Europe.

The land question, and the housing problem, remain very much where they were when I began my work in 1880. Indeed, the Scottish peasantry have been driven from their glens, and two hundred deer forests have been made at the expense of our national well-being under our eyes, while we have been asking for land-law reform. The drink trade has obtained a power in the country, defying all the efforts, unhappily the divided efforts, of Temperance reformers. And in the conflict with Germany we know how the drink paralyses us, robs us of hard-won victories, and threatens when the men return to devastate the land. But every one dreads to touch that palladium of our national life.

The declining birthrate—alas, in my own Hampstead it has fallen from thirty-three to seventeen while I have been here !—and the shocking revelations of the Commission on Venereal Diseases—force home on us the fact that the godliness of our country works out in the very moral corruption which destroys great nations. The whole work of Social Reform has yet to be done. Sanguine minds hope that the catastrophe of the war will set us upon the better way. But I am definitely convinced that the only sound hope is in God Himself. If we recover God, and believe in Him with all our hearts, if the truth of Christ grips the country again, and leads us to amend our personal lives and seek the power of God to reform and save society, a better day may come. But doubt has paralysed us, and the people who have any practical belief in God are few.

The last object which I have had before me, growing in importance year by year, has been the evangelization of the world. My purest joys have come from the part which I have been allowed to take in missionary work, and from the study of the facts which prove the rapid though silent spread of Christ's Kingdom throughout the world. When Griffith John went to China in the year that I was born, 1855, there were only five hundred converts to Christianity in the country, and now, even during the war, Mr. Sherwood Eddy has addressed eighty thousand Chinese students ; many hundreds of them have turned to Christ ; and China has appealed to the Christian Church for prayer in her national difficulties. His kingdom comes. The amazing progress of the work in India during the war shows plainly how the work is God's, rather than ours, and rouses, in me at any rate, the conviction that to have a part in it is a privilege which we shall duly estimate only in the future world. As I bring this record of my life to a close, and ask myself the question, " If you might have another life on earth following this, what would you do, what would you be? " I cannot help answering my question in this way : I should certainly choose to be a missionary, to follow in the footprints of Henry Martyn, or Mackay, or Gilmour. For I see now, what

I did not see at the beginning, that to be a pioneer of the Gospel, and to preach Christ where He has not been known, is the greatest thing that a man can do upon earth. This ministry at home has its opportunities, its joys, its rewards, as well as its toils and abundant trials ; but in the ordered hierarchy of God, in the circling ranks which Dante saw in Paradise, the Apostles come first. The Apostles are missionaries ; and we who come lower down in the scale—pastors, teachers, and evangelists—should eagerly recognize, and thank God for, those who are above us. We can only make up for our inferiority by frankly owning which order comes first, and by using all our opportunities and powers to send and to support the pioneers. This remains as the standing wonder to me, how the Church fails to see, that expansion is her first duty, and the extension of Christ's reign over the earth the condition of His intensive life in our souls. The closing verse of the first Gospel is to my mind the last will and testament of the Redeemer, and the word which epitomizes the whole truth of Christ for mankind : " All authority hath been given unto me in heaven and on earth. Go ye therefore and make disciples of all the nations, baptizing them into the name of the Father, and of the Son, and of the Holy Ghost, teaching them to observe all things whatsoever I commanded you, and lo, I am with you alway, even unto the end of the world."

Just as I write this closing page there comes to my hand the Chinese translation of my *Commandments of Jesus*. It gives me a faint but sweet thrill of satisfaction, to feel that even in so remote a way I have been allowed to teach those in the land of Sinim His holy commandments. But if, in those Oxford days, the Student Volunteer Movement had begun, if I had heard the call, if I had gone myself to China, where two of my boys, Walford Hart, and in direct succession to him, Meadows Turner, laid down their lives for Christ !— I can only think that I was not counted worthy to hear that call, and was sent to do the lower work for which I was better fitted. If the story of my life may bring some help and encouragement to those who are engaged in the home ministry—and it certainly shows how God can use and maintain through long years a very ordinary instrument—I trust, that by its poignant sense of that better and more honourable way it may summon a few young men, before it is too late, to answer their Master's call for the foreign field. And if the story of Lyndhurst Road impresses any reader with the sense of the blessing which has been on the Church, and the success that has attended its labours, let me record my own conviction, that the long prosperity of this Church has been due to these two things : first, that we have made the missionary claim the foremost responsibility of the Church ; and second, that a prayer-meeting every Saturday night prepares us for the worship and work of the Sunday, and a week of early prayer-meetings every July recruits and often re-creates the Church for its onward march.